Praise for *Amazing Words*

"Is there anyone alive who has more fun with words than Richard Lederer? In dozens of books, from *Crazy English* to *The Word Circus*, he has continually entertained and amazed us with his boundless knowledge of and enthusiasm for all things linguistic. Now, in *Amazing Words*, Lederer puts on yet another dazzling display, elucidating the wondrous stories and secrets that lie hidden in the language. There's an *ooh!* and an *ah!* and a hearty *ha-ha-ha!* on every page."
> —**Charles Harrington Elster**, author of *The Accidents of Style*

"Richard Lederer has outdone Richard Lederer. *Amazing Words* is clever, compelling, and totally captivating. This book is for anyone and everyone who loves the English language. It is one of a dozen books I would select to take along if I were exiled to a desert island."
> —**Paul Dickson**, author of *Words*

"This is not simply a book about *Amazing Words*, it is also an amazing book about words—and one that could have only been written by the inimitable Richard Lederer. Enjoy, word lovers, enjoy!"
> —**Dr. Mardy Grothe**, author of *I Never Metaphor I Didn't Like*

"*Amazing Words* is chock full of constant surprise. Each entry is a font of delight and knowledge. I had to keep reading because I unfailingly wanted to see how the next word would bedazzle, beguile, and bewitch me."
> —**Caroline McCullagh**, author of *American Trivia*

"Every page instructs, delights, and entrances readers—often all at once."
> —**Rod L. Evans**, author of *Tyrannosaurus Lex*

"Words are wonderfully interesting, yes, but only Richard Lederer makes them amazing."
> —**Robert Hartwell Fiske**, editor of *The Vocabula Review* and author of *The Best Words*

"Richard Lederer's *Amazing Words* is amazing indeed. He introduces you to new and unfamiliar words, and teaches you things you didn't know about familiar ones. You'll learn the surprising origins of words we use every day and the meanings of common expressions you probably took for granted. There's much more in these pages that will make you a better writer or reader: grammar and style advice, literary and rhetorical devices, vocabulary, slang. Best of all are the puns, games, wordplay, and other forms of recreational linguistics that reveal just how much fun our wonderful English language can be. It's a cliché (one of the topics discussed, of course) to say that something is 'as entertaining as it is educational.' But that description applies perfectly to *Amazing Words*."

—**Don Hauptman**, author of *Cruel and Unusual Puns*

Praise for Richard Lederer

"Columnist and punster Richard Lederer may be William Safire's only living peer at writing about grammar, word usage, and derivations."
    —*Washington Post Book World*

"Lederer beguiles and bedazzles."
    —*Los Angeles Times*

"Richard Lederer ought to be declared a national treasure."
    —*Richmond Times Dispatch*

"Richard Lederer is the true King of Language Comedy."
    —**Sidney Sheldon**, author of *After the Darkness*

"Columnist Extraordinaire."
    —*The New Yorker*

"Richard Lederer opens the treasure chest of English and delights in each shiny coin he finds."
    —**Rob Kyff**, a.k.a. "The Word Guy," nationally syndicated language columnist and author of *Once Upon a Word*

AMAZING
WORDS

AMAZING
WORDS

An Alphabetical Anthology of
Alluring, Astonishing, Astounding,
Bedazzling, Beguiling, Bewitching,
Enchanting, Enthralling, Entrancing,
Magical, Mesmerizing, Miraculous,
Tantalizing, Tempting, and Transfixing Words

RICHARD LEDERER

Marion Street Press

Portland, Oregon

to Jim Schuette and Kel Winter,
for the loving labors of Marion Street Press
in publishing my books

Acknowledgment

I thank Merriam-Webster, Inc. (www.Merriam-Webster.com), for permission to adapt entries from my book *The Word Circus* for *Amazing Words*.

Published by Marion Street Press
4207 SE Woodstock Blvd # 168
Portland, OR 97206-6267
USA
http://www.marionstreetpress.com/

Orders and review copies: (800) 888-4741

Printed in the United States of America
ISBN 978-1-936863-30-3

Back cover photo by Kim Treffinger

Library of Congress Cataloging-in-Publication Data pending

7INTRODUCTION

At seventy-four years of youth, I consider myself to be one of the luckiest men on the face of the earth. Looking back at my life, I can honestly say that I have pretty much closed the distance between who I am and what I do. When you love what you do, you never work a day in your life, and writing forty books has never felt like work.

Especially this one.

That's because the good people at Marion Street Press asked me to present to the world the approximately three hundred most amazing words I know. "O Frabjous day! Kaloo! Kalay!" I chortled in my joy. I've hung around with words my whole life, and many of them have become fast friends. Now I've been gifted with the opportunity to share with my readers the most logologically, etymologically, and linguistically amazing words among them.

Those three adverbs—*etymologically, logologically,* and *linguistically*—make for a mouthful, so I'll illustrate their uses with the word *usher.*

Like humanity, *usher* has a long history, going all the way back to the Latin *ostium,* "door," related to *os,* "mouth," because a door was likened to the mouth of a building. *Usher,* then, turns out to be a body metaphor for a person who stands at a door.

That's etymology. The Greek *étymon* (ἔτυμον) means "true, original," and the Greek-ending *logíā* (λόγια) means "science or study." Thus, etymology is the science or study of true and original word meanings. What unalloyed fun I've had auditioning a flash mob of amazing words for *Amazing Words* and spinning out the yarns of the origins of the most bedazzling, beguiling, and bewitching of those words in our glorious, uproarious, notorious, outrageous, courageous, contagious, stupendous, tremendous, end-over-endous English language.

Has there ever been another word as human as *usher?* In sound and meaning it is not a paragon among words, but it accommodates the full spectrum of humankind. Living in the house of *usher*, within its brief compass of five letters, we find, with the order of letters preserved, the pronouns *us, she, he,* and *her.*

That's an example of logology—the dance of the alphabet, the revelation, the showing forth, of letter patterns that cavort and caper inside words. Take it from me, *Riddler Reacher*, which is an anagram— a rearrangement—of all the letters in my name, *Richard Lederer.*

Usher winkingly reminds us that all words are created by people and that language unfailingly reflects the thrilling contradictions of our kind. Thus, even though writers write, bakers bake, hunters hunt, preachers preach, and teachers teach, grocers don't groce, butchers don't butch, carpenters don't carpent, milliners don't millin, haberdashers don't haberdash—and ushers don't ush. That's an area of linguistics, the scientific study of language, in this case taking words apart to analyze and play with their meaning-bearing elements.

As International Punster of the Year (no kidding; there really is such a title), I promise you that a fair piece of the wordplay in this book will be puns. After all, a good pun is like a good steak—a rare medium well done—and an excellent pun is its own reword.

I invite you to come through the *entrance* of this book; I guarantee it will *entrance* you. The entry for *entrance* will explain how we use both those words, which are made from the same letters but feature different etymologies, meanings, pronunciations, and accents. Like *usher* and *entrance*, the words you are about to meet in this book are seldom fancy or arcane or sesquipedalianly long. Rather, they are words you pal around with every day, and you're about to get to know a thousand of them a lot better.

Words are who we are. Words are what we do. Words inspire the heart, spark the mind, beget laughter. Words move the world. Words are as great a joy as food and drink and sex. May *Amazing Words* fill you with such tasty, palate-rinsing, and connecting pleasure.

Richard Lederer
San Diego, California
richard.lederer@pobox.com

A is an article, as in "a word," as well as the first letter of the alphabet. Turns out that quite the majority of our letters are also words or sound like words:

A: a	*I*: aye, eye, I	*N*: en	*T*: tea, tee
B: be, bee	*J*: jay	*O*: O, oh, owe	*U*: ewe, yew, you
C: sea, see	*K*: quay	*P*: pea, pee	*X*: ex
G: gee	*L*: el	*Q*: cue, queue	*Y*: why
	M: em	*R*: are	

And more than half our letters, when pluralized, sound like words:

B's: bees	*K*'s: quays	*P*'s: peas, pease, pees
C's: seas, sees, seize	*L*'s: els	*Q*'s: cues, queues
E's: ease	*M*'s: ems	*T*'s: teas, tease, tees
G's: geez	*N*'s: ens	*U*'s: ewes, use, yews, youse
I's: ayes, eyes	*O*'s: ohs, owes	*X*'s: exes
J's: jays		*Y*'s: wise, whys

(See EXPEDIENCY, I, Q-TIPS, S, SILENT, W, X.)

Abecedarian is a letter-perfect word that means "pertaining to the alphabet, or alphabetically arranged." This book is abecedarian in both senses of that definition.

The word *alphabet* is a joining of the first two letters of the Greek alphabet, *alpha* (άλφα) and *beta* (βήτα). The Greeks inherited their letters from the Phoenicians, who probably took their alpha from the Hebrew *aleph,* "ox."

> From alpha to omega,
>> You can bet the alphabet,
> Like a painting done by Degas,
>> Will leap and pirouette.
> See dancing words, entrancing words,
>> Sterling words unfurling.
> Watch prancing words, enhancing words,
>> Whirling, twirling, swirling.

The old Cambodian alphabet, with seventy-four letters, is the world's longest. Rotokas, spoken on the South Pacific island of Bougainville, uses only eleven letters.

Here's a look at the letters in our alphabet from different vantage points:

- BCDEGPTVZ, when sounded, all end with a long *e* sound, thus rhyming with each other.
- FHLMNRSX, when sounded, all end in consonant sounds.
- CDILMVX are Roman numerals.
- AEFHIKLMNTVWXYZ are made with straight lines.
- abcdefghjmnopqrstu include curves.
- AHIMOTUVWXY exhibit vertical left-right symmetry. They look the same in a mirror.
- BCDEHIKOX exhibit horizontal symmetry. Their top and bottom halves reflect each other.

Abracadabra is the longest common word with five *a*'s and features the four-letter *abra* at the beginning and the end, with a *cad* in between. The incantation may be derived from the Gnostic (early Christian) word *Abraxas* (ΑΒΡΑΞΑΣ), Greek for "God," the source of 365 emanations. Purportedly, the Greek letters for *Abraxas* add up to 365 when translated numerologically.

(See DEEDED, MISSISSIPPI, STRENGTHLESSNESS.)

Ace. In *ace,* the first, third, and fifth letters of the alphabet are joined. Ho hum, you yawn, and I agree because I haven't been playing with a full deck. I'm a jack ace who ought to be dealt with, you say to yourself. But think on this: if you add up the number of letters in that deck—*ace king queen jack ten nine eight seven six five four three two*—the total comes to fifty-two!

Here's a cute poser that involves *ace:* What is the pattern of the following names? The answer has nothing to do with the letters, syllables, or sounds in each name. Rather, the answer is "straightforward":

Eddie Rickenbacker, Elvis Presley, Elizabeth, John F. Kennedy, Bo Derek
Answer: *Ace, King, Queen, Jack, Ten*

And how is marriage like a deck of cards?
Answer: You start off with two hearts and a diamond—and pretty soon you want to grab a club and use a spade.

(See DIE, JACKPOT.)

Adam is a Hebrew name that means "mankind." *Adam's apple* is so called because many men, but few women, exhibit a bulge of laryngeal cartilage in front of their throats. According to male-dominated folklore, Eve swallowed her apple without care or residue, while a chunk of the fruit stuck in the throat of the innocent and misled Adam.

Adam and Eve were the happiest couple in history. That's because she couldn't tell him how many other men she could have married—and he couldn't tell her how much he loved his mother's cooking.

When was Adam created? A little before Eve ("eve"). Eve was the first palindromic word, so Adam introduced himself with the first palindromic sentence:

Name Me Man
Backward and forward, as you will perceive
Read Adam's first greeting to dear Mother Eve:
"Madam, I'm Adam." Now we can conceive
That her answer was simply, "Eve, mad Adam, Eve."

(See AGAMEMNON, BIBLE, CIVIC, KINNIKINNIK, NAPOLEON, PALINDROME, SENSUOUSNESS, WONTON, *ZOONOOZ*.)

Aegilops, meaning "an ulcer in part of the eye," is an eight-letter word in which all letters proceed in alphabetical order with no double letters. But let's admit that *aegilops* is pretty obscure. Using more common words, we can get up to six letters:

abhors	begins	biopsy	chinos
almost	bijoux	chimps	chintz

Agamemnon (Ἀγαμέμνων), the name of the mythical Greek king so prominent in the *Iliad* and other literary masterpieces, is constructed from three three-letter palindromes: *Aga, mem, non.*

(See ADAM, CIVIC, KINNIKINNIK, NAPOLEON, PALINDROME, SENSUOUSNESS, WONTON, *ZOONOOZ*.)

Ague is one of a few two-syllable words ("ay-gyoo") that become one-syllable words when letters are added at their beginning, as in *ague/vague* or *ague/plague*. Other examples include:

aged/paged	naked/snaked	ragged/bragged
rugged/shrugged	winged/twinged	

(See RODE.)

Ahoy originated as a word used to signal a ship or boat. Alexander Graham Bell, the inventor of the telephone, insisted on *ahoy* as the correct way of answering the telephone, but it was his rival, inventor Thomas Edison, who coined what became the universal word to answer the telephone—*hello*, itself an alteration of the earlier English *holla!*, "Stop! Pay attention!" Nowadays, only Montgomery Burns, *The Simpsons* superannuated scrooge, uses "Ahoy-hoy" to take a telephone call.

(See GOOD-BYE.)

Ai. The shortest two-syllable words are the rather obscure *aa,* a rough lava; *ai,* a three-toed sloth; and *Io,* a moon of Jupiter.

Air is a member of the most populous family of homophones, words that are spelled differently but sound the same:

air   aire   Ayr   Ayer   ere   err   Eyre   heir

Note that *err* is a member of *air* family. While many pronunciation experts would argue that "to 'air' is human, to 'ur' divine" (thank you, Alexander Pope), the airy sounding of *err* is firmly established in American English.

(See SCENT.)

Akimbo, "with hands on hip and elbows bent outward," may trace its ancestry to the Icelandic *kengboginn*, "bent hookwise, looking like a two-handled jug," because that's just what arms akimbo look like.

In addition to exciting the ear with its unusual sound, *akimbo* resides in two special categories of words:

First, *akimbo* is a deferential (or postpositive) adjective, one that must follow—and can never precede—the noun it modifies.

Second, *akimbo* is a prime example of a monogamous word—a word married to only one other word or phrase. Only arms can be *akimbo*, nothing else, just as only heroes can be *unsung*, breath can be *bated*, and thumbs *twiddled*. *Umbrage* can only be taken, *aspersions* cast, and *nothings* whispered (and sweet). These monogamous words have no life of their own beyond the specific idiom to which they are married.

(See GALORE.)

Alimony has been defined as "all the money" and "the bounty of mutiny." The word actually traces back to the Latin *alimonia*, "nourish." Hence, *alimony* is "eating money." Originally *alimony* was closer to a widow's pension or current welfare check than to a reluctant husband's subsidy.

My nephew phoned me and asked me, as a professional brand name concocter, to come up with a slogan for his business card and website.

"Okay," I said. "Let's review your basic life facts. You're a family lawyer who's involved in a lot of divorce cases, right?"

"Yes, Uncle Rich."

"And you live in San Antonio."

"Right."

"I've got it: *Remember the Alimony!*"

Alkaline. Can anyone ever top the combination of chemistry and a famous name in *alkaline?* Cleave *alkaline,* and you'll end up with *Al Kaline,* the Hall of Fame outfielder for the Detroit Tigers.

(See DAREDEVIL, MARSHALL, TEMPERAMENTALLY.)

Alone means "by oneself." Take away the first letter, and you get *lone,* which means "by oneself." Now take away the first letter of *lone,* and you get *one,* which means "by itself."

(See PASTERN, REACTIVATION, STARTLING.)

Amateur is derived from the very first verb that all students of Latin learn—*amo:* "I love." Amateurs do it for the love of it. Whether it be golf, fishing, quilting, or model trains, it can only be out of love that the amateur pours so many hours into an unremunerative pursuit.

(See VACCUUM.)

Ambidextrous, from Latin roots meaning "using both the left and right hands with equal ease," is a twelve-letter word in which the first six letters—*ambide*—are drawn from the left-hand side of the alphabet and the second six letters—*xtrous*—are from the right side. *Ambidextrous* is also a twelve-letter isogram, meaning that no letter is repeated. The word features all five major vowels, almost in order, and remains an isogram with a sixth vowel in *ambidextrously.*

The opposite of *ambidextrous* is *ambisinister:* "clumsy, as if possessing two left hands."

(See FACETIOUS, METALIOUS, RIGHT, ULYSSES SIMPSON GRANT, UNNOTICEABLY.)

Anagram. Can you create one word out of the letters in *new door?*

The answer is (yuck yuck) *one word.* The letters in *new door* are the same as those in *one word,* except in a different order.

When is enough not enough?

When you rearrange the letters in *enough,* you get *one hug.* Everybody knows that one hug is never enough!

To what commonality do the following words point: *thorn, shout, seat/sate/teas,* and *stew/wets?* The solution is that each is an anagram of a compass point: *north, south, east,* and *west.*

These riddles involve anagrams. An anagram (from Greek *ana gráphein* [ἀνά γράφειν], "to write over again") is a rearrangement of all the letters in a familiar word, phrase, or name to form another word, phrase, or name, as in the italicized words in this anagrammatical poem:

Arty Idol
Watch anagrams and you will see
That they inspire *idolatry.*
Please do not come *o tardily,*
And *dilatory* please don't be.
Adroitly anagrams will start
To alter *daily rot.* They're smart:
A *dirty lot,* an *oily dart,*
They'll change into the *doily art.*

Anagrams work best when there exists an *appropriate,* that is, *A-1, apt, proper* relationship between the two anagrams. If that connection is semantically powerful, we call the two items aptagrams:

aye = *yea*
desperation = *a rope ends it*
detour = *routed*
dormitory = *dirty room*
dynamite = *may end it*
evil = *vile*
insurgent = *unresting*

megalomania = *a main goal: me*
prosecutors = *court posers*
rescues = *secures*
ridiculous = *I? ludicrous!*
a shoplifter = *has to pilfer*
statement = *testament*
upholsterers = *restore plush*

No wonder that those who believe in the magical potency of words have hailed *the anagram* as *ah, an art gem* and *anagrams* as *ars magna* ("the great art").

(See COMPASS, DANIEL, EPISCOPAL, ESTONIA, SET, SILENT, SPARE, STAR, STOP, TIME, WASHINGTON, WILLIAM SHAKESPEARE.)

Anger, please remember, is only a single letter away from *danger.* That's why *angered* and *enraged* are anagrams of each other.

Anger kicks off the most pyrotechnic reverse bilingual palindrome ever concocted. Back in March 1886, there appeared in *Our Young Folks* magazine a magical, mesmerizing, miraculous Latin-English pairing, created by James C. P., that reads forward in English and backward in Latin. The two statements make sense in both directions and retain the same meaning in each language:

Anger? 'Tis safe. Never bar it. Use love! *Evoles ut ira breve neaps sit; regna!*

Danger is one of the most anagrammable words in the English language, as witness this little verse:

> *Ranged* in the *Garden* of *Danger*,
> A *serpent* at *present repents.*
> *Enter asp,* in slithers *a serpent.*
> Take a *gander.* Stay outside the fence.

Anthology. I am button-burstingly proud of a book of mine titled *Word Wizard* because it is an anthology of my best and most popular work and thus represents the arc of my writing career. The Greek forebear is *anthologia: ánthos* (ἄνθος), "flower" + *légein* (λέγω), "gather" = "a gathering or collection of flowers." I am so pleased to have grown enough literary blossoms that I could arrange them into a bouquet.

Our English language is made more exquisite and colorful by an anthology of flowery words:

- In Greek mythology, the blessed spent their afterlife in the Elysian fields, which were carpeted with a flower the Greeks named *asphódelos* (ἀσφόδελος). Over time the word acquired an initial *d* and eventually became *daffodil.* That's fortunate because we now have the best of all flower palindromes: *lid off a daffodil.*

- Also from ancient mythology we inherit *narcissus,* a handsome and usually white or yellow flower. The name echoes the myth of the handsome Narcissus and the doomed Echo, which you can read about in the entry for ECHO, below.

- The unusual double bulbs of the orchid bear an uncanny resemblance to male gonads. That's why the beautiful and expensive flower receives its name from the Greek word for "testicle," *órkhis* (ὄρχις). More than two thousand years ago, Pliny the Elder observed, "Mirabilis est órkhis herba, sive serapias, gemina radice, testiculis simili." Even if you don't know Latin, I'm confident that you can deduce the meaning of the first and last parts of that statement. Pliny believed that just holding an orchid in one's hand would expand sexual desire.

- Of the various plants associated with the Christmas season, the *poinsettia* possesses the most intriguing history etymologically. A Mexican legend tells of a penniless boy who presented to the Christ child a beautiful plant with scarlet leaves that resembled the Star of Bethlehem. The Mexicans named the plant *Flor de la*

Noche Buena ("Flower of the Holy Night"). Dr. Joel Roberts Poinsett, the first U.S. minister to Mexico, discovered the Christmas flower there in 1828 and brought it to this country, where it was named in his honor in 1836. The flaming poinsettia has become one of the most popular of Christmas plants—and one of the most misspelled and mispronounced words (*pointsettia, pointsetta, poinsetta*) in the English language.

- When we call someone *precocious,* we are complimenting a talent of theirs that they evince at an early age. *Precocious* literally means "cooked too early," from the Latin *prae-,* "before," and *coquere,* "to cook." The word was first used in English to describe plants that blossomed or produced fruit prematurely.

- The *tulip*'s cup-shaped "mouth" may remind you of "two lips," but that is not how the flower got its name. The Dutch borrowed *tulip* from the French (*tulipan*), who purloined it from the Turks (*tulbend*), who noted that the shape of the flower reminded them of a turban.

(See DANDELION, PHILODENDRON.)

Archetypical is the longest word with the most letters in alphabetical place. In *archetypical*, the letters *a, c, e, i,* and *l* occur as the first, third, fifth, ninth, and twelfth letters, just as they do in their foreordained alphabetic slots.

Arf. Lassie, Rin Tin Tin, and Snoopy bark *Arf!*, *Bow-wow!*, and *Woof!* but they do that only if they are English-barking dogs. The rest of the world, it appears, doesn't hear ear-to-ear with us:

- Brazilian   *au-au!*
- Chinese   *wang-wang!*
- French   *gnaf-gnaf!*
- German   *wau-wau!*
- Hebrew   *hav-hav!*
- Japanese   *wan-wan!*
- Russian   *gav-gav!*
- Swahili   *hu-hu-hu-huuu!*
- Swedish   *voff-voff!*

And fifty million Italians are convinced their dogs bark like Bing Crosby—*Boo-boo!*

Arm is one of more-than-you-might-guess body parts spelled with just three letters. Lend your ear to and cast your eye on *ear, eye, gum, hip, jaw, leg, lip, rib, toe,* and (more marginally) *fat, gut, lid,* and a plural, *ova.* Then there's *lap,* which disappears every time you stand up.

(See ELBOW, EYE.)

Ashtray. What do some folks empty into their trash? Their *ashtray,* which turns out to be pig latin for *trash.*

Other pig latin favorites of mine:

beast/East Bay   *devil/evil day*   *lover/overlay*   *true/outré*

Asinine. The meaning "stupid, silly" flows from an earlier meaning, "like an ass, donkey, or mule." You know that something catlike is *feline* and something doglike *canine.* Here are a dozen more animal adjectives to up the level of your semantic sophistication:

ape - *simian*	bull - *taurine*	fish - *piscine*	lion - *leonine*
bear - *ursine*	cow - *bovine*	fox - *vulpine*	pig - *porcine*
bee - *apian*	deer - *cervine*	horse - *equine*	sheep - *ovine*
bird - *avian*	eagle - *aquiline*	lamb - *ovine*	wolf - *lupine*

(See CONGRESS.)

Assassin descends from the Arabic *hashshashin,* literally "hashish eaters." The original hashshashin were members of a religious and military order located in the mountains of Lebanon. These fanatics would commit political murder after being intoxicated with great quantities of hashish.

Atone. The literal meaning of *atone* issues from what the word actually looks like—to be "at one," that is, united with God.

(See DAREDEVIL.)

@. Used for centuries in the sense of "each at the price of," the now-ubiquitous @, or *at-sign,* has recently taken on the locative sense of "at," especially in e-mail addresses. The @ predates the dawn of e-mail, by almost five hundred years, on Florentine trade documents dating back as far as 1536.

Informally and playfully, @ has taken on various names in other languages:

- Chinese   *little mouse*
- Danish   *a trunk*
- Dutch   *little monkey tail*
- Finnish   *meow meow*
- German   *cinnamon cake*
- Greek   *little duck*
- Hebrew   *elephant's ear, strudel*
- Hungarian   *worm*
- Korean   *sea snail*
- Russian   *dog*

Awful is one of a host of words whose noble meanings have degraded over time. In the year 1666 a great fire swept through London and destroyed more than half the city, including three-quarters of St. Paul's Cathedral. Sir Christopher Wren, the original designer of the cathedral and perhaps the finest architect of all time, was commissioned to rebuild the great edifice. He began in 1675 and finished in 1710—a remarkably short time for such a task. When the magnificent edifice was completed, Queen Anne, the reigning monarch, visited the cathedral and told Wren that his work was "awful, artificial, and amusing." Sir Christopher, so the story goes, was delighted with the royal compliment, because in those days *awful* meant "full of awe, awe-inspiring," *artificial* meant "artistic," and *amusing*, from the Muses, meant "amazing."

(See REEK.)

Aye can be anagrammatically looped into its own synonym, *yea.* These two English words share no letters with their French cousin *oui,* yet together they encompass the six most common vowels.

(See MANATEE.)

Balderdash reaches back to the time of William Shakespeare and originally meant "a hodge-podge of liquids," such as milk mixed with beer, beer with wine, and brandy with mineral water. Gradually, *balderdash* came to stand for "pretentious, bombastic, and senseless prose."

And, of course, *balderdash* can also mean "a rapidly receding hairline."

Words that describe words that befuddle and obfuscate possess some of the most fascinating etymologies in the English language:

- *gibberish.* In *Julius Caesar* (1604), Shakespeare wrote, "The graves stood tenantless and the sheeted dead / Did squeak and gibber in the Roman streets." As the sound of "gibber" indicates, the verb means "to utter incomprehensible prattle." From *to gibber* we get the verb *to jabber* (whence Lewis Carroll's "Jabberwocky") and the noun *gibberish.*

- *Double Dutch* is a Briticism that denotes a meaningless jumble of sounds. We say, "It's Greek to me," but the English loved to pick on the Dutch with such expressions as "Dutch treat" (no treat at all), "Dutch courage" (alcohol), and "in Dutch" (in trouble). From the Dutch *pappekak* we also get *poppycock*, literally "soft poop," or "baby poop."

- *Flapdoodle* is an American southernism. When you cook and then remove a bunch of pancakes ("flaps") from a cast-iron skillet that has not been properly seasoned, the designs ("doodles") are left at the bottom of the pan. Thus the complaint from Confederate troops: "If it wasn't for those damn Yankees making such a flapdoodle out of nothing, we'd be eating honey and homemade biscuits right now."

Let's shine the spotlight on three rhyming reduplications that signify meaningless prattle:

- *folderol*. Picture a medieval minstrel singing a ballad. He makes it up as he goes along, but every now and then his inspiration fails him. Rather than commit the faux pas of silence, he sings something like "fol-de-rol," the medieval equivalent of "la-la-la." In the late seventeenth century *folderol*, a nonsense word, came to mean "nonsense words."

- *Mumbo jumbo* was originally a word in Mandingo that denoted a magician who made the troubled spirits of ancestors go away.

- *Hocus-pocus* is said to issue from the Latin *hoc est corpus meum*—"this is my body"—from the Roman Catholic mass. From *hocus* has issued the words *hoax*, "a mischievous trick," and *hokum*, "nonsense."

In truth, one could compile an entire book of "stuff and nonsense" words—*baloney, blarney, bosh, bunk, cockamamie, claptrap, cock-and-bull story, codswallop, doublespeak, fiddle-faddle, flimflam, hogwash, hooey, humbug, malarkey, piffle, twaddle,* and *tommyrot*. That so many people have been able to come up with so many words to identify and describe nonsensical, insincere, and misleading language shows that there is still hope that one day we may create a pollution-free verbal environment.

(See GOBBLEDYGOOK, HORSEFEATHERS, SUPER DUPER.)

Bash. What do these words have in common: *bash, clash, crash, dash, gash, gnash, hash, lash, mash, slash, smash, thrash,* and *trash*?

"The words all rhyme," you answer.

Right. But can you spot what it is that the thirteen words share in their content?

Faces are bashed, gashed, slashed, and smashed. Cars crash. Hopes are dashed. Armies clash. Teeth gnash. Beef is hashed. Potatoes are mashed. Rooms are trashed. And prisoners are lashed and thrashed.

Now the pattern becomes clearer. All these -*ash* words are verbs that express repeated actions of great violence. Why, over the more than the fifteen-hundred-year history of the English language, have speakers seized on the -*ash* sound cluster to create words that describe mutilation?

Listen closely to the *a*, and you will hear that it sounds like a drawn-out human scream. Now listen closely to the hissing sound of *sh*, and note that it too takes a long time to expel. The eighteenth century English poet Alexander Pope once wrote that "The sound must seem an echo of the sense." It appears that the agonizing, hissy, drawn-out sound of -*ash* is particularly well suited to the sense of violent actions that unfold over seconds, minutes, or even longer periods of time.

(See MOTHER, SNEEZE.)

Bated. In the context of "bated breath," *bated* is a form of *abated* and means "reduced in force or intensity, restrained." *Bated* is also a monogamous word, one that can be used with only one other word, in this instance *breath*. You may have heard about the cat who chewed on some strong-smelling cheese, breathed into a mousehole, and waited with baited breath. Under all other circumstances, it's *bated*.

Speaking of mice, it's easy to see why our word *muscle* descends from the Latin word *musculus,* "little mouse." Certain muscles appeared to move beneath surface of the skin like small mice running.

The *baited/bated* confusion illustrates the difficulties that we English speakers can experience with homophones—words that sound alike but have different spellings and meanings. How many times have we read about menus guaranteed to "wet your appetite"? Great expectorations! If writers would bear (not bare) in mind the knife's edge metaphor—the menu is the whetstone upon which the knife's edge of the appetite is sharpened—they would always spell the verb correctly as *whet*.

(See AKIMBO.)

Bathroom. Despite the two halves of this word, most bathrooms don't have any baths in them. In fact, a dog can go to the bathroom under a tree—no bath, no room; but it's still going to the bathroom. And doesn't it seem a little bizarre that we go to the bathroom so that we can go to the bathroom?

Bear/Bull. As descriptions of investors, both terms have been around since the early 1700s. The bear market metaphor seems to have arisen out of a story common to many cultures that tells about a man who sold a bearskin before he caught his bear. On this analogy, certain speculators in London's Exchange, the Wall Street of its day, became known as bearskin jobbers. These financial dice rollers gambled on a falling market, selling stock they didn't own in the hope that it would drop in value, before they had to deliver it to the purchaser.

The bestial analogy in a bull market is to the habit aggressive bulls have of pushing forward and tossing their heads upward, an apt emblem for a market characterized by investors who believe that stock prices will go up.

Bible. The word *bible* derives from the Greek *biblía* (βιβλία), which means "books." Indeed, the Bible is a whole library of books that contain many different kinds of literature—history, narrative, short stories, poetry, philosophy, riddles, fables, allegories, letters, and drama.

The thirty-nine books of the Old Testament, the twenty-seven books of the New Testament compose the champion bestseller of all time. Translated into more than two thousand languages, the Bible is available to about 80 percent of the world's people and outsells all other popular books. Each year in the United States alone, approximately 44 million copies are sold and 91 million distributed.

While the spiritual values of the Bible are almost universally recognized, the enduring effect of the Bible on the English language is often overlooked. In truth, a great number of biblical words, references, and expressions have become part of our everyday speech, so that even people who don't read the Bible carry its text on their tongues.

Here's a sampling of biblically inspired words:

- *talent.* In ancient times, a talent was a unit of weight, and this weight of silver or gold constituted a monetary unit, one that figures prominently in a famous parable of Jesus: "For the kingdom of heaven is as a man travelling into a far country, who called his own servants, and delivered unto them his goods. And unto one he gave five talents, to another two, and to another one; to every man according to his several ability" (Matthew 25:14–15).

  The most common modern meaning of the word *talent*—some special, often God-given ability or aptitude—is a figurative extension of the parable.

  An undeveloped ability is a *latent talent*, a two-word anagram achieved by simply transposing the first and third letters.

- *maudlin.* In Mark 16: 9–10, we read, "Now when Jesus was risen early the first day of the week, he appeared first before Mary Magdalene, out of whom he had cast seven devils. And she went and told them that she had been with him, and they mourned and wept." Medieval and Renaissance painters portrayed a tearful Mary Magdalene so sentimentally that, over the years, her name was transformed into the word *maudlin*, which now means "tearfully sentimental."

- *shibboleth.* In the Book of Judges 12:5–6, we learn about a conflict between the peoples of Gilead and Ephraim: "And the Gileadites took the passages of Jordan before the Ephraimites; and it was so, that when those Ephraimites which were escaped said, Let me go over; that the men of Gilead said unto him, Art thou an Ephraimite? If he said, Nay; then they said unto him, Say now shibboleth." Because the Ephraimites didn't have the *sh* sound in their language, they could not pronounce the word correctly, and 42,000 of them were slain. That's how the word *shibboleth* has acquired the meaning that it has today: a password, catchword, or slogan that distinguishes one group from the other.

(See CARNIVAL, GOOD-BYE.)

Bikini. Those skimpy two-piece swimsuits for women are named after the Marshall Islands atoll, where the first hydrogen bombs were tested after World War II. Quite possibly the name *bikini* was chosen as a metaphor comparing the explosive effect of the swimsuit on men to the bombs detonated on that Pacific atoll.

(See HAMBURGER, LACONIC, SANDWICH.)

Bildungsroman, stitched together from two roots that mean "education novel," doesn't denote an office complex in Italy but rather "a story in which the main character matures and gains an education." Charles Dickens's *Great Expectations*, Mark Twain's *The Adventures of Huckleberry Finn,* and J. D. Salinger's *The Catcher in the Rye* are prominent examples of the genre.

Blooper first appeared in American English in the mid-1920s as a baseball term describing a wounded fly ball looped just past the reach of the infielders. Just as bloopers in baseball can make fielders look like bumbling clowns, verbal bloopers can mortify those who make them. Almost at the same time, the verb *to bloop* began to signify the operating of a radio set to cause it or other sets to emit howls and whistles, perhaps an echo of our reactions to physical or verbal howlers. About a decade later, the nouns *bloop* and *blooper* came to signify pratfalls of the body and tongue.

Of the thousands of specimens of inspired gibberish that I've captured and put on display, my favorite is this gem that gleamed out from a student essay: "Sir Francis Drake circumcised the world with a one-hundred foot clipper." The statement is hysterically unhistorical, and we have no trouble believing that a student actually wrote it. How blunderful that one young scholar's innocent malapropizing of *circumnavigate* and accidental pun on *clipper* can beget such nautical naughtiness.

The all-time best teacher response to a student blooper happened during the 1960s. A professor received a composition in which one of his students enthusiastically described his adventures in Venezuela, where he had worked the previous summer. One error kept appearing throughout the narrative: the student consistently misspelled the word *burro* as *burrow.*

Seizing the delicious opportunity, the professor wrote at the end of the essay, "I thoroughly enjoyed your enthusiastic narrative about your adventures in Venezuela and your love of its fauna. But it is apparent to me from your spelling that you do not know your ass from a hole in the ground."

(See MALAPROPISM, MONDEGREEN, SPOONERISM.)

Blossom is a seven-letter noun and verb with a double letter in the middle. Pluck that double letter, and you end up with the five-letter word *bloom*, with a different double letter in the middle, but with the same meaning as *blossom*, as a noun and as a verb.

Being a marsupial, a mother kangaroo carries her young in her pouch. Kangaroo words do the same thing: Within their letters they conceal a smaller version of themselves—a "joey," which is what a kangaroo's offspring is called. The joey must be the same part of speech as the mother kangaroo, and its letters must appear in the same order.

The special challenge of kangaroo words is that the joey must be a synonym; it must have the same meaning as the fully grown kangaroo. A *plagiarist* is a kind of *liar*. A *rapscallion* is a *rascal*. On the job, your *supervisor* is your *superior*. And (one of the best pairings) people who are *rambunctious* are also *raucous*.

I've trained as many kangaroo words as I could to hop through this poem:

Ab-Original Words

Hop right up to those kangaroo words,
    Slyly concealing whiz-bangaroo words,
Accurate synonyms, *cute* and *acute,*
    Hidden *diminutive* words, so *minute.*

Lurking inside of *myself* you'll find *me.*
    Just as inside of *himself* you'll find *he.*
Feel your mind *blossom*; feel your mind *bloom*:
    Inside a *catacomb*'s buried a *tomb.*

Kangaroo words are *precocious* and *precious,*
    Flourishing, lush words that truly refresh us.
We're *nourished*; they *nurse, elevate,* and *elate* us.
We're so *satisfied* when their synonyms *sate* us.

Kangaroo words both *astound* us and *stun.*
    They're so darned *secure* that we're *sure* to have fun!
With *charisma* and *charm,* they're a letter-play wonder.
    They *dazzle* and *daze* with their treasures, down under.

(See SYNONYM.)

Bolt. The fastest man in the world at the time this book was published is Usain Bolt. Louis Jean and Auguste Marie Lumière created the first movies that told stories. In French, *Lumière* means "light."

Names such as *Bolt* and *Lumière* that are especially suited to the profession or a characteristic of their owners are called aptronyms. Believe it or not, Daniel Druff is a barber, C. Sharpe Minor a church organist, and James Bugg an exterminator. Some aptronymic personages are famous:

- champion tennis player Margaret Court
- football star Jim Kiick
- baseball stars Early Wynn, Herb Score, Johnny Bench, and Cecil and Prince Fielder
- golf stars Gary Player and Tiger Woods (woods are golf clubs)
- astronaut Sally Ryde
- presidential spokesperson Larry Speakes
- Romantic poet William Wordsworth
- World Series of Poker champions Jamie Gold and Chris Moneymaker
- American judge Learned Hand
- manufacturer of toilets Thomas Crapper
- and (joke alert!) spouse snipper Lorena Bobbitt (Get it? "Bob it").

While we're on the topic of spot-on appropriate surnames, it wasn't that long ago that Steve Jobs, Johnny Cash, and Bob Hope were alive. But now we have no Jobs, no Cash, and no Hope.

Here's a cute game that employs aptronymic first names: these days, we often attend conferences, parties, and other gatherings where we are asked to wear name tags that say, "Hello, I'm _____."

The object of our game is to match a real first name with a real profession to spark a punny connection, as in "My name is Homer, and I'm a baseball player," "My name is Jimmy, and I'm a safecracker," and "My name is Mary, and I'm a justice of the peace."

Even more spectacular are serial puns on names and professions. *Hello, our names are*:

- Alexis, Carmen, Chevy, Jack, Mercedes, Otto, Phillip, and Rusty, and we work on cars.
- Annette, Bob, Brooke, Eddie, Gil, and Tad, and we're fishermen.
- Beech, Sandy, Shelly, and Wade, and we're lifeguards.
- Bill, Buck, and Penny, and we work at the mint.

- Bud, Daisy, Holly, Iris, Lily, Pansy, Petunia, Rose, and Violet, and we sell flowers.
- Case, Courtney, Sue, and Will, and we're lawyers.

Bookkeeper is the only common word that features three consecutive pairs of double letters. It is easy to imagine the bookkeeper's assistant, a *subbookkeeper,* who boasts four consecutive pairs of double letters.

Now let's conjure up a zoologist who helps maintain raccoon habitats. We'd call that zoologist a *raccoon nook keeper*—six consecutive sets of double letters!

Not done: Now let's imagine another zoologist who studies the liquid inside chickadee eggs. We'd call this scientist a *chickadee egg goo-ologist*—and into the world is born three consecutive sets of triple letters!

(See SWEET-TOOTHED.)

Boss. We can thank early Dutch settlers for our word *boss*, which began as *baas*, "master." Noting the English spelling, it's apparent that your *b-o-s-s* is a backward double s.o.b!

(See BRAND, DESSERTS, FILIBUSTER.)

Brand. Brand names spring from the practice of branding animals—and human beings—to indicate ownership. A product that is *brand new* is as fresh as a newly branded calf. A number of trademarked items lend themselves to letter play:

- *Wal-Mart* (retail megastores) spoonerized becomes a *Mall Wart.*
- *Tylenol* (analgesic), *Pepsi* (cola), and *Yamaha* (motorcycles) are among the product names that cry out to be palindromed: *lonely Tylenol, Pepsi is pep,* and *Ah, May, a Yamaha.*
- Reversing another brand name, we wonder are the purveyors of *Evian* bottled water trying to put something over on us? No? Then why is the *Evian* brand name *naive* spelled backwards?
- Even more infelicitous are the reversals of the products *Tums* (antacid tablets), *Dial* (soap), and *Tulsa* (gasoline).
- If you chew a *Tic Tac* (breath mint) switching the two halves of the pellet, that could be a wise social *TacTic.*

- If you tack an *s* onto the end of *Saltines* (crackers), you get *saltiness.*

- *Advil* (analgesic) anagrams into *valid* and *spandex* (stretch fabric) into *expands.*

- *Avis* (car rental) with the first letter looped to the back becomes *Visa* (credit card).

- *Avon* (cosmetics) reversed becomes *Nova* (a car manufactured by Chevrolet).

- *Camry* automobile, yields, with letters in order, *my* and then, from what's left, *car.* The name of the manufacturer of the Camry is Toyota. Capitalized, A TOYOTA is not just a palindrome; every letter therein features left-right symmetry and is itself palindromic. *Civic* automobile is a palindrome composed of Roman numerals.

Here are a dozen more palindromic brand names:

Aviva (insurance)	*Mum* (deodorant)	*S.O.S.* (scouring pads)
Aziza (cosmetics)	*Noxon* (silver polish)	*TNT* (TV channel)
Elle (magazine)	*Pep* (cereal)	*Tat* (insect repellant)
Eve (cigarettes)	*See's* (candies)	*Xanax* (sedative)
(See XEROX.)		

Buffalo. *Buffalo buffalo buffalo Buffalo buffalo* is a possible sentence, and it raises the question why *buffalo* (from a Latin word for "wild oxen") has become a verb denoting "to confuse, baffle, frustrate." The answer is that, despite the slaughter of tens of millions in the United States, the animal is hard to kill individually. Buffalo are swift, tough, and belligerent.

Products made from buffalo were plentiful in the nineteenth century, including strips of buffalo hide that were used to bring metals to a high polish. That's where we get the verb *to buff.* Firemen wore buffalo robes as their winter gear. Dandies who had nothing better to do than to rush to fires and watch the burning, emulated the firefighters by donning the same buffcoats, as they were called. These men became known as buffs, and, by extension, a *buff* is anyone avidly devoted to a pursuit or hobby. And because these buffcoats were the color of human skin, *in the buff* arose as a synonym for "naked."

The vogue meaning of *buff* as "well built, muscular, hunky" also reflects *buffalo,* an image of rugged strength.

Buffalo is one of more than fifty animal names that can function as a verb:

ape	clam (up)	flounder	lion(ize)	rook
badger	cow	(out) fox	louse (up)	skunk
bird	crane	(leap) frog	monkey (with)	snake
bird dog	crow (about)	goose	parrot	snipe (at)
bitch	dog	grouse	pig (out)	sponge
buck	duck	gull	pigeon(hole)	squirrel (away)
bug	eagle	hawk	pony (up)	toady
bull	fawn	hog	quail	weasel (out of)
carp	ferret	horse (around)	ram	wolf
chicken (out)	fish	hound	rat (out)	worm (out of)

(See BUTTERFLY, CANARY, CAPER, CLAM, CRESTFALLEN, DACHS-HUND, DANDELION, HORSEFEATHERS, OSTRACIZE, PARTRIDGE, PEDI-GREE, TAD, TURKEY, VACCINATE, ZYZZYVA.)

Butterfly. Behold the convergence of etymology and entomology. The butterfly may take its name from the medieval belief that these insects stole milk and butter in the dark of night. Or it may be that the creature is simply the color of butter, and it flies.

What we can be sure of is that a butterfly will flutter by—and a dragonfly will drink its flagon dry.

(See BUFFALO, CANARY, CAPER, CLAM, CRESTFALLEN, DACHS-HUND, DANDELION, HORSEFEATHERS, OSTRACIZE, PARTRIDGE, PEDI-GREE, TAD, TURKEY, VACCINATE, ZYZZYVA.)

Cabbage. Lewis Carroll once wrote to a little girl: "With the first seven letters of the alphabet, I can make a word." That word was *big-faced (ABCDEFG* with an *I).* Clever, clever, but *big-faced* has questionable status as a word.

The more familiar *cabbage* is one of a number of seven-letter *piano words*, ones that can be spelled out using the musical notes ABCDEFG. Other seven-letter examples are *acceded, baggage, defaced,* and *effaced.* The ten-letter *cabbage-bed,* listed in at least one dictionary, is a tempting possibility.

Cabbage-headed (thirteen letters), meaning "stupid," has been suggested as the longest recognizable word cobbled entirely from letters in the first half of the alphabet. Other candidates include the reduplications *diddle-daddled* and *fiddle-faddled.*

Boldface and *feedback* are the shortest words (eight letters) that contain each of the first six letters of our alphabet.

Finally, note that cabbage is one of a number of slangy culinary metaphors for money: *beans, bread, cabbage, candy, chicken feed, clams, dough, gravy, kale, lettuce, peanuts, spinach,* and *sugar.*

(See COCKAMAMIE, METAPHOR, NONSUPPORTS.)

Cakewalk. The cakewalk was originally a nineteenth-century dance invented by African-Americans in the antebellum South. It was intended to satirize the stiff ballroom promenades of white plantation owners, who favored the rigidly formal dances of European high society.

Cakewalking slaves lampooned these stuffy moves by accentuating their high kicks, bows, and imaginary hat doffings, mixing the cartoonish gestures together with traditional African steps. Likely unaware of the dance's derisive roots, the whites often invited their slaves to participate in Sunday contests, to determine which dancers were most elegant and inventive. The winners would receive *a piece of cake*, a prize that became the dance's familiar name. Doesn't that just *take the cake*?

After Emancipation, the contest tradition continued in black communities; the *Oxford English Dictionary* dates the widespread adoption of *cakewalk* to the late 1870s. It was around this time that the *cakewalk* came to mean "easy"—not because the dance was particularly simple to do but because of its languid pace and association with weekend leisure.

(See COMPANION, COUCH POTATO, DACHSHUND, HAMBURGER, PUMPERNICKEL, SALARY, TOAST.)

Caliber. At the end of the nineteenth century, a crisis occurred in the Barnum and Bailey Circus. The man who was shot out of the cannon every day was asked by his wife to quit his high-risk profession, much to the distress of the great Phineas Taylor Barnum. PT, whose wit was equal to his showmanship, summoned the fellow and said, "I beg you to reconsider. Men of your caliber are hard to find."

Barnum, of course, was perpetrating a playful pun on the word *caliber*, which, from its earliest beginnings, meant "the diameter of a bullet or other projectile."

Our high-caliber English language is going great guns, so let's go gunning for the guns and cannons that stand ready to fire when we speak and write:

- *bite the bullet.* Visit a Revolutionary War battle site such as Fort Ticonderoga, and you may see some gruesome artifacts in its museum—bullets with teeth marks in them. Possessing no real anesthesia to ease the agony of amputation, long-ago surgeons offered wounded soldiers the only pain reducer they could—a bullet to bite hard on. Just thinking about such trauma is enough to make one *sweat bullets*. After anesthesia was introduced in the United States in 1844, the expression came figuratively to mean "to deal with a stressful situation resolutely," as in Rudyard Kipling's lines:

> Bite the bullet, old man
> And don't let them think you're afraid.

- *a flash in the pan*. This phrase sounds as if it derives from the way prospectors pan rivers for gold. In truth, though, *a flash in the pan* refers to the occasional misfiring of the old flintlock muskets when the flash of the primer in the pan of the rifle failed to ignite the explosion of the charge. It is estimated that such misfirings ran as high as 15 percent, leading *a flash in the pan* coming to mean "an intense but short-lived success or a person who fails to live up to his or her early promise."

- *go off half-cocked*. Muzzle loaders, then as now, had a half cock, or safety position, for a gun's hammer that back-locked the trigger mechanism so that the weapon couldn't be fired. The half-cock position doesn't generate enough power to make sparks to fire the pistol, so when a person *goes off half-cocked* (or *at half cock*), he or she is not in control of the situation.

- *skinflint*. In many parts of early America, necessities such as flint were scarce. When one side of a flint used in a flintlock weapon had worn away, it lost proper contact with the frizzen and caused inadequate sparking to set off the powder charge. Faced with this problem, some gun owners would skin, or sharpen, the flint with a knife, creating a bevel in the flint, which could then make full contact and generate an adequate shower of sparks. A fellow who *skinned his flint* was looked upon as being a parsimonious, penny-pinching, frugal, stingy cheapskate—a veritable *skinflint*.

- *ramrod*. A ramrod is a long piece of metal or wood that rams the ball and patch down the barrel of a muzzle-loading firearm and sets them against the main powder charge. Eventually, *ramrod* took on the added meaning "a person marked by rigidity, stiffness, and severity."

- *snapshot*. Shutterbugs have long been partial to gun terminology, seeing parallels between shooting with a camera and shooting with a gun. *Snapshot* is borrowed from hunting—a shot fired quickly without deliberate aim.

- *point blank.* In ballistics, a weapon fired point blank is one whose sites are aimed directly at a target so that the projectile speeds to its destination in a flat trajectory. By extension, a point-blank question or accusation is one that is direct, blunt, and straight to the mark.

- The opposite of *point blank* is *hanging fire*, which means "undecided, up in the air, delayed." In munitions, *hanging fire* describes a delay in the explosion or discharge of a firearm.

- *to stick to one's guns.* When we stick to our guns, we "hold firmly to our position." To stand and continue firing cannon when under heavy attack on the battlefield took courage because artillerymen usually lacked infantry weapons. But when a cannoneer broke and ran, the enemy could turn the guns to their own use. Thus, many a soldier was actually chained to his gun to ensure bravery.

- *loose cannon.* Muzzle-loading cannons on old-time warships were mounted on a wheeled carriage so that they could be hauled outboard for firing. Now imagine a warship rolling and pitching in a violent storm. The cannon breaks loose from its lashings and becomes a ton or more of metal on wheels careering unpredictably about the deck—maiming or killing any sailors unfortunate enough to get in the way and perhaps smashing through the ship's side. Human *loose cannons* are dangerous in the same way to their associates and bystanders. If unrestrained, such unpredictable people can sink the entire ship.

I've just shot my bolt on the subject of guns and cannons in our everyday parlance—lock, stock, and barrel. Please don't label me a trigger-happy son of a gun if I shoot you one last pistol-packing explanation.

The lock, stock, and barrel are the three main components of a gun that together compose essentially the entire weapon. Thus, *lock, stock, and barrel* has come to mean the entirety of something—the whole shooting match.

(See FIRED, METAPHOR.)

Canary. From what creature did the Canary Islands derive their name? Dogs, of course. The Canary Islands were so dubbed after the large dogs (*canes grandes*) found there. The familiar yellow songbirds, also native creatures thereabout, were named after the islands, rather than the other way around.

(See BUFFALO, BUTTERFLY, CAPER, CLAM, CRESTFALLEN, DACHS-
HUND, DANDELION, HORSEFEATHERS, OSTRACIZE, PARTRIDGE, PEDI-
GREE, TAD, TURKEY, VACCINATE, ZYZZYVA.)

Candidate. When he went to the Forum in Roman times, a candidate
for office wore a bleached white toga to symbolize his humility, purity of motive, and candor. The original Latin root, *candidatus*, meant
"one who wears white," from the belief that white was the color of
purity and probity. There was wishful thinking even in ancient Roman politics, even though a white-clad Roman *candidatus* was ac-
companied by *sectatores*, followers who helped him acquire votes by
bargaining and bribery. The Latin parent verb *candere*, "to shine, to
glow," can be recognized in the English words *candid, candor, candle,*
and *incandescent.*

We know that candidates are ambitious; it's also worth knowing
that *ambition* developed from the Latin *ambitionem*, "a going about,"
from the going about of candidates for office in ancient Rome.

(See FILIBUSTER, GERRYMANDER, IDIOT, OSTRACIZE, POLITICS.)

Caper. When someone is *capricious* and *capers* about, he or she is
acting like a frisky, playful billy goat. *Caprice, capricious, caper,* and
Capricorn all come to us from the Latin *caper,* "goat." Goats caper
through our English vocabulary:

- A *goatee* is trimmed chin beard that resembles the tufts of hair on
  a goat's chin. Perhaps the most famous goatee adorns the chin of
  Uncle Sam.

- A *cabriolet*, originally was a light, two-wheeled vehicle drawn
  by one horse. The jaunty motion of the small carriage reminded
  some of the frisky leaps of a goat. Hence, *cabriole,* ultimately
  shortened to *cab.*

- And goats caper in one very common expression in American
  English. High-strung race horses are sometimes given goats as
  stablemates to calm them, and the two animals can become insep-
  arable companions. Certain gamblers have been known to steal
  the goat attached to a particular horse that they wanted to run
  poorly the next day. By extension, when we *get someone's goat*, we
  upset that person and throw off his or her performance.

(See BUFFALO, BUTTERFLY, CANARY, CLAM, CRESTFALLEN, DACHS-
HUND, DANDELION, HORSEFEATHERS, OSTRACIZE, PARTRIDGE, PEDI-
GREE, TAD, TURKEY, VACCINATE, ZYZZYVA.)

Carnival. We think of carnivals as traveling entertainments with rides, sideshows, games, cotton candy, and balloons; but the first carnivals were pre-Lenten celebrations—a last fling before penitence. The Latin word parts, *carne*, "meat, flesh," and *vale*, "farewell," indicate that the earliest carnivals were seasons of feasting and merrymaking, "a farewell to meat," just before Lent.

Carnival is one of hundreds of words and expressions that began in religion (from Latin *religionem*, "respect for what is sacred"). Because our society has become secularized, we overlook the religious foundation of our everyday parlance:

- *bonfire.* Originally the bone fires that consumed the bodies of saints burned during the English Reformation.

- *enthusiastic.* From the Greek *enthousiasmós* (ἐνθουσιασμός), "a god within," first meant "filled with God," as did *giddy*, from Anglo Saxon *gydig*, "god-held man."

- *excruciating.* The Latin word for "cross," *crux*, is embedded in the words *crux, crucial,* and *excruciating*, which has broadened from denoting the agony of the crucifixion to any kind of torturous pain.

- *fan.* A clipping of *fanatic*, "inspired by the temple." The opposite, *profane*, describes a person who is irreverent and sacrilegious, from the Latin *pro*, "outside," and *fanum*, "the temple."

- *holiday.* Originally a "holy day," descending from the Old English *haligdaeg*. With the change in pronunciation has come a change in meaning so that holidays, such as Independence Day and Labor Day, are not necessarily holy.

- *red-letter day.* So called because of the practice of calendar and almanac publishers of printing the numbers of saints' days and religious feast days in red ink. Such days now describe any distinctive day in a person's life, such as birthdays, graduation days, and the day the local sports team wins the championship.

- *short shrift.* In bygone days, political offenders, military captives, and heretics were executed almost out of hand. There was but a thin pretense of justice in which the prisoner could confess (*shrive*) his sins to a priest and prepare his soul for death. Those who kept these unfortunate souls in thrall often allotted but a short time for confession, and this hurried procedure became known as *short shrift*. Nowadays, this compound means "to give scant attention, to make quick work of."

(See BIBLE, GOOD-BYE.)

Casino. Start with the *i* in the middle and move left. When you get to the *c*, loop to the back and proceed left for two letters. You'll come up with *is a con.* Hmm.

Catch-22. The working title for the late Joseph Heller's modern classic novel about the mindlessness of war was *Catch-18*, a reference to a military regulation that keeps the pilots in the story flying one suicidal mission after another. The only way to be excused from flying such missions is to be declared insane, but asking to be excused is proof of a rational mind and bars excuse.

Shortly before the appearance of Heller's book in 1961, Leon Uris's *Mila 18* was published. To avoid confusion with the title of Uris's war novel, Heller and his editor decided to change *Catch-18* to *Catch-22*. The choice turned out to be both fortunate and fortuitous as the *22* more rhythmically and symbolically captures the double duplicity of both the military regulation itself and the bizarre world that Heller shapes in the novel. ("That's some catch, that Catch-22," observes Yossarian. "It's the best there is," Doc Daneeka agrees.)

During the more-than-five decades since its literary birth, *catch-22*, generally lower-cased, has come to mean any predicament in which we are caught coming and going and in which the very nature of the problem denies and defies its solution. So succinctly does *catch-22* embody the push-me-pull-you absurdity of modern life that the word has become the most frequently employed and deeply embedded allusion from all of American literature.

Here's a small shelf of words and expressions that started out in twentieth-century literature:

- "So it goes."—Kurt Vonnegut, *Slaughterhouse Five*
- "Not with a bang, but a whimper."—T. S. Eliot, "The Hollow Men"
- "Big Brother is watching you."—George Orwell, *Nineteen Eighty-Four*
- "the perfect storm"—Sebastian Junger, *The Perfect Storm*
- "I have promises to keep."—Robert Frost, "The Road Not Taken"
- "Do not go gentle into that good night."—Dylan Thomas, "Do Not Go Gentle Into That Good Night"

(See CHARACTONYM, CHORTLE, DOGHOUSE, NERD, OZ, PANDE-MONIUM.)

Catchphrase is the most frequently used English word containing six consonants in a row, an internal pattern that also marks *borschts, latchstring, watchspring, weltschmerz,* and *Knightsbridge,* a district in London.

(See CHRISTCHURCH.)

Charactonym. The name of a literary character that is especially suited to his or her personality. The enormous and enduring popularity of Charles Dickens's works springs in part from the writer's skill at creating memorable charactonyms—Scrooge, the tightfisted miser; Mr. Gradgrind, the tyrannical schoolmaster; Jaggers, the rough-edged lawyer; and Miss Havisham ("have a sham"), the jilted spinster who lives in an illusion. John Bunyan's Mr. Wordly Wiseman, Susanna Centlivre's Simon Pure, and Walter Scott's Dr. Dryasdust are other famous fictional charactonyms.

Modern examples include Willie Loman ("low man") in Arthur Miller's *Death of a Salesman* and Jim Trueblood in Ralph Ellison's *Invisible Man.* Not that many years ago, a doctor show named "Marcus Welby" ruled the television ratings. The title of the show and name of the lead character were purposely designed to make us think of "make us well be."

(See CATCH-22, CHORTLE, DOGHOUSE, NERD, OZ, PANDEMONIUM.)

Chargoggagoggmanchauggagoggchaubunagungamaugg is the Algonquian name for a lake near Webster, Massachusetts. The word means "You fish on your side; I fish on my side; nobody fish in the middle." Fifteen of its forty-five letters are *g*'s, and not one is an *e* or *i.*

(See FLOCCINAUCINIHILIPILIFICATION, HIPPOPOTOMONSTROSES-QUIPEDALIAN, HONORIFICABILITUDINITATIBUS, LLANFAIRPWLL-GWYNGYLLGOGERYCHWYRNDDROBWLLLLANTYSILOGOGOCH, PNEUMONOULTRAMICROSCOPICSILICOVOLCANOKONIOSIS, SUPER-CALIFRAGILISTICEXPIALIDOCIOUS.)

Chiasmus. "Success is getting what you want; happiness us wanting what you get." That's not only a profound statement and a common-sense truth. It's also an example of chiasmus—a reversal in the order of words in two otherwise parallel phrases in order to produce a rhetorical or humorous effect. The *chi* in *chiasmus* stands for the letter *X* in the Greek alphabet, and the word comes from the Greek *khiasmós* (χιασμός), meaning "crossing; to mark with a *X*." In most chiastic statements, if you stack the first clause on the second and then draw straight lines from the key words in the first to the second, you will draw an *X*. Try it with a chiastic quotation like "When the going gets tough, the tough get going."

Chiasmi (the formal plural form) show up in some of the most clever, thought-provoking, and memorable pronouncements in history:

- "One should eat to live, not live to eat."—Cicero
- "If guns are outlawed, only outlaws will have guns."—unofficial slogan of the NRA
- "Ask not what your country can do for you; ask what you can do for your country."—John F. Kennedy

Quotations like these have been used for centuries by the world's greatest thinkers, leaders, and entertainers—from Aristotle ("We should behave to our friends as we would wish our friends to behave to us") to Shakespeare ("Fair is foul, and foul is fair") to Mae West ("It's not the men in my life that count; it's the life in my men"). From ancient Sanskrit to this very moment, chiasmi have been employed to inspire, insult, seduce, teach, and provoke.

And above all, please remember: it's better to leave the house and kiss your wife good-bye than to leave your wife and kiss the house good-bye.

(See HYSTERON PROTERON, IRONY, METAPHOR, METONYMY, OXY-MORON, PARADOX, ZEUGMA.)

Chocoholic. From the Arabic word *al-koh'l* and the Latin ending *–ic* we cheerfully sever *-aholic* and create a spanking new suffix that means "one addicted to." Among the *-aholic* clones recorded by linguistic observers we find *workaholic, chocoholic, Cokeaholic, newsaholic, wordaholic, sexaholic, shopaholic*, and *spendaholic*. Perhaps we shall one day see and hear *aholaholic* to describe someone who succumbs to the irresistible impulse to use the suffix *-aholic* to describe irresistible impulses.

(See HAMBURGER.)

Chortle. Lewis Carroll made his stories a wonderland of wordplay. The verbivorous author of *Alice in Wonderland* and *Through the Looking-Glass,* Carroll evinced a prodigious talent for merging two words and beheading parts of one or both. He called these inventions portmanteau words because he loved to scrunch two words into one as clothes are crammed into a portmanteau, or traveling bag. The most famous example of Lewis Carroll's facile gift for blending is his "Jabberwocky" poem, which begins:

> 'Twas brillig, and the slithy toves
> Did gyre and gimble in the wabe;
> All mimsy were the borogoves,
> And the mome raths outgrabe.

When Alice asks Humpty Dumpty to explain the word *slithy,* he answers: "Well *slithy* means 'lithe and slimy.' You see, it's like a portmanteau—there are two meanings packed into one word." Dumpty later interprets *mimsy*: "Well, then, *mimsy* is 'flimsy and miserable' (there's another portmanteau for you)." Two words that appear later in "Jabberwocky" have become enshrined in dictionaries of the English language—*chortle* ("chuckle" + "snort") and *galumph* ("gallop" + "triumph"). When we today eat *Frogurt*, quaff *Cranapple* juice and *Fruitopia*, have *brunch* ("breakfast" + "lunch"), take a *staycation* ("stay" + "vacation") rather than stay at a *motel* ("motor" + "hotel"), ride our *moped* ("motor" + "pedal"), lament the *smog* ("smoke" + "fog"), learn from *webinars* ("web" + "seminars"), play the game of *Fictionary* ("fiction" + "dictionary"), and save with *groupons* ("group" + "coupons"), we are sharing Lewis Carroll's *ginormous* ("giant" + "enormous") delight in portmanteau words.

(See CATCH-22, CHARACTONYM, DOGHOUSE, NERD, OZ, PANDEMONIUM.)

Christchurch, the most British city in New Zealand, contains ten consonants (clustered 3-4-3) and only two vowels, an astonishing 5-1 ratio. Note the three occurrences of *ch.*

(See CATCHPHRASE.)

Chthonic ("relating to the spirits of the underworld") is among the handful of tongue-tangling, ear-rinsing words that begin with four consonants, joined by *phthisis* ("tuberculosis") and *pschent* ("an Egyptian double crown").

Quatri-consonantial words that begin with the letter *s* are usually of German or Yiddish origin and begin with *sch*—*schlemiel, schlep, schlimazel, schlock, schlump, schmaltz, schmatte, schmear, schmo, schmooze, schmuck, schmutz, schnapps, schnauzer, schnitzel, schtick, schtupp,* and *schwa.*

Circus. When you speak a *three-ring circus*, you are actually repeating yourself because *circus* echoes *kírkos* (κίρκος), the Greek word for "ring, circle."

"Hey, First-of-May! Tell the butcher in the back yard to stay away from the bulls, humps, stripes, and painted ponies. We have some cherry pie for him before doors and spec." Sound like doubletalk? Actually, it's circus talk—or, more technically, circus argot, argot being a specialized vocabulary used by a particular group for mutual bonding and private communication. Communities are most likely to develop a colorful argot when they have limited contact with the world outside of their group. The circus community is a perfect example of the almost monastic self-containment in which argot flourishes. Big top people travel in very close quarters, and because they usually go into a town, set up, do a show, tear down, and leave, they have little contact with the locals. They socialize with each other, they intermarry, and their children acquire the argot from the time they start to talk.

First-of-May designates anyone who is brand-new to circus work. That's because circuses used to start their tours around the first day in May. A *candy butcher* is a concessionaire who sells cotton candy (*floss*) and other food, along with drinks and souvenirs, to the audience during the show. The *backyard* is the place just behind the circus entrance where performers wait to do their acts. A *bull* is a circus elephant, even though most of them are female. Among other circus beasts, *humps, stripes,* and *painted ponies* are, respectively, camels, tigers, and zebras. *Cherry pie* is extra work, probably from *chairy pie,* the setting up of extra chairs around the arena. *Doors!* is the cry that tells circus folk that the audience is coming in to take their seats, and *spec* is short for *spectacle,* the big parade of all the performers.

Trust me: This topic ain't no *dog and pony show*—the designation for a small circus with just a few acts, also known as a *mud show.*

What we call the toilet circus folk call the *donniker,* the hot dog or grill concession trailer where the circus can snag a snack is a *grease joint,* and a circus performer is a *kinker.* The townspeople are *towners* or *rubes.* In the old days, when large groups of towners who believed (sometimes accurately) that they had been fleeced by dishonest circus people, they would come back in a mob to seek retribution. The cry *Hey rube!* went out, and everyone knew that the fight was on.

A full house is called a *straw house* from the days when straw would be laid down in front of the seats to accommodate more people than the seats could hold. Distances between engagements were called *jumps.* Thus, an old circus toast rings out: "May your lots be grassy, your jumps short, and your houses straw."

> Nothing now to mark the spot
> But a littered vacant lot.
> Sawdust in a heap, and where
> The center ring stood, grass worn bare.
> But remains the alphabet,
> Ready to leap and pirouette.
> May the spangled letters soar
> In your head forevermore.

(See NUT.)

CIVIC. It's not just a palindrome, but, along with *CIVIL, LIVID, MIMIC,* and *VIVID,* the longest word (five letters) composed entirely of Roman numerals. If we assign each letter its Roman numerical value, *mimic* yields the highest total—2,102—and *civil* the lowest—157.

(See ADAM, AGAMEMNON, KINNIKINNIK, NAPOLEON, PALINDROME, SENSUOUSNESS, WONTON, *ZOONOOZ.*)

Clam. Many a word maven has been asked, "In the comparison *happy as a clam,* why are clams so happy?"

To arrive at an answer, one needs to know that the expression is elliptical, that is, something is left out. When we discover the missing part, we unlock the origin and true meaning of the phrase. As it turns out, *happy as a clam* is little more than half of the original saying, the full simile being *happy as a clam at high tide.* A clam at high tide is sensibly happy because, in high water, humans can't capture the shellfish to mince, steam, bake, stuff, casinoed, or Rockefeller it, and high tide brings small yummy organisms to the mollusk.

Similarly, although we usually say, *the proof is in the pudding,* the full explanation is that *the proof of the pudding is in the eating.* And *to harp on*, meaning "to dwell on the same topic," is in fact a shortening of the old phrase *to harp on one string*, which meant "to play the same note on a harp string over and over."

Finally, we may well wonder why people say *naked as a jaybird* when jaybirds are covered with feathers. Here's the first printed citation of *naked as a jaybird*, as it appeared more than a century ago, in 1893: "He will have the humbug qualifications of cow-boy stripped from his poor worthless carcass so quickly that he would feel like a jay bird with his tail feathers gone." Turns out, therefore, that a jaybird is naked only when some of its nether plumage is missing.

(See BUFFALO, BUTTERFLY, CANARY, CAPER, CRESTFALLEN, DACHS-HUND, DANDELION, HORSEFEATHERS, OSTRACIZE, PARTRIDGE, PEDI-GREE, TAD, TURKEY, VACCINATE, ZYZZYVA.)

Cliché comes to us from the Old French *cliquer*, "to click." That's the sound printers used to make when they took a wood engraving and struck it into molten lead to make a cast. This mold was a *stereotype,* from the Greek *stereós* (στερεός), "solid," which was used to reproduce a picture over and over. Hence, the metaphorical stereotype, which forms a fixed, unchangeable image in the mind's eye.

Clichés begin their lives as imaginative expressions and comparisons. That's how they become clichés. Like a phonograph needle, our words settle into the grooves that the clichés have worn into our speech and writing. Phrases that once possessed power become trite, hackneyed, and lifeless—words that themselves are clichés for clichés.

Using clichés is as easy as ABC, one-two- three, pie, falling off a log, shooting fish in a barrel, and taking candy from a baby. They make us happy as a clam, lark, kid in a candy shop, and a pig in ... slop.

But if you want to hit a bull's eye, the spot, the jackpot, the ground running, the ball out of the park, and the nail on the head, then you should avoid clichés like the plague.

(See METAPHOR.)

Clue. In ancient Greek mythology, a dreadful monster called the Minotaur lived in a labyrinth on the island of Crete. Theseus, the founder-king of Athens, volunteered to enter the labyrinth and slay the beast in order to stanch the constant slaughter of Athenian youth fed to the creature. Ariadne, the daughter of the Cretan king, had fallen in love with Theseus and provided him with a *clewe* (Middle English), a ball of thread, that he unwound as he went into the maze. After Theseus decapitated the Minotaur, the thread guided him out of the heart of the maze.

Gradually *clewe*, now *clue*, came to mean anything that helps us to solve a baffling situation, something that leads us from the unknown to the known.

(See ECHO, JOVIAL, TANTALIZE, WEDNESDAY.)

Cockamamie hails from *decalcomania*, the process of making superficial tattoos or affixing decals to windows and walls. Because this practice was seen as fake art, *cockamamie* broadened to describe anything that was phony or worthless.

The odd letters of our alphabet—*ACEGIKMOQSUWY*—include all the major vowels, along with *Y*. I'm not being cockamamie when I say that the longest, unaffixed word that can be strung together from such odd letters is the ten-letter *cockamamie*.

(See BALDERDASH, GOBBLEDYGOOK, METAPHOR.)

Cockney. In the *Oxford Dictionary of Slang,* editors John Simpson and John Ayto identify slang as "English with its sleeves rolled up, its shirttails dangling, and its shoes covered with mud." One of the hardest-working and most earthy of slangs is that of London's East End cockneys.

The word *cockney* originally meant an odd or misshapen egg. Traditionally, a cockney is anyone born within the sound of Bow Bells, the bells of Bow Church, also called St. Mary-le-Bow Church. By Victorian times, the cockney dialect had spread well beyond the tintinnabulation of those bells.

Rhyming slang was first officially recorded in the mid-nineteenth century. In a series of articles published in the *Morning Chronicle* in 1849–50, Henry Mayhew called it "the new style of cadgers' cant, all done on the rhyming principle." Mayhew suggested that cockney slang originated in the language of beggars and thieves and was fabricated to baffle the police.

It is an indirect sort of slang that substitutes a rhyme for the word in mind. Thus, in "Pass the Aristotle," the last word, as you can guess, stands for *bottle*. In "Be sure to get the brass tacks," *tacks* stand for *facts*, leading some word sleuths to deduce cockney as the source of the cliché "Let's get down to brass tacks." "It's all as plain as the I suppose on your boat race"—the nose on your face.

A greater number of such expressions substitute not a word but a phrase.

- "I'm going down the frog and toad"—road.
- "I'm going up the apples and pears"—stairs.
- "'E's gone into the soup and gravy"—Navy.
- "She's gone out for saint and sinner"—dinner.
- "She's at the near 'n' far"—bar.
- "'E's on the off 'n' on"—John.
- "Would ye loik Lilian Gish, Jack the Ripper, or Kate and Sidney for Jim Skinner"—fish, kipper, or steak and kidney for dinner?
- "Do you get it now, me briny marlin'"—darlin'?

The process of substitution does not stop with rhyme. In clipped speech, the actual rhyming word is often omitted. Only the first part of the phrase is spoken, and the rhyme and the word in mind are both assumed. Thus, in "'Ow ye doin', me old china?" "my old china" means "my old friend: china plate"—*mate*. I'll bet you can't hardly Adam it. "Adam and Eve"—*believe*.

Companion originates from the Latin *com*, "together," and *panis,* "bread." You and I are companions in our love of language because together we break the bread of words. That wage earners are called breadwinners reminds us of the importance of bread in medieval life. Not surprisingly, both *lord* and *lady* are well-bread words. *Lord* descends from the Old English *hlaf*, "loaf," and *weard*, "keeper," and *lady* from *hlaf*, "loaf," and *dige*, "kneader."

In days of yore, housewives often needed to scrimp, even on essentials. Whenever wheat was in short supply, the bottom crust of pies was made with rye meal. Wheat was used only for the upper crust. Soon *upper crust* entered everyday speech to mean the socially select.

(See CAKEWALK, COUCH POTATO, DACHSHUND, HAMBURGER, HOAGIE, METAPHOR, PUMPERNICKEL, SALARY, SANDWICH, TOAST.)

Compass. Read this quatrain, and answer the question "What am I?":

> In my front a twisted thorn.
>   On my right a scrambled seat.
> Behind me is a broken shout,
>   And on my left a shattered stew.

The answer is: I am a compass. *Thorn, seat, shout,* and *stew* anagram into *north, east, south,* and *west.*

(See ANAGRAM, DANIEL, EPISCOPAL, ESTONIA, SET, SILENT, SPARE, STAR, STOP, TIME, WASHINGTON, WILLIAM SHAKESPEARE.)

Congress. People love to make fun of members of Congress. Mark Twain sneered, "Suppose you were an idiot. And suppose you were a member of Congress. But I repeat myself." Others have snickered, "If *pro* and *con* are opposites, is *congress* the opposite of *progress*?"

The following anti-congressional item whizzes around the Internet: "Baboons are the noisiest, most obnoxiously aggressive of all primates. So what group noun do we assign to these creatures? A *congress* of baboons!" This claim is bogus. A bunch of baboons is usually a *troop* and occasionally a *rumpus.*

We all know that a bunch of sheep crowded together is a flock, that a group of antelope loping together is a herd, and that a bevy of bees buzzing together is a swarm. But have you ever heard of a *covey* of quail, a *cowardice* of curs, a *labor* of moles, a *cete* of badgers, a *covert* of coots, a *flush* of mallards, a *kindle* of kittens, or a *plump* of wildfowl? Most of these collective nouns evolved during the Middle Ages, when the sophisticated art of hunting demanded an equally sophisticated vocabulary to name the objects of the chase.

Here are some more of the most beguiling of these group nouns:

a *barren* of mules	a *murder* of crows
a *charm* of finches	a *murmuration* of starlings
a *clowder* of cats	an *ostentation* of peacocks
a *convocation* of eagles	a *parliament* of owls
a *crash* of rhinoceroses	a *shrewdness* of apes
an *exaltation* of larks	a *skulk* of foxes
a *gaggle* of geese	a *sounder* of swine
a *leap* of leopards	an *unkindness* of ravens

RICHARD LEDERER

Convict. Have you noticed that a great number of two-syllable words are nouns when their first syllable is stressed and verbs when their second syllable is stressed, as in "If they conVICT me, I'll become a CONvict"? This phenomenon is sometimes known as Phyfe's rule. The person who wrote the following ad apparently had not mastered the subtleties of this pattern: "Unmarried women wanted to pick fruit and produce at night."

Similarly, on the side of my recycling bin is emblazoned:

> City of San Diego
> Environmental Services
> Refuse Collection

What a waste of resources!

Other examples of first-syllable stress = noun; second-syllable stress = verb include:

addict	digest	permit	refund
combat	impact	present	reject
conduct	import	progress	suspect
contract	object	rebel	transfer
decrease	perfume	record	transplant

A few three-syllable examples, such as ATtribute/atTRIbute, DISconnect/disconNECT, and INterrupt/ interRUPT, fill out this category.

Cool. Nobody is quite sure where the word *slang* comes from. According to H. L. Mencken, *slang* developed in the eighteenth century (it was first recorded in 1756) either from an erroneous past tense of *sling* (*sling-slang-slung*) or from the word *language* itself, as in *(thieve)s'lang(uage)* and *(beggar)s'lang(uage)*. The second theory makes the point that jargon and slang originate and are used by a particular trade or class group, but slang words are slung around to some extent by a whole population.

Slang words generally lead mayfly lives—here today, gone tomorrow. Yet *cool*, a slang adjective that means "excellent," has hung around for more than seventy years and shows no sign of retiring. And *cool* remains cool even in the face of competition from more than seventy competitors that stepped up into our slanguage after the birth of *cool*—*ace, awesome, bad, bangin', beast, bitchin', blazin', bomb-ass, chill, chunky, cool beans, copacetic, corny, cretaceous, cruisin', da bomb, def, dope, ducky, endsville, epic, fantabulous, far out, fetch, flipville, fly, fresh, frickin' A, gear, groovy, hip, hot, ice cold, ill, kick-ass, kickin', killer, large, mint, like wow!, nasty, neato, nifty, outasight, peachy keen, phat, pimpin', primo, rad, righteous, sassy, scoopin', sick, sickening, slammin', smokin', smooth, stylin', super, sweet, the max, the most, tite, tops, totally tubular, tuff, uber, unreal, whoa,* and *wicked.*

How cool is that?

Cop. The standard explanation traces *cop* or *copper*, meaning "police," to copper buttons worn on early police uniforms, or to copper police badges supposedly issued in some cities, but there is no convincing evidence for this conjecture.

Another theory explains *cop* as an acronym standing for "constable on patrol" or "chief of police." But these acronymic etymologies almost always turn out to be spurious, after-the-fact explanations. Another inconvenient truth is that acronyms were virtually unknown in English before the twentieth century, while *cop* itself was well-established by the mid-nineteenth century.

In reality, the law enforcement sense of *cop* and *copper* harks back to the Latin word *capere,* meaning "to seize," which also gives us *capture. Cop* as a slang term meaning "to catch, snatch, or grab" took its place in English in the eighteenth century. Criminals apprehended by the police were said to have been "copped"—caught by the "coppers" or "cops."

(See POSH.)

Corpse. Subtract an *e* from *corpse,* a word that ends with a silent letter, and you'll come up with *corps,* a word characterized by two silent letters.

Couch potato compares lumpish watchers of television to lumpy potatoes: The longer couch potatoes sit, the deeper they put down their roots and the more they come to resemble potatoes. But there's more than just a vegetable image here; *couch potato* is a pun on the word *tuber.* A potato is the *tuber* of a plant, and *boob tuber* was an early term for someone watching television, i.e. the *boob tube.*

(See CAKEWALK, COMPANION, COUCH, DACHSHUND, HAMBURGER, PUMPERNICKEL, SALARY, SANDWICH, TOAST.)

Covivant. What do you call the person with whom you are romantically entangled and with whom you are living? *Friend, boyfriend,* and *girlfriend* are too coy and do not identify the live-in arrangement, nor do *lover, mistress,* and *paramour,* even though they are fine, old words. *Cohabitor* is a mouthful that is cold and passionless, while *partner* has recently narrowed to describe only gay couples (and sounds too businesslike to me). *Roommate* and *POSSLQ* ("persons of opposite sex sharing living quarters") identify the joint living arrangement but not the emotional arrangements, while *significant other* suggests a close, caring relationship but not necessarily the cohabitation.

My candidate for the bon mot to catch and crystallize the person living with you in what used to be called "sin" is *covivant.* The word captures and coalesces the intimacy of *lover* and *significant other* and the cohabitational accuracy of *roommate* and *POSSLQ.* Fashioned from the Latin *co,* "together," and the French *vivant,* "living," *covivant* is bilingually endearing. Its Latinness communicates a sense of permanence and stability, and its Frenchness sprays the perfume of romance.

Viva *covivant!*

(See GAY.)

Crestfallen. The sport of cockfighting contributes to the poetry of our everyday prose. From the cockpit (yes, the modern meaning of the word comes from the cramped arena of flying feathers) we gain several common metaphors. A *well-heeled* fighting cock is fitted with sharp spurs on its feet designed to inflict maximum damage. Nowadays, to be *well-heeled* means to be equipped with the most powerful of weapons: money.

A hackle is a long, narrow, shiny feather on the necks of certain birds, gamecocks among them. In the heat of battle, a fighting cock's hackles become erect as a demonstration of its fury. That's why, when the going gets tough, people *get their hackles up.*

If that going gets too tough, people can become crestfallen. *Crestfallen,* meaning "dispirited or defeated," does not refer to the act of dropping one's toothpaste. As victory approaches, the crest of a fighting cock rises, deep red and rigid. But when defeat is imminent, the crest droops, and the bird becomes crestfallen.

(See BUFFALO, BUTTERFLY, CANARY, CAPER, CLAM, DACHSHUND, DANDELION, HORSEFEATHERS, OSTRACIZE, PARTRIDGE, PEDIGREE, TAD, TURKEY, VACCINATE, ZYZZYVA.)

Crossword is the reverse of its original form. The first such puzzle was concocted by one Arthur S. Wynne, a journalist from Liverpool and games section editor of the *New York World.* On December 21, 1913, Wynne's poser appeared in the Sunday edition of the *New York World,* radiating into a diamond and containing no black squares. He modeled the puzzle after the traditional British word square, a group of words whose letters are arranged so they will read the same horizontally and vertically. No surprise, then, that Wynne christened his creation *word-cross.*

Four weeks later, typesetters at the newspaper inadvertently switched the two halves of *word-cross,* and—presto! change-o!—the *crossword* puzzle was born.

Nobody utters a cross word about crossword puzzles. In fact, the genre has gone on to become the most popular word game on earth.

(See SIDEBURNS.)

Dachshund. The dachshund is one of the most popular and beloved breeds of dog in the U. S. of A. Many a caninophile has decided to "get a long little doggie."

The dachshund is also one of the oldest dog breeds in history, dating back to ancient Egypt. The name and the low, sleek body come from one of its earliest uses—flushing badgers and other underground animals from their holes. In German, *Dachs* means "badger" and *Hund* means "hound."

In nineteenth century United States, some folks suspected that sausages were made from dog meat, as evidenced by this popular ditty:

> Oh where, oh where has my little dog gone?
> Oh where, oh where can he be?
> Now sausage is good, baloney, of course.
> Oh where, oh where can he be?
> They make them of dog, they make them of horse.
> I think they made them of he.

When hot sausages in a bun became popular, it was but a short leap to the term *hot dog*. That the sausage looks a little like the body of a dachshund helped *hot dog* to cleave to the American palate.

(See BUFFALO, BUTTERFLY, CANARY, CAPER, CLAM, CRESTFALLEN, DANDELION, HAMBURGER, HORSEFEATHERS, OSTRACIZE, PARTRIDGE, PEDIGREE, TAD, VACCINATE, ZYZZYVA.)

Daffynition. Some waggish genius once defined *hootenanny* as what you get when you cross an owl with a goat, and another verbathlete defined *relief* as "what trees do each spring." Punderful definitions like these take a fresh approach to the sounds and meanings of words. You won't find such entries in dictionaries, only in fictionaries, but they do have a name—*daffynitions*. Here are some of my favorites:

- *alarms.* What an octopus is;
- *apologist.* A short summary of the first moon landing;
- *baloney.* Where some hemlines fall;
- *bigamist.* A fog over Italy;
- *buccaneer.* The cost of a two-dollar pair of earrings;
- *bulldozer.* Somebody who sleeps through political speeches;
- *diploma.* Whom to call when the pipes leak;
- *fungi.* The life of the party;
- *information.* How geese fly;
- *mutilate.* What cats do at night;
- *oboe.* A cockney tramp;
- *pasteurize.* Too far;
- *shampoo.* A fake bear;
- *specimen.* Astronauts;
- *vitamin.* What you do when guests come to your home.

(See PHILODENDRON, PUN, SPOONERISM, SWIFTY.)

Dandelion. The English used to call the yellow, shaggy weed a "lion's tooth" because the jagged, pointed leaves resemble the lion's snarly grin. During the early fourteenth century, the lion's-tooth plant took on a French flavor and became the *dent-de-lion,* "tooth-of-the-lion." Then it acquired an English accent: *dandelion.*

The toothsome *dent* adds bite to our English language in other ways. When we indent a paragraph (from the Latin *dens*, "tooth," by way of the French *dent*), we take a chunk, or small bite, out of the beginning. *Indenture*, from the same root, strictly means "a document with serrated edges," referring to the once-common practice of cutting contracts into halves with jagged edges—one half for each party. By fitting the edges together, one could authenticate the document.

(See ANTHOLOGY, PHILODENDRON.)

Daniel. Often, the more demanding the restrictions, the more fun I have making a poem. I had an exhilarating time writing this little ditty, in which each of the eleven lines is composed of just the six letters in the name *Daniel*:

An idle
Lead-in
Ad line:
DANIEL,
Nailed
In deal
(i.e., land
In dale),
Led in a
Denial
And lie.

(See ANAGRAM, COMPASS, EPISCOPAL, ESTONIA, SET, SILENT, SPARE, STAR, STOP, WASHINGTON, WILLIAM SHAKESPEARE.)

Daredevil *dared evil.* In the game of charades, we act out a big word by dividing it into smaller words. I have just charaded the word *daredevil*. Everybody loves a charade, especially when the cleaving becomes clever (see SCINTILLATING):

- *Alienation* characterizes *a lie nation.*
- *Barflies* live in an atmosphere of *barf, lies.*
- Your adventures in *brokerage* could lead you into a *broke rage.*
- A *caravan* often includes a *car, a van.*
- A *conspiracy* is a *cons' piracy.*
- A *generation* is a *gene ration.*
- Your *identity* is your *i.d. entity.*

- An *island is land.*
- When governments *overtax* us they wield an *overt ax* to chop up our wallets.
- Why is so much of our hard-earned money *theirs*? Because they are *THE IRS*.
- A *soap opera* makes us sigh, *"So, a pop era."*
- Is it *significant* that I don't *sign if I can't*?
- Don't *assume* because it makes an *ass* out of *u* and *me*.
- Carelessly set fires are the forest's *prime evil.*
- And, razzle-dazzlingly: If a boy and a girl are *amiable together*, he may wonder, *"Am I able to get her?"*

Dr. Samuel Johnson, who built the first famously great dictionary of the English language, created a charade in this punderful verse:

> I should be punishéd
> For every pun I shed.
> Please don't leave a puny shred
> Of my punnish head!

(See ALKALINE, MARSHALL, TEMPERAMENTALLY.)

Deadline. Writers, students, workers, and business people constantly face deadlines—dates when manuscripts and homework must be submitted and orders filled. When such deadlines are not met, penalties result, such as lower grades or loss of business. But the punishment for passing beyond the original deadlines were more deadly.

During the American Civil War, a deadline was a line of demarcation around the inner stockade of a prison camp, generally about seventeen feet. At the notorious Confederate camp in Andersonville, Georgia, a line was actually marked out some distance from the outer wire fence. Any prisoner crossing this line was shot on sight.

Writer Douglas Adams quips, "I love deadlines. I like the whooshing sound they make as they fly by."

Deeded is the longest word consisting of two letters each used three times. *Deeded* can be typed with just one finger, along with *ceded, mummy, muumuu,* and *yummy.*

(See INDIVISIBILITY, LOLL, MISSISSIPPI, SLEEVELESSNESS.)

RICHARD LEDERER

Denouement. Playwrights, novelists, and other storytellers involve their characters in a plot in which they become tied in a knot woven from the complicated threads of the storyline. The denouement, from the French *desnouer,* "to untie," is the outcome of the plot complications that have bound the characters.

(See BILDUNGSROMAN, METAPHOR.)

Desserts. The most apt of all reverse palindromic pairs. When you are *stressed,* you should eat *desserts.* In *Roma* you may discover *amor,* but watch out: too much *eros* can make you *sore.*
Other lengthy reversals:

deliver/reviled	diaper/repaid	drawer/reward
stinker/reknits	warder/redraw	

(See BOSS, WONTON.)

Die. The noun *die,* meaning "a cube used for gambling," is the only common English word that forms its plural by adding a consonant in the middle—*dice.*

Dice roll across the table of our language. A *high roller* is a craps player who will roll the dice for big stakes. If that player experiences a lucky streak, he or she will be *on a roll,* meaning "unbeatable with the dice; very successful in one undertaking after another."

Make no bones about it, meaning "direct; uncomplaining," may refer to the behavior of not yakking or complaining about the roll of the dice, or bones, as they are often called. *At sixes and sevens,* "all disorder and confusion," began in the old dice game of hazard, played with two dice, like craps, in which *sinque* and *sice* ("five" and "six") were the most risky bets to make. Anyone who tried to throw these numbers was considered careless and confused. Although the two words meant "five" and "six," they became *sixes and sevens,* a jocular shift to a total of the unlucky thirteen.

(See JACKPOT.)

Disaster. In William Shakespeare's *Julius Caesar,* Cassius warns Brutus that fate lies "not in our stars, but in ourselves." Nevertheless, for centuries, people have believed that the stars and their heavenly positions govern events here on earth. In the ghostly opening scene of *Hamlet,* Horatio speaks of "stars with trains of fire and dews of blood, / Disasters in the sun. . . ."

If a conjunction of the heavenly bodies is not propitious, disaster will strike. Cobbled from the Latin *dis*, "bad, against," and *astrum*, "star," *disaster* literally means "against the stars, ill-starred, star-crossed."

Astrum is a prolific root that gives us *aster* (a star-shaped flower), *astrology* ("star study"), *astronomer* ("star arranger"), *asteroid* ("star form"), and *astronaut* ("star sailor"). Then there's the *asterisk*, the symbol that looks like a "little star." You may wish to dispute my celestial etymologies, but I think you'd be an asterisk it:

- *lunatic.* Luna, the Roman goddess of the moon, is memorialized in *lunatic.* That's because when the moon is full, it is said to render us daft—*moonstruck* or *loony.* Some studies show that more crimes are committed during the full moon than any other lunar phase. Is that because there is more light to perpetrate transgressions, or because our long-ago ancestors were right all along?

- *honeymoon.* We moon around about somebody, we moonlight with a second job that we perform at night, we take a long trip once in a blue moon, and newlyweds go on honeymoons. The ancients customarily drank mead, or honey wine, for the first thirty days of marriage. *Honeymoon* joins together *honey,* used figuratively to mean "love," and *moon* as a synonym for "month." The idea is that the honeymoon is the sweetest month of a marriage, which, like the moon itself, will wane.

- *eccentric.* Derived from Greek *ékkentros* (ἔκκεντρος), "out of the center," from *ek*, "out of" + *kentron*, "center," *eccentric* first appeared in English in 1551 as an astronomical term describing "a circle in which a heavenly body deviates from its center." Modern-day astronomers still use *eccentric* in that way.

- *dog days.* The ancients believed that the influence of the stars generated the dog days, summer periods of triple-*h* weather—hazy, hot, and humid. In the days of the Romans, the six or eight hottest weeks of the summer, roughly July through the first half of August, were known colloquially as *caniculares dies,* or "days of the dog." According to Roman lore, the dog star Sirius rose with and added its heat to the sun, making a hot time of the year even hotter.

(See METAPHOR, STAR.)

Disgruntled. When a pig gets laryngitis, is it then disgruntled?

But seriously . . .

What do you make of the fact that we can talk about certain things and ideas only when they are absent? Once they appear, our blessed English language doesn't allow us to describe them. Have you ever run into someone who was combobulated, sheveled, gruntled, chalant, plussed, ruly, gainly, maculate, kempt, pecunious, peccable, or souciant?

English is a language populated with a lot of heads without tails and odds without ends. Have you ever met a sung hero or experienced requited love? I know people who are no spring chickens, but where, pray tell, are the people who are spring chickens? Where are the people who actually would hurt a fly? All the time I meet people who *are* great shakes, who actually *did* squat, who *can* cut the mustard, who *can* fight City Hall, who *are* my cup of tea, who *would* lift a finger to help, who *would* give you the time of day, who *do* have a mean bone in their body, and whom I *would* touch with a ten-foot pole, but I can't talk about them in English—and that *is* a laughing matter.

(See DISGRUNTLED.)

Doghouse. The first appearance of the phrase *in the doghouse* to mean "out of favor with the powers that be" occurs in James Barrie's play *Peter Pan* (1904). Mr. Darling, the father of the three children, is punished for his shabby treatment of Nana, the Newfoundland dog, who is also the children's nurse. And where does he spend his exile? In Nana's doghouse, of course.

It's sad how dogs, those most loyal and companionable of creatures, are treated so shabbily in our English language. It's easy to think of common words and expressions that are negative about dogs: *hangdog, underdog, dog tired, a dog's life, dog days, you dirty dog, sick as a dog, in the doghouse, you're dogging it, going to the dogs, you're dog meat*—on and on it goes. But why don't we say *cute as a dog, amiable as a dog, loyal as a dog, loving as a dog*? How many positive canine words and phrases leap to mind? Not many.

(See CATCH-22, CHARACTONYM, NERD, OZ, PANDEMONIUM.)

Doldrums. The doldrums are those parts of the ocean near the Equator that are noted for calm and neutral weather. They pose no difficulty for fuel-driven vessels, but for sailing ships they mean a dead standstill. When we are stuck in boredom or depression, we are in the doldrums.

Moreover, *doldrums* is an example of an unplural—a plural word that has no singular. We can never be in just one doldrum. So, like *gruntled, sheveled,* and *combobulated* (see *gruntled*), we behold another category of heads without tails.

Doesn't it seem just a little wifty that we can make amends but never just one amend; that no matter how carefully we comb through the annals of history, we can never discover just one annal; that we can never pull a shenanigan, consume an egg Benedict, or get just one jitter, willy, delirium tremen, or heebie-jeebie? Why, sifting through the wreckage of a room blown to smithereens, can we never find just one smithereen?

Indeed, this whole business of plurals that don't have matching singulars reminds me to ask this burning question, one that has flummoxed scholars for decades: if you have a bunch of odds and ends and you get rid of or sell off all but one of them, what do you call that single item you're left with?

(See DISGRUNTED, SCUTTLEBUTT.)

Doornail. Many a bibliophile knows the opening paragraph of Charles Dickens's classic *A Christmas Carol*:

> Marley was dead: to begin with. There is no doubt whatever about that. The register of his burial was signed by the clergyman, the clerk, the undertaker, and the chief mourner. Scrooge signed it; and Scrooge's name was good upon 'Change, for anything he chose to put his hand to. Old Marley was as dead as a door-nail.
>
> Mind! I don't mean to say that I know, of my own knowledge, what there is particularly dead about a door-nail. I might have been inclined, myself, to regard a coffin-nail as the deadest piece of ironmongery in the trade. But the wisdom of our ancestors is in the simile; and my unhallowed hands shall not disturb it, or the Country's done for. You will therefore permit me to repeat, emphatically, that Marley was as dead as a door-nail.

The phrase *dead as a doornail* reaches back well before the Victorian Age, back to the fourteenth-century *Vision of Piers Plowman*. But, as the narrator of *A Christmas Carol* wonders, what's so dead about a doornail? To find out, we must look at the craft of carpentry.

Long-ago carpenters would drive big-headed metal nails into the heavy studs surrounding doors to strengthen or beautify them. Because metal nails were precious then, the carpenters would hook the tip of the nail back to "clinch" the nail (as we clinch a deal). The nail was "dead," meaning "fixed, rigid, immovable," as in *deadline* and *deadlock*. Carpenters today still use the term "dead-nailing."

It didn't take long for the pun on "fixed, rigid, immovable" and "not alive" to become clinched in our language.

(See HALLMARK, METAPHOR.)

Doublespeak. In 1948, political author George Orwell reversed the last two numbers of the year and created a dystopian novel titled *1984,* a dark vision of a totalitarian society that controlled everyone, including their language. Formed from a melding of two words that Orwell created for that novel—*doublethink* and *newspeak*—*doublespeak* became in the 1950s a label for language in the public sector that is deliberately deceptive, euphemistic, dishonest, and inhumane.

For example, Florida-based airline Spirit, a pioneer in charging fees for carry-on luggage, installed in its new Airbus 320 planes seats that don't recline. The name they conferred on these rigid, unadjustables: *pre-reclined seats.*

Here's a small selection of real-life doublespeak terms from various sectors of our society:

- *What's my line?* "utensil maintainer" = dishwasher, "interment excavation expert" = gravedigger, "sex industry worker" = prostitute
- *commercial doublespeak.* "previously distinguished vehicle" = used car, "interdental stimulator" = toothpick, "social expression product" = greeting card
- *military doublespeak.* "enhanced radiation device" = nuclear bomb, "governmental unconsolidation" = overthrow, "collateral casualties" = civilian deaths
- *economic doublespeak.* "revenue enhancement" = tax increase, "negative investment increment" = loss, "equity retreat" = stock market crash

And keep in mind that nothing in life is certain except terminal living and revenue enhancement.

(See EUPHEMISM, FIRED, GOBBLEDYGOOK.)

Drunk. My fellow verbivore and tireless researcher Paul Dickson has uncovered 2,964 synonyms for *drunk*. The entries range from the euphemistic *tired* to the comical *plastered*, from the nautical *afloat* to the erudite *Bacchi-plenus*, from the elegant *inebriated* to the scatological *shit-faced*, from the rhyming *whiskey frisky* to the time-bound *Boris Yelstinned*, and from the terminal *stiff* to the uncategorizable *zoozled*. Surely a world record for synonyms.

Another fancy synonym for *drunk* is *intoxicated*. The Greek word *tóxon* (τοξικόν) meant "bow" (as in "arrow launcher"). The poison Greek warriors used to tip their arrows took on the name *toxikón*. Ultimately that poison became embedded in our word *intoxicate,* having traveled from the Greek military through late Latin *intoxicatus* to the drunken fellow who slurs, "Name your poison."

I've always thought that English is a truly intoxicating language, so I'm not surprised at the findings of scientists in India who discovered a way to convert old newspapers into alcohol. The cellulose in the newsprint is broken down by a fungus into glucose and then fermented with yeast. Although they can't explain why, the inventors of the process have discovered that old copies of the upscale English-language daily *Hindustan Times* yield the most intoxicating results, more mind-spinning than the Indian-language newspapers.

Language holds the great power to intoxicate us, as Emily Dickinson proclaimed so vividly:

> I taste a liquor never brewed—
> From Tankards scooped in Pearl—
> Not all the vats upon the Rhine
> Yield such an Alcohol!
>
> Inebriate of Air—am I—
> And Debauchee of Dew—
> Reeling—thro endless summer days—
> From inns of Molten Blue.

(See SYNONYM.)

Ecdysiast. When exotic dancer Gypsy Rose Lee asked H. L. Mencken to coin a dignified word for a stripper, the author and critic came up with *ecdysiast*, from the Greek *ecdysis* (ἐϰδύω), "to molt." The metaphoric comparison to a bird losing its feathers is appropriate, clear, and vivid.

Echo. Of all the literary sources that flow into our English language, mythology is one of the richest. We who are alive today constantly speak and hear and write and read the names of the ancient gods and goddesses and heroes and heroines, even if we don't always know it.

Echo, for example, is an echo of a story that is more than two millennia old. Echo was a beautiful nymph who once upon a time aided Zeus in a love affair by keeping Hera, his wife, occupied in conversation. As a punishment for such verbal meddling, Hera, the queen of the gods, confiscated Echo's power to initiate conversation and allowed her to repeat only the last words of anything she heard.

Such was a sorry enough fate, but later Echo fell madly in love with an exceedingly handsome Greek boy, Narcissus, who, because of Echo's peculiar handicap, would have nothing to do with her. So deeply did the nymph grieve for her unrequited love, that she wasted away until nothing was left but her voice, always repeating the last words she heard.

The fate that befell Narcissus explains why his name has been transformed into words like *narcissism* and *narcissistic*, "pertaining to extreme self-love." One day Narcissus looked into a still forest lake and beheld his own face in the water, although he did not know it. He at once fell in love with the beautiful image just beneath the surface, and he, like Echo, pined away for a love that could never be consummated.

(See CLUE, JOVIAL, TANTALIZE.)

Eerie is the most common example among five-letter words with just one consonant. Add *audio*—five letters, four vowels, three syllables—*adieu*, and *queue*. Then there's *Ouija*—the name of a popular Parker Brothers board game of divination that is still used for fun and fraud. *Ouija* is a conjunction of *yes* in French and German. The trademark is usually pronounced *weeja*, yet the spelling of *Ouija* includes every major vowel but *e*.

(See AI, DEEDED, RODE.)

Egress, from the Latin *e,* "out" + *gress,* "step," is a fancy word for *exit*, and P. T. Barnum, the Greatest Showman on Earth, made creative use of it.

Barnum's American Museum in Lower Manhattan was so popular that it attracted up to fifteen thousand customers a day, and some would spend the entire day there. This cut into profits, as the museum would be too full to squeeze another person in. In classic Barnum style, PT put up above a cage holding a mother tiger and her cubs a sign that read, "TIGRESS." Then, over a doorway next to that sign, he put up another sign that said, "TO THE EGRESS." Many customers followed that sign, looking for an exhibit featuring an exotic female bird. What they found instead was themselves out the door ("the egress") and back on the street. Once they had exited the building, the door would lock behind them, and if they wanted to get back in, they had to pay another admission charge.

(See CALIBER.)

Einstein. You don't have to be an Einstein to see that the name *Einstein* is a double violation of the "*i* before *e*, except after *c*" rule.

Among the dozens of instances in which *e* precedes *i* in uncapitalized words are this dozen:

caffeine	feisty	kaleidoscope	seize
counterfeit	heifer	leisure	sovereign
either	height	protein	therein

And among words in which *c* is immediately followed by *ie* we note:

ancient	fancier	omniscient	species
concierge	financier	science	sufficient
conscience	glacier	society	tendencies

E-I, I-E—Oh?

There's a rule that's sufficeint, proficeint, efficeint.
For all speceis of spelling in no way deficeint.
While the glaceirs of ignorance icily frown,
This soveriegn rule warms, like a thick iederdown.

On words fiesty and wierd it shines from great hieghts,
Blazes out like a beacon, or skien of ieght lights.
It gives nieghborly guidance, sceintific and fair,
To this nonpariel language to which we are hier.

Now, a few in soceity fiegn to deride
And to forfiet thier anceint and omnisceint guide,
Diegn to worship a diety foriegn and hienous,
Whose counterfiet riegn is certain to pain us.

In our work and our liesure, our agenceis, schools,
Let us all wiegh our consceince, sieze proudly our rules!
It's plebiean to lower our standards. I'll niether
Give in or give up—and I trust you won't iether!

(See GHOTI, HICCOUGH.)

Elbow anagrams into another body part, *bowel*, a category that seems to attract somewhat unmentionable regions, including *spine/penis* and *ears/arse.* The most arcane of these is the *suture,* defined not only as "the stitching of a wound or other opening," but also as "the juncture of two bones, especially of the skull." If we accept *suture* as a body part, it becomes an anatomical anagram of *uterus.*

(See ANAGRAM, EYE.)

Electric sparks from the Greek *ēlektron* (ἤλεκτρον), "beaming sun." The second *c* in *electric*, *electricity*, and *electrician* all make different sounds.

Elizabeth, that popular, royal English name, sparks forth more nicknames than any other: *Babette, Bess, Bessie, Bessy, Bet, Beth, Bethina, Betsey, Betsy, Betta, Bette, Bettie, Bettina, Bettine, Betty, Buffy, Elisa, Elise, Elissa, Elisse, Eliza, Ella, Ellie, Elsa, Else, Elsie, Ilse, Lib, Libbie, Libby, Lil, Lillian, Lillie, Lilo, Lily, Lilybet, Lilybeth, Lis, Lisa, Lisabet, Lisabeth, Lisbet, Lisbeth, Lise, Lisette, Lissa, Liz, Liza, Lizabeth, Lizbet, Lizbeth, Lize, Lizette, Lizolet, Lizza, Lizzie,* and *Lyssa.* That's more than fifty transmutations.

Encyclopedia glows from the Greek *enkyklopaideiā* (ἐγκύκλιος παιδεία): *en*, "in" + *kyklos*, "circle" + *paideia*, "education, child-rearing." Altogether, the first meaning of *encyclopedia* was "to circle a child with learning."

Enervate. After I spoke at a conference for teachers of English in a large state, one of the officers of the group stood up and effused, "Thank you, Doctor Lederer, for your most enervating performance." She apparently thought that *enervating* means "energizing," but it doesn't. *Enervating,* from the Latin *e*, "out of" + *nervus,* "nerve, sinew," means "to weaken," which is what I hope I didn't do to those English teachers.

Enervate is what I call a confusable word, one that doesn't turn out to mean what it looks and sounds like. Here's a tower of babbling words:

- *Anchorite* means "a person who lives in seclusion," not "a sailor."
- *Antebellum* means "before the war," not "against war."
- *Cupidity* means "a strong desire for wealth," not "a strong desire for love."
- *Friable* means "easily crumbled," not "easily fried."
- *Fulsome* means "offensive to the senses," not "full, abundant."
- *Meretricious* means "falsely attractive," not "worthy."
- *Penultimate* means "next to the last," not "last, final."
- *Presently* means "soon," not "now."
- *Prosody* means "the study of verse," not "the study of prose."

- *Restive* means "fidgety," not "serene."
- *Risible* means "disposed to laugh," not "easily lifted."
- *Scarify* means "to criticize cuttingly," not "to frighten."

And *wherefore* means "why," not "where." When Juliet sighs, "O Romeo, Romeo! Wherefore art thou Romeo?" she is not trying to locate her new squeeze. Rather she is lamenting that the young man she's jonesing for turns out to be a member of a rival and despised family, the Montagues. This interpretation is clarified by the lines that follow:

> Deny thy father and refuse thy name;
> Or, if thou wilt not, be but sworn my love,
> And I'll no longer be a Capulet.

English. The rise of English as a planetary language is an unparalleled success story that begins long ago, in the middle of the fifth century A.D. At the onset of the Dark Ages, several large tribes of sea rovers—the Angles, Saxons, and Jutes—lived along the continental North Sea coast, from Denmark to Holland. They were a fierce warrior people who built beaked galleys and fought with huge battle-axes and battle hammers, burning towns, and carrying off anything they happened to want.

Around A.D. 449, these Teutonic plunderers sailed across the water and invaded the islands then known as Britannia. They found the land pleasant and the people, fighting among themselves, very easy to conquer, so they remained there. They brought with them a Low Germanic tongue that, in its new setting, became Anglo-Saxon, or Old English, the ancestor of the English we use today. During the reign of King Egbert in the ninth century, the land became known as *Englaland*, "the land of the Angles," and the language *Englisc*, because the Angles were at that time the chief group.

Entrance. Note the unusual pattern of the end-rhymes in this poem:

> Listen, readers, toward me bow.
> Be friendly; do not draw the bow.
> Please don't try to start a row.
> Sit peacefully, all in a row.
> Don't squeal like a big, fat sow.
> Do not the seeds of discord sow.

Even though each couplet ends with the same word, the rhymes occur on every other line. That's because *bow, row,* and *sow* each possess two different pronunciations and meanings. These rare pairings of etymologically unrelated look-alike words are called heteronyms:

A Hymn to Heteronyms

Please come through the *entrance* of this little poem.
    I guarantee it will *entrance* you.
The *content* will certainly make you *content,*
    And the knowledge gained sure will enhance you.

A boy *moped* around when his parents refused
    For him a new *moped* to buy.
The *incense* he burned did *incense* him to go
    On a *tear* with a *tear* in his eye.

He *ragged* on his parents, felt they ran him *ragged.*
    His just *deserts* they never gave.
He imagined them out on some *deserts* so dry,
    Where for water they'd search and they'd rave.

At *present* he just won't *present* or *converse*
    On the *converse* of each high-flown theory
Of circles and *axes* in math class; he has
    Many *axes* to grind, isn't cheery.

He tried to play baseball, but often *skied* out,
    So when the snows came, he just *skied.*
But he then broke a leg *putting* on his ski boot
    And his *putting* in golf was in need.

He once held the *lead* in a cross-country race,
    Till his legs started feeling like *lead,*
And when the pain *peaked*, he looked kind of *peaked.*
    His *liver* felt *liver*, then dead.

A *number* of times he felt *number*, all *wound*
    Up, like one with a *wound*, not a wand.
His new TV *console* just couldn't *console*
    Or *slough* off a *slough* of despond.

The *rugged* boy paced 'round his shaggy *rugged* room,
    And he spent the whole *evening* till dawn
Evening out the wild *winds* of his hate.
    Now my anecdote *winds* on and on.

RICHARD LEDERER

He thought: "*Does* the prancing of so many *does*
Explain why down *dove* the white *dove*,
Or why *pussy* cat has a *pussy* old sore
And *bass* sing in *bass* notes of their love?"

Do they always sing, "*Do* re mi" and stare, *agape*,
At eros, *agape*, each *minute*?
Their love's not *minute;* there's an *overage* of love.
Even *overage* fish are quite in it.

These bass fish have never been in short *supply*
As they *supply* spawn without waiting.
With their love fluids bubbling, abundant, *secretive*,
There's many a *secretive* mating.

(See CAPITONYM.)

Episcopal. How sweet it is: Rearrange every letter in *Episcopal*, and you end up with *a Popsicle* and *Pepsi-Cola*. Pepsi-Cola was invented in 1893 in New Bern, North Carolina, by a pharmacist named Caleb Bradham, who owned a drug store just across the street from the town's Episcopal church. According to town lore, the concoction went by the name "Brad's Drink" for several years, but the inventor wasn't completely happy with that. One day, according to the story, he glanced across the street and looked at the sign in front of the Episcopal church in a whole new way.

Presbyterian brings forth *best in prayer*, and *Presbyterians* yields *Britney Spears*, which could be the denomination's *best PR in years.*

(See ANAGRAM, COMPASS, DANIEL, ESTONIA, SET, SILENT, SPARE, STAR, STOP, TIME, WASHINGTON, WILLIAM SHAKESPEARE.)

Estonia is not only a Baltic country in northern Europe. It is an anagram of the first seven letters in *Etaoin Shrdlu*. While *Etaoin Shrdlu* looks like somebody's name, it is actually a letter sequence produced by running the finger down the first two vertical rows of the old Linotype machine keyboards. The order of letters in *Etaoin Shrdlu* is determined by what was perceived to be the frequency that each letter appeared in print, with *e* being the most ubiquitous member of the alphabet.

(See ANAGRAM, COMPASS, DANIEL, EPISCOPAL, SET, SILENT, SPARE, STAR, STOP, TIME, WASHINGTON, WILLIAM SHAKESPEARE.)

Euphemism. Prudishness enjoyed (if that's the word) its golden age in the straitlaced Victorian era. Take the widely read *Lady Gough's Book of Etiquette.* Among Lady Gough's social pronouncements was that under no circumstances should books written by male authors be placed on shelves next to books written by "authoresses." Married writers, however, such as Robert and Elizabeth Barrett-Browning, could be shelved together without impropriety.

So delicate were Victorian sensibilities that members of polite society would blush at the mention of anything physical. Instead of being pregnant, women were in a delicate condition, in a family way, eating for two, or expectant. Women did not "give birth"; they experienced "a blessed event." Their children were not "born"; rather, the little strangers were "brought by the stork," "came into the world," or "saw the light of day."

Such words and expressions are called euphemisms. From Greek, a euphemism (ευφημία) is literally "the practice" (*-ism*) of using happy (*eu-*) speech (*pheme*)." A euphemism is a mild, indirect word or phrase used in place of one that is more harsh or direct or that may have an unpleasant, distasteful connotation. A euphemism is calling a spade a heart—or telling it like it isn't.

In the Victorian Age, euphemisms extended even to animals and things. *Bull* was considered an indecent word, and the proper substitute was "he cow," "male cow," or (gasp!) "gentleman cow." Victorian standards were so exacting that Victorians couldn't refer to something as vulgar as "legs." Ladies and gentlemen of that era had to call them "limbs," even when talking about the legs on a piano; they went so far as to cover up piano legs with little skirts. It's not surprising, then, that Victorians never requested something as shocking as a leg or breast of chicken; they asked for "a drumstick" or "dark meat" or "light meat."

At a Richmond, Virginia, reception in his honor, Winston Churchill, then a Member of Parliament, was served cold fried chicken along with the champagne. When he reached the buffet table, the great man asked his hostess for a breast. The woman, a lady of considerable Victorian sensibility and maternal endowment, gently chided him: "We southern ladies use the term 'white meat.'"

The day after the event, the ever-chivalrous Churchill sent his hostess a corsage, with a card attached: "I hope you will display these flowers on your delicate white meat."

RICHARD LEDERER

The opposite of a euphemism is a *dysphemism,* the intentional use of harsh, rather than polite, language, as in calling one's spouse *the old man* or *the ball and chain,* labeling postal letters and packages *snail mail,* or referring to dying as *croaking.*

(See DOUBLESPEAK, FIRED, GOBBLEDYGOOK, HORSEFEATHERS, ZOUNDS.)

Expediency. What characteristic do the following words share: *any, arty, beady, cagey, cutie, decay, easy, empty, envy, essay, excel, excess, icy, ivy, kewpie, seedy,* and *teepee?* Turns out that each word is cobbled from the sounds of two letters—*NE, RT, BD, KG, QT, DK, EZ, MT, NV, SA, XL, XS, IC, IV, QP, CD,* and *TP.* Such words are labeled grammagrams.

Gaze upon some three-syllable grammagrams:

cesium (CZM)	enemy (NME)	odious (ODS)
devious (DVS)	envious (NVS)	opium (OPM)
effendi (FND)	escapee (SKP)	tedious (TDS)

And behold grammagrams of four syllables:

anemone (NMNE)	Arcadian (RKDN)
eminency (MNNC)	excellency (XLNC)

Finally, I introduce the three longest grammagrams—the pentasyllabic *effeminacy (FMNSE), expediency (XPDNC),* and *obediency (OBDNC).*

Here's a swatch of letter-perfect verse, with accompanying translation. Keep in mind that the same letter twice in a row sounds like a plural. For example, *II* means "eyes."

	Translation
YURYY	Why you are wise
Is EZ to C	Is easy to see.
U should be called	You should be called
"XLNC."	"Excellency."
U XEd NE	You exceed any
MT TT.	Empty tease.
I NV how U	I envy how you
XL with EE.	Excel with ease.

(See REBUS.)

Eye is the only palindromic body part. *Eye, I,* and *aye* are all homophones, yet each starts with a different letter.

When it comes to words and phrase origins, the eyes have it:

- *Daisy* was created in Old English from the poetical "day's eye." The flower is indeed a metaphor waiting to be born, with its sunburst center, its radiating white petals, and its sensitivity to the progress of the day, opening during the sunny hours and closing in the evening and extinguishing its brightness. The poet Geoffrey Chaucer, without benefit of any linguistic manual, referred to the sun as "the day's eye, or else the eye of day."

- *Daylights* is timeworn slang for the human eyes, dating back to at least the early eighteenth century. This makes a certain amount of sense since the eyes are the "source" of all the light we see. The practice of equating the eyes with lights or windows is even older; one Latin word for *eye* was *lumen,* meaning "light." "To beat (or scare) the daylights out of" someone first meant to pummel or frighten him or her so badly that the person's eyes, at least figuratively, popped out.

- Have you heard about the cross-eyed teacher? She couldn't control her pupils. That pun plays on the two meanings of the word *pupil.* The first, "a student," is borrowed from the Latin *pupillus,* "orphan, ward, minor." A second meaning boasts the more enchanting etymology: In ancient Rome, the *pupilla,* "little doll," was a diminutive of *pupa,* "girl." When the Romans looked deep into each other's eyes, they used the same word for the tiny doll-like images of themselves reflected there. They called the part of the eye that the image could be seen in the *pupil.*

- The adjective *supercilious,* literally "with raised eyebrows," comes from the Latin *super,* "above," and *cilium,* "eyelid" or "eyebrow." A supercilious person is one who shows arrogance by figuratively or literally raising an eyebrow.

- An *autopsy*—Greek *autós* (αυτος), "self" + *opsy* (όψις), "eye"—is an examination of a dead person in which the coroner sees with his or her own eyes.

- *Iris* was originally the Greek word for "rainbow" and the goddess of rainbows and messenger of the gods. Later her name was applied to the colorful flower and to the thin, circular structure in our eyes that gives them color.

- *Window* started out as "the wind's eye," a feature of a home that would let out the eye-stinging smoke and odor of bodies and damp fur.

(See FINGER, HAND, HUMERUS, HYSTERICAL.)

Facetious. What did one of the poet A. E. Housman's debtors write to him?: "AE: IOU." The shortest (nine letters) and most accessible word that contains all five major vowels in sequence is *facetious*. AEIOU words that test the outer limits of the English language include *abstemious, abstentious, acheilous, acheirous, adventitious, aparecious, areious* (the shortest), *annelidous, arsenious, arterious, atenisodus, bacterious, caesious, fracedinous, lamelligomphus* (the longest), *lateriporous,* and *parecious.*

The five major vowels each appear once in alphabetic order in the words *lawn tennis court.*

Unnoticeably is the shortest word (eleven letters) that contains the major vowels in reverse order, each occurring only once. Other exhibits include *subcontinental* and *uncomplimentary,* at fifteen letters the longest such word.

(See AMBIDEXTROUS, METALIOUS, SEQUOIA, ULYSSES SIMPSON GRANT, UNCOPYRIGHTABLE.)

Fathom. When we try to fathom an idea, we are making poetic use of an old word that originally meant "the span between two outstretched arms." Then it came to mean "a unit of six feet used for measuring the depth of water." By poetic extension, the verb *to fathom* now means "to get to the bottom of" something, and that something doesn't have to be the ocean.

(See DOLDRUMS, METAPHOR.)

Filibuster. I love the sounds of words like *whippersnapper, persnickety, flibbertigibbet,* and *filibuster.* The last of these words is borrowed from the Dutch *vrijbuiter,* "freebooter," which first meant "pirate, adventurer" in English. That sense is retained in the current denotation of *filibuster*: "holding a piece of legislation captive by making long and windy speeches."

I have a special interest in Dutch words that have sailed into our language because I am married to Simone van Egeren, my Dutch treat, born in Rotterdam. My time with Simone has been a succession of saucy Holland days.

When the Dutch came to the New World, the figure of St. Nikolaas, their patron saint, was on the first ship. The pronunciation of *St. Nikolaas* became folk etymologized, and the English in New York heard their Dutch neighbors saying *Sinterklaas.* They recognized the Dutch name Klaas and thought they were hearing "Santa Klaas." After the Dutch lost control of New Amsterdam to the English in the seventeenth century, *Sinterklaas* gradually became anglicized into *Santa Claus* and acquired some of the features of the British Father Christmas.

It is time to cut through the poppycock (from the Dutch *pappekak,* "soft dung") by noting the enormous contributions that the Dutch language has made to our English tongue. A partial list of gifts from our Netherfriends embraces *barracks, bedspread, boodle, boor, booze, boss, boy, brandy, bully, bulwark, bumpkin, buoy, bush, caboose, coleslaw, cookie, cruise, cruller, cuspidor, date, deck, decoy, dingus, dope, dumb, excise, furlough, gas, gin, golf, groove, halibut, hay, hobble, hop* (plant), *hose* (stockings), *huckster, husk, hustle, jib, kit, knapsack, landscape, loiter, luck, mangle, mart, pickle, pit* (in fruit), *placard, rack, school* (of fish), *scow, skate, sketch, sled, sleigh, sloop, slur, smuggle, snap, snatch, snoop, snort, snow, snuff, splint, spook, spool, stoker, stoop* (porch), *tackle* (fishing), *uproar, waffle, wagon, walrus, wiseacre,* and *yawl.*

(See BOSS, CANDIDATE, IDIOT, INAUGURATE, POLITICS.)

Finger entered our language through a very old Germanic etymon that means "one in five." "Hold on," you might object. "The thumb is not a finger, so a finger can't be one in five." *Au contraire.* The just-about-as-old Old English ancestor to *thumb, thuma,* meant "swollen finger."

Despite what you may read on the Internet, the phrase *rule of thumb* has nothing to do with any law enjoining a husband from using a stick thicker than his thumb to beat his wife.

What a horrible thought!

Rule of thumb actually harks back to days of old, when rulers of the measuring kind were uncommon and woodworkers used the length of the thumb from the knuckle to the tip as an approximate measure of one inch—inexact, but better than nothing. Nowadays, "rule of thumb" signifies any rough-and-ready method of estimating.

We can put our finger on *prestidigitator.* As impressive as that word looks and sounds, its derivation is quite simple, from the Italian *presto,* "nimble," and the Latin *digitus,* "finger." A prestidigitator radiates the illusion of possessing magical powers through skill with his or her quick hands.

(See EYE, HAND, HUMERUS, HYSTERICAL.)

Fired. The meaning of *fired* as "to discharge someone from a job" is an extension of applying fire to gunpowder.

Nobody gets fired anymore. Nowadays, when people lose their jobs, they are "reclassified," "rightsized," "deselected," "outplaced," "nonpositively terminated," or any other of dozens of euphemistic verbs that really mean axed, canned, sacked, or given the heave-ho.

In the continuing search for newer, softer, and more ambiguous verbs with which to administer the final blow to helpless jobholders, Laurence Urdang, longtime editor of *Verbatim, the Language Quarterly,* came up with a new pun game:

If clergymen are defrocked and lawyers are disbarred, then alcoholics are delivered, hairdressers are distressed, manicurists are defiled, models are disposed, and pornographers are deluded.

Employing the *de-* and *dis-* prefixes, I offer my own multiple verbs for getting rid of members of other professions:

- Bankers are distrusted and disinterested.
- Cowboys are debunked, deranged, and decaffeinated.

- Elks Clubbers are dislodged and dismembered.
- Judges are disrobed, dishonored, disappointed, and defined.
- Magicians are dispelled and disillusioned.
- Mathematicians are deciphered, disfigured, discounted, and dissolved.
- Preachers are demoralized, decreed, distracted, and dissected.
- Songwriters are denoted and decomposed.
- Tailors are depressed, depleted, and dispatched.
- Teachers are declassified, detested, and degraded.
- Tennis players are deduced, disadvantaged, deserved, and defaulted.

(See CALIBER, DOUBLESPEAK, PUN.)

First is the only ordinal number whose letters appear in alphabetical order. The only alphabetic cardinal number that matches the alphabetic order of *first* is *forty*. A number of other "figure-ative" words do a number on us:

- *One* generates the homophone *won.*
- Double *one* and get *two,* which generates two homophones, *to* and *too.*
- Double *two* and get *four* and the two homophones *for* and *fore.*
- Double *four* and get *eight* and its homophone *ate.*
- *Three* generates three full anagrams—*three, there,* and *ether.*
- *Four* is the only numeral with a number of letters that matches its value.
- *FIVE.* Take from *FIVE* the first, second, and fourth letters an—oh, fie!—you end up with *V,* which still signifies "five."
- *Ten* is the only number that spells a common word when its letters are reversed.
- *Eleven* is the longest number word that alternates vowels and consonants.
- *Thirteen. Eleven + Two = Twelve + One* is not only mathematically accurate. Each side of the equal sign is an anagram of the other side.
- *Fifteen.* Amazingly, the same idea works twice in Spanish for the number fifteen in that language: *Catorce + Uno* (14 + 1) = *Once + Cuatro* (11 + 4), and *Doce + Tres* (12 + 3) = *Trece + Dos* (13 + 2).

- *TWENTY-NINE* is capitalized with all straight lines—twenty-nine of them!

- *Eighty-one* is one of only two square-root words, in which the number of letters (nine) is the square root of the number signified by the word itself. The other square-root number word is the ten-letter *one hundred.*

- *One thousand.* Quick: You have two minutes to rattle off a series of words that are completely devoid of the letter *a.* Actually, all you have to do is start counting "one-two-three-four-five" and so on. You could progress all the way through *nine hundred ninety-nine* and never use an *a*—not until you reached *one thousand.*

- *Five thousand* is the longest and highest number that can be spelled isogrammatically—no letter repeated.

- *One million.* Starting from the number one, you'll have to get to a million before you sound the letter *m*, and you'll have to reach *one billion* before you sound a *b.*

Floccinaucinihilipilification, meaning "the categorizing of something as worthless or trivial," is a twenty-nine-letter, twelve-syllable word that dates back to 1741. Until 1982, *floccinaucinihilipilification* was the longest word in the *Oxford English Dictionary.* While it contains nine *i*'s, it is the longest word devoid of *e*'s. It also conceals the seven-letter palindrome *ilipili.*

(See CHARGOGGAGOGGMANCHAUGGAGOGGCHAUBU-NAGUNGAMAUGG, HIPPOPOTOMONSTROSESQUIPEDALIAN, HONORIFICABILITUDINITATIBUS, LLANFAIRPWLLGWYNGYLL-GOGERYCHWYRNDDROBWLLLLANTYSILOGOGOCH, PNEUMONOUL-TRAMICROSCOPICSILICOVOLCANOKONIOSIS, SUPERCALIFRA-GILISTICEXPIALIDOCIOUS.)

Focus is a Latin word that meant "hearth, fireplace." As the focal point for life in the Roman home, the place that kept family warm and cooked the family's food, *focus* wound up as a word for any place where people or things converge.

Focus is also the focal point of a triple-double homophonic pun:

Have you heard about the man who gave his male offspring a cattle ranch and named it *Focus*? It was the place where the sun's rays meet—and the sons raise meat.

Forecastle. A ship's *forecastle* is sometimes written as *fo'c's'le*, making it the most apostrophied of our words. Just ask the ship's bo's'n.

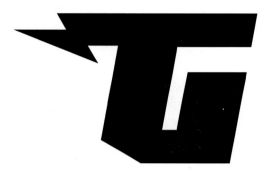

Galore. What do these words have in common: *galore, extraordinaire, akimbo, aplenty, aweigh, incarnate, fatale, royale, par excellence, immemorial, aforethought,* and *manque?* The answer is that the dozen are "deferential words." While the vast majority of adjectives usually precede the nouns they modify, the words in this list always come after the noun they modify.

    Galore can also be internally spoonerized as *Al Gore.*

    (See AKIMBO.)

Gargoyle. According to *The Da Vinci Code* author Dan Brown, the words *gargoyle* and *gargle* are related because of the gargling sound cathedral waterspout heads make. Both *gargoyle* and *gargle* derive from an Old French root, *gargouille,* meaning "throat," apparently from the water passing through the mouths of the grotesque figures.

Gay came to life seven hundred years ago from Old French *gai,* "merry." I grew up with *gay* as an adjective that meant "exuberant, high spirited," as in the *Gay Nineties* and *gay divorcee.* Starting as early as the 1930s in the mass media, *gay* began traveling the linguistic path we linguists call specialization, making the same journey as words such as *discrimination, segregation, partner, comrade,* and *colored.* In 1938 in the movie *Bringing Up Baby*, the character David, played by Cary Grant, when asked why he is wearing women's clothing replies, "Because I just went gay all of a sudden."

In the 1960s, activists popularized the concept of Gay Liberation—occasioning much hand-wringing among some heterosexuals, who lament that a perfectly wonderful word has been lost to general usage, wordnapped by the homosexual community. But as much as some heteros believe they need *gay,* the gay community needs it more—as an emblem of self-esteem, as a more fulfilling word than *homosexual* because it communicates a culture rather than concentrating on sexual orientation. For those who decry the loss of *gay* to general discourse, I recommend that henceforth they be merry.

(See COOL.)

Gerrymander. Elbridge Gerry (1744–1814), a vice president to James Madison, is the inspiration for a political term in our English language. In 1812, in an effort to sustain his party's power, Gerry, who was then governor of Massachusetts, divided that state into electoral districts with more regard to politics than to geographical reality.

To a drawing of one of the governor's manipulated districts Gilbert Stuart—the same fellow who had painted the famous portrait of George Washington—added a head, eyes, wings, and claws. According to one version of the story, Stuart exclaimed about his creation, "That looks like a salamander!" "No," countered the editor of the newspaper in which the cartoon was to appear, "better call it a Gerrymander!" The verb *gerrymander* (now lowercased and sounded with a soft *g*, even though Gerry's name began with a hard *g*) is still used today to describe the shaping of electoral entities for political gain.

Historically, *gerrymander* is the first American word to be born in a cartoon. A special kind of populist literature is the comic strip, and characters and stories we encounter in our newspapers and comic books and on movie screens have exerted an influence on our language.

- In 1928, Walt Disney gave the world a Mickey—an all-American rodent who performed heroic deeds and squeaked his undying love for Minnie. Soon after World War II, international markets were flooded with wristwatches bearing Mickey's likeness. Because these watches were generally cheap affairs subject to chronic and chronological mainspring breakdowns, people started calling anything shoddy or trivial *mickey mouse.*

- The name of H. T. Webster's wimpy comic-strip character, Caspar Milquetoast, has become a synonym for a wimpy, unassertive man.

- Speaking of *wimpy,* some linguists trace *wimpy* and *goon* to Elzie Segar's cartoon strip *Thimble Theatre,* which, when animated became *Popeye.*

- *On the fritz,* meaning "not operating properly," may have started with one of the earliest comic strips, *The Katzenjammer Kids.* Typically, the two hyperactive German boys, Hans and Fritz, caused all sorts of troubles for the Captain and other grownups in the story.

- For more than eight decades, Blondie's husband has been creating culinary masterpieces in the kitchen, yet he doesn't appear to have gained an ounce (for which I hate him). Dagwood carries the cornucopia of ingredients from the refrigerator to the kitchen table on his arms and head, and the massive repasts he concocts are now known as *Dagwood sandwiches.*

(See CANDIDATE, MAVERICK, POLITICS, SANDWICH, SIDEBURNS, SILHOUETTE, SPOONERISM.)

Ghoti. George Bernard Shaw, who championed the cause of spelling reform, once announced that he had discovered a new way to spell the word *fish.* His fabrication was *ghoti—gh* as in enou*gh, o* as in w*o*men, and *ti* as in na*ti*on.

There are many other "fish" in the A-B-Sea—*phusi: ph* as in *ph*ysic, *u* as in b*u*sy, *si* as in pen*si*on; *ffess: o*ff*, pretty, i*ss*ue; *ughyce:* la*ugh,* h*y*mn, o*c*ean; *Pfeechsi: Pf*eiffer, be*e*n, fu*ch*sia; *pphiapsh:* sa*pph*ire, marr*i*age, p*sh*aw; *fuiseo: f*at, g*ui*lt, nau*seo*us; *ftaisch:* so*f*ten, vill*ai*n, *sch*wa; *ueiscio:* li*eu*tenant (British pronunciation), forf*ei*t, con*sci*ous.

I stop here only because the game has become in-*f*-able.

(See EINSTEIN, HICCOUGH.)

Gobbledygook. Back in 1942, a blackout order came across the desk of President Franklin D. Roosevelt: "Such preparations shall be made as will completely obscure all Federal buildings and non-Federal buildings occupied by the Federal government during an air raid for any period of time from visibility of internal or external illumination."

Roosevelt fired back: "Tell them that in buildings where they have to keep the work going to put something across the windows."

Inflated and abstract writing such as that 1942 blackout order is called *gobbledygook*. The word was cobbled by one-time Texas congressman Maury Maverick, who compared the forbidding prose of Washington bureaucrats to the senseless gobbling of turkeys that echoes in the public mindspace. Gobbledygook, according to semanticist Stuart Chase, means "using two or three or ten words in the place of one, or using a five-syllable word where a single syllable would suffice. Gobbledygook doesn't call a spade a spade. Gobbledygook calls a spade "a manual excavation device." That's why the one-syllable, three-letter word *now* has been replaced by the five-word, seventeen-letter "at this point in time." Lest we forget, it is language that separates the human beings from the bureaucrats.

(See BALDERDASH, DOUBLESPEAK, EUPHEMISM, FIRED.)

Golf. Mark Twain is said to have called it a good walk spoiled, and Oscar Wilde defined it as a man fanning a ball with a stick.

Bob Hope quipped, "If you watch a game, it's fun. If you play it, it's recreation. If you work at it, it's golf." Arthur Daley added, "Golf is like a love affair: If you don't take it seriously, it's no fun; if you do take it seriously, it breaks your heart."

Right off, please know that *golf* does not stand for "gentlemen only; ladies forbidden" any more than *posh* is formed from "port out starboard home" or *cop* from "constable on patrol" or *tip,* as a gratuity, from "to insure promptness" or *news* from "north-east-west-south" or you-know-what from "for unlawful carnal knowledge" and you-know-what from "ship high in transport." Do not trust acronymic explanations of word origins.

Truth be told, the word *golf* is derived either from the German *kolbe,* which like the Dutch *colf* and French *chole,* means "stick, club," or from the Scottish *gowf,* meaning "to strike."

Personally, I don't play this sport for two linguistic reasons: First, the word *golf* is, appropriately, *flog* spelled backward. Second, I have dedicated my life to being above par and don't wish to flog myself trying to be subpar.

I also try to avoid being stymied. *Stymie* was originally a situation in which a player's golf ball rested between the cup and another ball, obstructing its path. Some suggest that *stymie* issues from the Gaelic *stigh mi,* meaning "inside me," while others point to the Dutch *stuit mij,* "it stops me." Now that players mark their balls and remove the impediment, the word has soared off the fairway of golfing parlance and into general use to mean "frustrated, thwarted, blocked in reaching an objective."

(See LOVE, SOUTHPAW.)

Good-bye. In our greetings when we meet someone and our farewells when we part repose hidden messages. *Howdy* is a shortening of "How do you do," while *good-bye* is an elision of "God be with you" and *so long* of "Don't let it be so long till I see you again."

AT&T used to use the slogan "Make your every hello a real good buy."

(See AHOY, CARNIVAL.)

Groak is a real verb that means "to stare at another's food in hopes that he or she will offer you some, in the manner of dogs and certain people we know."

Gry. The most pervasive, invasive, and evasive of all word puzzles that make the rounds of cyberspace is this challenge: "There are three words in the English language that end in *g-r-y.* Two of them are *angry* and *hungry.* What is the third?"

The greatest service this book can perform for you is to announce that the *-gry* question is a time-wasting linguistic hoax. This poser first slithered onto the American scene in 1975 on the Bob Grant radio talk show on WMCA in New York City. Word mavens have tried to bury *-gry* before, but it keeps rising, like some angry, hungry monstrosity from *Tales From the Crypt.*

The answer to the infernal question is that there is no answer—at least no satisfactory answer. I advise anybody who happens upon the *angry + hungry + ?* poser to stop burning time and to move on to a more productive activity, like counting the number of angels on the head of a pin or the reductions in your property taxes.

In unabridged dictionaries are enshrined at least fifty -*gry* words in addition to *angry* and *hungry*, and every one of them is either a variant spelling, as in *augry* for *augury*, *begry* for *beggary*, and *bewgry* for *buggery*, or exceedingly obscure, as in *anhungry*, an obsolete synonym for *hungry*; *aggry*, a kind of variegated glass bead much in use in the Gold Coast of West Africa; *puggry*, a Hindu scarf wrapped around the helmet or hat and trailing down the back to keep the hot sun off one's neck; or *gry*, a medieval unit of measurement equaling one-tenth of a line.

A more realistically challenging puzzle of this type is "Name a common word, besides *tremendous*, *stupendous*, and *horrendous*, that ends in -*dous*."

At least thirty-two additional -*dous* words repose in various dictionaries: *apodous, antropodous, blizzardous, cogitabundous, decapodous, frondous, gastropodous, heteropodous, hybridous, iodous, isopodous, jeopardous, lagopodous, lignipodous, molybdous, mucidous, multifidous, nefandous, nodous, octapodous, palladous, paludous, pudendous, repandous, rhodous, sauropodous, staganopodous, tetrapodous, thamphipodous, tylopodous, vanadous,* and *voudous.*

But these examples are as arcane as those that purport to solve the -*gry* problem.

Still, there is a fourth common word ending in -*dous*—*hazardous.*

Had. Here's the record for the number of repeated uses of a word in a sentence—eleven, one right after the other:

Mary and John are students in an English class, and they each are asked to write a sentence on the blackboard. In his offering, John uses the verb "had," while, in hers, Mary uses "had had." Here is the result:

Mary, where John had had "had," had had "had had"; had "had had" had the teacher's approval, Mary would have been correct.

Hallmark. In long-ago England, gold was appraised at a building named the Goldsmiths' Hall. If the gold content was acceptable, the gold was stamped with a seal that became known as a *hallmark*. That's why today any mark, object, or action denoting quality and excellence is termed a *hallmark*.

Another golden word is *touchstone*, a criterion or standard, whose meaning goes straight back to goldsmiths, who kept hard stones in their shops. When a customer brought in some gold, the goldsmith would rub it against the stone, usually composed of jasper or basalt, With his practiced eye, the goldsmith could determine from the streak left on the stone the purity and quality of the gold. Hence, *touchstone*.

And here's a compound that's as good as gold: In bygone days, wandering peddlers were a familiar part of the American scene. A typical member of the class carried a few household items in a pack, while better-established peddlers pushed or drove wagons.

An essential part of the peddlers' business was the buying and selling of old gold. If the traveling salesman had the slightest doubt about the value of an item, he would file a shallow groove in that item and touch it with nitric acid. Color reactions from the acid would reveal the approximate gold content, and inferior metals would be decomposed by the treatment. This procedure was known as the *acid test*; by extension, any exacting method designed to reveal hidden flaws has come to be known by this term.

To the ledger of words once reserved for business alone we can add a number of verbal products now shared in our common language:

- *retail*. To transport lumber, long-ago French woodcutters hacked logs into small, moveable pieces called tail, from the Latin *talea*, "a cutting." The lumbermen delivered the tail, or cut wood, to village dealers, who would cut the wood again—that is, retail it for sale to customers. Eventually *retail* was adopted by other merchants who had to "cut up" spices, barrels of wine, or bales of cloth into smaller, salable quantities.

- *masterpiece*. Commercial life in medieval times was organized by guilds and crafts. An English apprentice who wished to be recognized as a master, with the right to work without supervision, was required to submit some article of metal, wood, stone, or leather. Like today's academic dissertations, the quality of the work determined the artisan's future, and it came to be known as a *master piece*.

- *cut and dried*. Certain herbs sold in herbalists' shops were prepared ahead of time and thus lacked the freshness of herbs newly picked. Since the early eighteenth century these herbs have been labeled *cut and dried*. It's easy to see how that phrase came to signify anything boring and lacking in spontaneity.

- *millstone*. When people say they feel they've been *put through the mill*, they echo a metaphor from the trade of milling. Grain fed to the jaws of a great stone mill is subjected to heavy and thorough grinding. By figurative extension, any person receiving rough treatment is said to be *put through the mill*. Related words and expressions include *milling around, run-of-the-mill,* and *millstone,* a circular stone used for grinding, but now any heavy burden.

* *the whole nine yards.* The fact that no printed citation exists for *the whole nine yards* prior to 1967 renders dubious the nautical theory that the expression refers to the nine sails on a three-square-masted rigger. Nor could *the whole nine yards,* which means "the whole shootin' match," "whole hog," "the whole ball of wax," issue from football, in which a team must gain ten, not nine, yards to reach a first down. Equally unproven or provably wrong are dozens of other etymological explanations, including the material to make a dress, bridal veil, or Scottish kilt; the length of a machine-gun belt in World War II fighter planes; the height of a prison retaining wall; and the volume of mined ore.

My research indicates that *the whole nine yards* refers to the revolving barrels on the backs of concrete mixing trucks. These barrels held a volume of nine cubic yards (they're now twelve cubic yards) in the early 1960s, a fact that explains why I never heard the phrase when I was growing up in the 1950s. Emptying the entire contents was one humungous road job—and, in most states, illegal because the weight of such a load would exceed the per-axel limits.

As you can see, my explanations are never in the abstract—and always in the concrete.

(See DOORNAIL, METAPHOR.)

Hamburger. Somebody once defined a hamburger as "a humble immigrant hunk of meat that came to this country and soared to fame on a bun." That somebody was right. In its native land, the dish was originally called "Hamburg steak," taking its name from the West German city of Hamburg.

After the Hamburg steak arrived in the United States midway in the nineteenth century with the first great wave of German immigrants, its name began to change. Ultimately the Hamburg steak lowercased its capital *H*, acquired the suffix *-er*, lost the s*teak*, and, in 1891 in Tulsa, Oklahoma, first snuggled into a bun. The result was the hamburger.

The adventure in creative word formation didn't stop there. Somewhere along the way, speakers of English interpreted *-burger* as a suffix that means "sandwich made with a bun." Once -*burger* became a new word part, *cheeseburger, beefburger, baconburger, fishburger, chiliburger, veggieburger*, and a trayful of other burgers entered the American gullet and dictionaries.

Starting out as a *Frankfurt sausage*, the frankfurter took a similar geographical and etymological odyssey. Nowaday*s -furter* can be used to denote any kind of sandwich made with an elongated bun, as in *chickenfurter* and *fishfurter*.

And speaking of frankfurters, do you know that Charlemagne mustered his Franks and set out with great relish to assault and pepper his enemies, but he couldn't ketchup? Frankly, I never sausage a pun. It's the wurst!

(See BIKINI, COMPANION, DACHSHUND, LACONIC, SANDWICH, TOAST.)

Hand. I always try to be even-handed in my approach to writing. On the one hand, I try not to be highhanded, underhanded, or heavy-handed. On the other hand, I don't want you to handcuff me or force my hand or reject my writing out of hand.

Because handedness—the tendency to favor one hand over the other—and language seem to be uniquely human traits, biologists have assumed that they are closely linked. Whether or not this is true, I hope you'll lend me a hand, give me a hand, and give me a free hand to show my hand but not force my hand. I present for your consideration a handy, hand-picked, and handy-dandy topic about which I possess firsthand knowledge.

Now open this handbook, a manual of manual words and expressions that lend a hand to our English language and leave it anything but shorthanded.

President Harry Truman loved to tell a joke about the dismal science of economics: "All my economists say, 'on the one hand . . . on the other hand.' Just give me a one-handed economist!" The quip depends on one's sense of the hand as a dominant metaphor in our English language. Apparently, Truman rejected out-of-hand, two-handed economists whose hands were tied, even as they served him hand and foot. Talk about a left-handed compliment. You really have to give a hand to and hand it to Mr. Truman.

Some words with *hand* in them go hand and glove with handedness while others are more oblique. In the fourteenth century a game was played involving the passing of money by hand into a cap held by an umpire. The game came to be called *hand i' cap* ("hand in cap"), whence our word *handicap*. In the fifteenth century one of the meanings of *handsome* was "easy to handle."

Many of our common words play right into our hands by deriving from *manus,* the Latin word for "hand": *manacle, maneuver, manicure, manipulate, manual, manufacture, manumit, manuscript,* and *emancipate* ("to remove one's hands from").

The hand figures in many of our common folk sayings: A bird in the hand is worth two in the bush. Many hands make light work. The hand that rocks the cradle rules the world. Idle hands are the devil's workshop.

And hands reach out from many of our most intriguing expressions:

- *Caught red-handed* means caught with blood on one's hands.
- *To win hands down* refers to a jockey who has a comfortable lead. He doesn't need to lift his hands to whip the horse, so he lets his hands drop.
- *Hand over fist* was originally a seafaring term referring to the hand-over-hand movements made by an old hand during rapid ascent into the rigging of a sailing ship.
- *Wash one's hand of the matter* alludes to Pontius Pilate's statement in the Book of Matthew that Christ's death was out of his hands because his hands were tied.

(See EYE, FINGER, HEART, HUMERUS, HYSTERICAL.)

Harrowing. Among farm equipment is a cultivating implement set with spikes or spring teeth that pulverizes the earth by violently tearing and flipping over the topsoil. That's why we identify an emotionally lacerating experience as *harrowing.*

Harrowing is one of a crop of down-to-earth metaphors that stimulate the *fertile* minds of the *cultivated* geniuses who read wordbooks like this one:

- *Haywire* gives us another agricultural metaphor. Anyone who has ever tried to use tightly stretched wire to bind bales of hay knows how inefficient and ornery the stuff can be. When someone or something behaves in an uncontrolled manner, we say that he, she, or it goes *haywire.*
- *by hook or by crook.* A custom in medieval England allowed peasants to collect from royal forests whatever deadwood they could pull down with a shepherd's crook or cut with a reaper's billhook. By extension, *by hook or by crook* has come to signify "by whatever means."

- *windfall.* European peasants, forbidden to cut down or pick fruit from trees, were allowed to gather gratuitous fuel and food blown down by acts of nature, a bounty that required little effort on the part of the lucky recipients. By extension, we today use a *windfall* to describe an unexpected stroke of good luck.

- The arduous job of hoeing long rows in uncooperative terrain makes for *a tough row to hoe*, that is, "a difficult task."

- Late spring frosts or pests of the insect or human variety can kill an aborning tree or flower before it has a chance to develop. When we terminate a project in its early stages, we say that we *nip it in the bud*.

- Hay is made by setting mown grass out in the sun to dry. When we want to make the most of an opportunity, we try to *make hay while the sun shines*.

(See METAPHOR.)

Hear is the only verb in English not ending in *e* that becomes past tense by adding just a *d* to its present-tense form.

(See VERB.)

Heart. In the English language, the heart is often used to denote the seat of passion, com-passion, courage, and intelligence. Of all the parts of the body, the heart is the one that throbs most pervasively through our daily conversation.

If, for example, we are deeply saddened, we might say that we are *heartsick, heartbroken, downhearted, heavy-hearted,* or *discouraged.* At the heart of *discouraged* beats the Latin *cor,* "heart," giving the word the literal meaning of "disheartened." Or if we wish to emphasize our sincerity, we might say *heartfelt, with all my heart, from the bottom of my heart,* or *in my heart of hearts.*

If something pleases us greatly, we might drag out *heart's delight* or *it warms the cockles of my heart.* The latter is a somewhat redundant statement; a cockle is a bivalve mollusk of the genus *cardium* (Latin "heart") that takes its name from its shape, which resembles that of a human heart.

Heart is also a letter-playful word. Loop the *h* from the front to the back and, behold, *earth.* Or simply add an *h* to the end of *heart* and get *hearth,* the heart of the home.

(See EYE, FINGER, HAND, HUMERUS, HYSTERICAL.)

Hiccough. Take the word *cough*, where the *-ough* letter string sounds like "off," and place *hic* in front, and you'll get *hiccough*, in which the *-ough* is now pronounced "up." Those are two of ten possible soundings of the string *-ough*:

bough	cough	hiccough	tough	through
bought	dough	lough	thoroughbred	trough

Now take the word *tough*. Insert an *r* after the first letter and you get *trough*. Go back to *tough* and insert an *h* after the first letter and you get *though*. Now insert an *r* after the first two letters and you get *through*. Finally, insert an *o* after the first two letters and you get *thorough*. Because of the protean properties of *-ough*, none of these words rhyme with each other.

Here's a poem that illustrates how tough English spelling can be:

> **Tough Stough**
> The wind was rough.
> The cold was grough.
> She kept her hands
> Inside her mough.
>
> And even though
> She loved the snough,
> The weather was
> A heartless fough.
>
> It chilled her through.
> Her lips turned blough.
> The frigid flakes
> They blough and flough.
>
> They shook each bough,
> And she saw hough
> The animals froze—
> Each cough and sough.
>
> While at their trough,
> Just drinking brough,
> Were frozen fast
> Each slough and mough.
>
> It made her hiccough—
> Worse than a sticcough.
> She drank hot cocoa
> For an instant piccough.

(See EINSTEIN, GHOTI.)

RICHARD LEDERER

Hijinks is the only common lowercase word that sports three consecutive lowercase dotted letters. *Beijing* and *Fiji* are the two most famous place names that share this dotty letter pattern. Less renown is Lake *Mijijie*, in Australia, which includes a five-dotted embedded palindrome.

Hippopotomonstrosesquipedalian is a very long word that means "pertaining to a very long word" and is, hence, self-referential. This mouthful breaks down into Greek word parts that signify "like a monstrous hippopotamus with half again as many feet."

May you have some fun absorbing this hippopotomonstrosesquipedalian passage:

In promulgating your esoteric cogitations and articulating your superficial sentimentalities and philosophical, pseudopsychological observations, beware of platitudinous ponderosity, circumnavigatory circumlocutions, and windy suspiration. Let your conversational communication possess a clarified conciseness, a compacted comprehensibility, a coordinated consistency, and a concatenated cogency.

Eschew all conglomerations of obfuscatory oratory, bilious bloviation, garrulous gobbledygook, and attenuated affectation. Let your extemporaneous descantings and unpremeditated expostulations possess incontrovertible intelligibility, unburdened by bombastic babblement, polysyllabic prolixity, and loquacious, longiloquent logorrhea.

In other words, say what you mean, mean what you say, and don't use big words.

(See CHARGOGGAGOGGMANCHAUGGAGOGGCHAUBU-NAGUNGAMAUGG, FLOCCINAUCINIHILIPILIFICATION, HONORIFICABILITUDINITATIBUS, LLANFAIRPWLLGWYN-GYLLGOGERYCHWYRNDDROBWLLLLANTYSILOGOGOCH, PNEU-MONOULTRAMICROSCOPICSILICOVOLCANOKONIOSIS, SUPERCALIFRA-GILISTICEXPIALIDOCIOUS, WORD.)

Hoagie. I was born and grew up in Philadelphia a coon's age, a blue moon, and a month of Sundays ago—when Hector was a pup. *Phillufia,* or *Philly,* which is what we kids called the city, was where the epicurean delight made with cold cuts, cheese, tomatoes, pickles, and onions stuffed into a long, hard-crusted Italian bread loaf was invented.

The creation of that sandwich took place in the Italian pushcart section of the city, known as Hog Island. Some linguists contend that

Hog Island easily transmogrified into *hoagie,* while others claim that the label *hoagie* arose because only a hog had the appetite or the technique to eat one properly.

As a young adult I moved to northern New England ("N'Hampsha," to be specific), where the same sandwich designed to be a meal in itself is called a grinder, because you need a good set of grinders to chew them. But my travels around the United States have revealed that the hoagie or grinder is called at least a dozen other names—a *bomber, Garibaldi* (after the Italian liberator), *hero, Italian sandwich, rocket, sub, submarine* (which is what they call it in California, where I now live), *torpedo, wedge, wedgie,* and, in the deep South, a *poor-boy* (usually pronounced "poh-boy").

(See CAKEWALK, COMPANION, COUCH POTATO, DACHSHUND, HAMBURGER, PUMPERNICKEL, SALARY, SANDWICH, TOAST.)

Honorificabilitudinitatibus is a Latin ablative plural that literally means "with honor." Shakespeare uses the noun in *Love's Labor's Lost,* where Costard says: "I marvel thy master hath not eaten thee for a word; for thou art not so long by the head as *honorificabilititu-dinitatibus:* thou are easier swallowed than a flap-dragon." The word appears only in Shakespeare's *Love's Labor's Lost* and is thus a *hapax legomenon,* a verbal form that shows up in just one venue.

Like *floccinaucinihilipilification, honorificabilitudinitatibus* is an *i-*full (seven *i*'s) that within its thirteen syllables contains nary a single *e.*

In addition, *honorificabilitudinitatibus* has the honorable distinction of being the longest dictionary entry that alternates consonants and vowels throughout. Distant runners-up include *supererogatorily* (sixteen letters), *overimaginative* (fifteen letters), *verisimilitude* (fourteen letters), and *ineligibility* (thirteen letters).

Sweetheart is a sweetheart of a word that alternates consonant pairs and vowel pairs. *Cloakrooms* and *steamboats* are the only other common ten-letter examples.

Among nations in this category, the eighteen-letter *United Arab Emirates* is the world's reigning superpower.

(See CHARGOGGAGOGGMANCHAUGGAGOGGCHAUBU-NAGUNGAMAUGG, FLOCCINAUCINIHILIPILIFICATION, HIP-POPOTOMONSTROSESQUIPEDALIAN, LLANFAIRPWLLGWYN-GYLLGOGERYCHWYRNDDROBWLLLLANTYSILOGOGOCH, PNEUMONOULTRAMICROSCOPICSILICOVOLCANOKONIOSIS, SUPER-CALIFRAGILISTICEXPIALIDOCIOUS.)

Horsefeathers. In modern life, horses are no longer crucial in helping us to hunt, do battle, draw vehicles, round up livestock, or deliver mail and goods. Nevertheless, our equine friends still figure prominently in the figures of speech that canter—neigh, gallop—through our English language.

"Horsefeathers!" you respond, bridling at my suggestion and working yourself into a lather. "Now hold your horses and get off your high horse, you horse's ass. You're just trying to spur me on to the end of my tether and beat a dead horse." The meanings of these words and expressions are generally clear, although the equine expletive *horsefeathers* deserves an etymological exegesis.

Rows of tapered boards are laid on roofs to provide flat surfaces for asphalt shingles, called "feather strips." Old-timers in New England and New York, noting the feather-like pattern, called the clapboards *horsefeathers*. Why the *horse* in the word? Because the boards were large, and large things sometimes attract the designation *horse*, as in *horse chestnut, horse radish, horsefly*, and *horse mackerel.*

But why has *horsefeathers*—like *tommyrot, balderdash, codswallop,* and *poppycock*—become a three-syllable explosion of derision? Because it has evolved into a euphemism for a shorter barnyard epithet.

Check your dictionary and you'll discover a paddock of disguised words that descend from the world of horses, including *cavalier, cavalcade, chivalry, hackneyed, henchman, hippopotamus, marshal,* and any variation on the name *Philip.*

I'm full of horsepower and feeling my oats—champing (not chomping) at the bit and eager to give free rein to talking horse sense with you about the English language. So prick up your ears and listen to how often we compare people with horses—disk jockeys, coltish lasses with ponytails, dark horse candidates who are groomed to give the frontrunners and old warhorses a run for their money, and workhorses who, although saddled with problems of galloping inflation, can't wait to get back in harness each Monday at the old stamping (not stomping) ground.

I've tried to lead a horse to language *and* make you think. I'm trusting that you won't look this gift horse in the mouth.

Don't look a gift horse in the mouth is one of the oldest proverbs known to humankind, whinnying back at least 1,500 years. You can ascertain the age and health of a horse by examining the condition and number of its teeth. Although an animal may appear young and frisky, a close inspection may reveal that it is *long in the tooth* and ready for the glue factory. Still, it is considered bad manners to inspect the teeth of a horse that has been given you and, by extension, to inquire too closely into the cost or value of any gift.

But if you are buying a horse from a trader, however, you are advised to determine its age and health by examining the teeth *straight from the horse's mouth,* the precise source of this entry.

(See BALDERDASH, BUFFALO, BUTTERFLY, CANARY, CAPER, CLAM, CRESTFALLEN, OSTRACIZE, PARTRIDGE, PEDIGREE, TAD, TURKEY, VACCINATE, ZYZZYVA.)

Hotshots. A number of words contain two adjacent sets of the same three letters. These are sometimes labeled internal tautonyms, but I'll simplify and call them double triples. Excluded are reduplicative words that are specifically constructed of repeated elements, such as *cancan, cha-cha,* and *fifty-fifty.*

Common words that contain double triple patterns include:

*alfalf*a	ins*tantan*eous	po*ssessed*	stom*achach*e
*assass*in	*kinkin*ess	re*deeded*	su*perper*fect
*barbar*ic	*murmur*	ri*nging*	*testes*
con*tented*	para*llelled*	sa*tiation*	*tinting*

The fairly common word exp*ression*le*ssness* includes three occurrences of the same three letters.

The hotshot word *hotshots* is the only common one that consists of two touching sets of the same four letters.

(See INTESTINES, RESTAURATEURS, SHANGHAIINGS, UNDERGROUND.)

Humerus. Technically the so-called funny bone is the ulnar nerve that causes that tingly sensation when we strike our arm. But the source of that feeling is the knob on the end of the bone running from the shoulder to the elbow. The medical name for that bone is the *humerus*, and back in 1840 some wag seized upon the homophonic similarity of *humerus* and *humorous* and dubbed the humerus the *funny bone,* a learned pun that has become part of our language.

One of the amazements of language is that it seeks to name everything. Here are more little-known labels for body parts:

* *canthus.* The point at either end of each eye where the upper and lower lids meet;

- *frenum.* The thin muscle under the tongue;
- *lunula.* The half-moon pale area at the base of your fingernails and toenails;
- *opisthenar.* The back of the hand, opposite the palm;
- *philtrum.* The indentation that runs from just below your nose to the middle of your upper lip;
- *purlicue.* The web of flesh between your thumb and forefinger;
- *thenar.* The fleshy pad just below the thumb;
- *tragus.* The fleshy bump of the ear between the side of the face and the ear cavity;
- *uvula.* The thing that hangs down from the back of the throat;
- *vomer.* The slender bone that separates the nostrils.

(See EYE, FINGER, HAND, HEART, HYSTERICAL.)

Humor. There was nothing the least bit funny about the word *humor* when it was born. Ancient philosophers believed that four fluids coursed through each person's body—blood, phlegm, choler (or yellow bile), and melancholy (or black bile)—and that our health and temperament (Latin *temperamentum,* "mixture") were controlled by the proportion of these fluids. An imbalance of these constituents, which the ancients called *humors,* could cause odd, or *humorous,* behavior. We still use *humor* in the old way when we say, "He's in a bad humor."

Hurricane blows in from an Arawakan (West Indies) word that means "evil spirit." In 1953 the National Weather Service began conferring female first names on all hurricanes, categorizing those devastating winds as female. When I was a boy, we bandied about a little riddle: "Why do they give hurricanes female names?" "Because otherwise, they'd be himicanes!"

Har har. Chuckle, chuckle.

That riddle doesn't make sense any longer because, in 1979, the service started identifying hurricanes by both male and female names alternately: Alma, Bertram, Charlotte, Donald, Elaine, and so on. That's one small step for humankind. It's the right thing that those meteorological "evil spirits" not be exclusively female.

Hysterical. The ancients, in their finite wisdom, believed that the womb—*hystéra* (ύστερος) in Greek, "of the womb"—was an unfixed organ that floated around inside a woman's body, tickling her and making her emotionally unstable, or *hysterical.* In that sense, *hysteria* is a subtle dig at women, stereotyping them as flighty and emotionally volatile. It was Sigmund Freud who first popularized the notion that men could be hysterical, too.

And why is it that a man gets a *her*nia and a woman a *hys*terectomy?

(See EYE, FINGER, HAND, HEART, HUMERUS.)

Hysteron proteron is a Greek figure of rhetoric that "the latter earlier," or more familiarly, the cart before the horse. In hysteron proteron the logical order or sequence of objects or events is reversed. If you bear this concept in mind, you'll find examples all around you:

- You don't go *back and forth* between places. You must go forth before you can go back.

- You don't put on your *shoes and socks* each morning. That is an exceedingly difficult maneuver. You put on your socks first, then your shoes.

- You aren't *head over heels* in love. You're head over heels in love because when you flip, literally or metaphorically, your heels are over your head.

- It's not that you can't *have your cake and eat it, too.* If you think about it, it should be that you can't eat your cake and have it, too.

- It isn't a *hit-and-run* play. If you know your baseball, you know that the sequence constitutes a run-and-hit play.

- And, closely related to hysteron proteron, it shouldn't be *ass backward*, which is the proper arrangement of one's anatomy, to describe things all turned around. For that state of disarray the expression should be *ass frontward.*

(See CHIASMUS, IRONY, METAPHOR, METONYMY, OXYMORON, PARADOX, ZEUGMA.)

I. What is the shortest word in the English language? Any letter of the alphabet qualifies as a word, but *a, I,* and *o* are also words with meanings other than designations for letters. An argument can be made that *I* is the shortest word among these because it is the skinniest. In fact, the reason that the dot was added to the lowercase *i* and the *I* was capitalized when used as a pronoun is that the letter was so small and skinny that it looked like a stray speck on the page.

I am here to tell you that English is the only major language to capitalize its first-person singular pronoun. Some observers believe that such capitalization brings about a linguistic ethnocentrism, a sort of "beauty is in the *I* of the beholder" complex. As evidence, *I* stands at the top of the list of English words most frequently spoken.

Now that you know the shortest word in English, what is the shortest sentence? The answer is "I am"—only three letters.

And now that you know the shortest sentence in English, what is the longest sentence? The answer is "I do."

(See A, EXPEDIENCY, I, Q-TIPS, S, SILENT, W, X.)

Idiot. The original Greek meaning of the word *idiótēs* (ἰδιώτης) was not nearly as harsh and judgmental as our modern sense. Long before the psychologists got hold of the word, the Greeks used *idiótēs*, from the root *idiós*, "one's own, personal, private," as in *idiom* and *idiosyncrasy*, to designate those who did not hold public office. Because such people possessed no special status or skill, the word *idiot* gradually fell into disrepute.

The vote that we cast is really a "vow" or "wish." And this is the precise meaning of the Latin *votum*. People in our society who fail to exercise their democratic privilege of voting on election day are sometimes called idiots.

(See CANDIDATE, FILIBUSTER, GERRYMANDER, INAUGURATE, OK, OSTRACIZE, POLITICS.)

Inaugurate literally means "to take omens from the flight of birds." In ancient Rome, augurs would predict the outcome of an enterprise by the way the birds were flying. These soothsayer-magicians would tell a general whether or not to march or to do battle by the formations of the birds on the wing. They might even catch one and cut it open to observe its entrails for omens. Nowadays, presidential candidates use their inauguration speeches to take flight on an updraft of words, rather than birds—and they do often spill their guts for all to see.

(See CANDIDATE, FILIBUSTER, GERRYMANDER, IDIOT, OK, OSTRACIZE, POLITICS.)

Indivisibility. The *i*'s have it. The vowel *i* is repeated more frequently in single words than any other letter, such as in the four-*i*'ed *civilizing, infinitive,* and *initiation;* the five-*i*'ed *initializing, invincibility,* and *invisibility;* and the six-*i*'d *indivisibility.* There are those who would catch your eyes with seven *i*'s in *indivisibilities,* a word that strikes me as jerry built and jury rigged.

The letter *s* clearly wins the prize for frequency of a consonant, showing up five times in the likes of *assesses*, six times in *possessiveness,* and eight times in *possessionlessness.*

Here's a parade of the other twenty-four letters, with examples of words in which each letter pops up and out most frequently. Note how *j, q, v,* and *x* don't like hanging out with their own kind:

RICHARD LEDERER

A: abracadabra (5)	*J:* jejune (2)	*R:* referrer (4)
B: babble (3)	*K:* knickknack (4)	*T:* statuette (4)
C: concupiscence (4)	*L:* hillbilly (4)	*U:* muumuu (4)
D: fuddy-duddy (5)	*M:* mammogram (4)	*V:* valve (2)
E: beekeeper (5)	*N:* nonintervention (5)	*W:* powwow (3)
F: riffraff (4)	*O:* photocomposition (5)	*X:* executrix (2)
G: giggling (4)	*P:* pepper-upper (5)	*Y:* syzygy (3)
H: hashish (3)	*Q:* quinquennial (2)	*Z:* pizzazz (4)

Another five-*n* word is *inconveniencing,* in which all the *n*'s appear three letters away from each other.

(See DEEDED, MISSISSIPPI, SLEEVELESSNESS.)

Infantry. If adults commit adultery, do infants commit infantry? Chuckle chuckle, snort snort—but we are led to ask what is the relationship, if any, between *infants* and *infantry?*

Infant was born from the Latin *in-*, "not" + *fari*, "speak" = "one who is not yet capable of speech." In Italian, *infante* came to mean "boy" or "foot soldier"; hence, our word *infantry.*

Infinite means "immeasurably large." Add the five letters *simal* and you get *infinitesimal*—a word that means "immeasurably small." Thus, you make the word greater to make it smaller.

Inflammable. Derived from the French *enflamer, inflammable* used to appear as a warning meaning "Don't light a match here." Despite the fact that nobody was befuddled by the adjective *inflammatory,* a number of unfortunate souls, seeing *inflammable* as a fuel tank label, reasoned that the *in-* meant "not" and was thus the equivalent of "incombustible." As a result, *flammable* has been adopted, with its clear meaning "combustible," and is opposed by the equally clear *nonflammable.* But *inflammable* survives, so that *flammable* and *inflammable* now mean the same thing.

Flammable and *inflammable* are the two most notorious examples of apparent opposites that turn out to mean the same thing, but they are not alone: *A slim chance* and *a fat chance* are the same, as are *a caregiver* and *a caretaker, a good licking* and *a bad licking, passive* and *impassive, heritable* and *inheritable,* and *What's going on?* and *What's coming off?*

This whole business of opposition and sameness makes the head spin and the mind boggle. How can *sharp speech* and *blunt speech* be the same, while *a wise man* and *a wise guy* are opposites? How can *quite a lot* and *quite a few* be the same, while *overlook* and *oversee* are opposites?

If *button* and *unbutton* and *tie* and *untie* are opposites, why are *loosen* and *unloosen* and *ravel* and *unravel* the same? How can *invaluable* objects be more valuable than *valuable* ones? And why are *pertinent* and *impertinent*, *canny* and *uncanny*, and *famous* and *infamous* neither opposites nor the same?

(See DISGRUNTLED.)

Intestines is the most logologically exciting of all body components. Its first five letters are an anagram of its second five, and both halves are anagrams of the word *inset*. With its letter order intact, *testes* hides inside *intestines*.

(See ARM, ELBOW, EYE, HOTSHOTS, RESTAURATEURS, SET, SHANGHAIINGS.)

Iota, the ninth letter of the Greek alphabet, is the name for what we call the letter *i*. Because that letter is so thin, the word has come to signify the smallest of things, a jot. *Iota* is also a rare four-letter word crammed with three syllables. Choice lowercase examples include *area, aria, idea, oleo,* and *olio.* Capital examples include *Oreo, Iowa, Iona, Oahu,* and *Ohio.*

(See AGUE, RODE.)

Irony is a rhetorical and literary device that involves an incongruity between two elements. You can't have too many ironies in the fire:

Verbal irony is an incongruity between what is said and what is meant. Bayed about by his enemies, Marc Antony praises those who have assassinated Julius Caesar as "honorable men. So are they all, all honorable men." Gradually, and too late for Caesar's killers to intercede, the Roman rabble come to see that Antony really means that Brutus and his co-conspirators are the opposite of honorable men.

Situational irony exploits a discrepancy between what we expect and what happens in a work of art. It is ironic that the oiler, the strongest of the men in Stephen Crane's short story "The Open Boat," is the one who drowns while the others, weaker and sicker, survive.

It is ironic that Edwin Arlington Robinson's rich and shining Richard Cory "one calm summer night, / went home and put a bullet through his head."

The heartrending, gut-wrenching gulf between what we know and what a literary character knows is *dramatic irony*—watching that character advance toward and walk off a cliff and not being able to cry out and help. We know well before Oedipus discovers it that he has married Jocasta, the girl just like the girl who married dear old dad. We know well before Shakespeare's Romeo and Juliet and Hamlet about the sleeping potion and poison sword that will extinguish their young lives. But we cannot help them.

Now that you know that irony is a discrepancy that illuminates the human condition, please don't use *ironic* to mean a simple coincidence. It is ironic that a nation of our wealth should also incarcerate the highest percentage of prisoners in the world. That on the street the other day I happened to bump into a superannuated classmate from elementary school is in no way ironic; it's just coincidental.

(See CHIASMUS, HYSTERON PROTERON, METAPHOR, METONYMY, OXYMORON, PARADOX, ZEUGMA.)

Irregardless may be the word that, aside from dirty, sexist, and racist terms, lands you in the deepest and most scalding hot water. *Irregardless* is a semiliterate blend of *irrespective* and *regardless* and is inhabited by the two-headed Hydra of *ir-* and *-less*, two negative-affixes. Use *irregardless* in speech or (gasp!) in print, and you will not reap the full fruits of English-speaking civilization. That's my story, and I'm sticking to it, disirregardless of what the permissive grammarians say.

Jackpot originally described the reward to the big winner in a game of progressive poker, in which you need a pair of jacks or better to "open the pot." Because the stakes grow higher until the requisite pair is dealt, *jackpot* has gradually expanded to include the pots of gold in slot machines, game shows, and state lotteries.

The great American game of poker is so embedded in our national consciousness that it deals us a number of everyday words and expressions:

- *four-flusher.* A cardsharp who is out to cheat you may be dealing from the bottom of the deck and giving you a fast shuffle, in which case you may get lost in the shuffle. You might call such a low-down skunk a *four-flusher. Flush,* a hand of five cards that are all of one suit, flows from the Latin *fluxus* because all the cards flow together. *Four-flusher* characterizes a poker player who pretends to such good fortune but in fact holds a worthless hand of four same-suit cards and one that doesn't match.

- *blue-chip.* Now that I've laid my cards on the table, let's see what happens when the chips are down. Why do we call a gilt-edged, sure-thing stock a *blue-chip stock?* Because poker chips were white, red, and blue, and the blue were traditionally the most valuable.

- *stack up.* Why, when we compare the value and power of two things, do we often ask how one *stacks up* against the other, as in "How do the Red Sox stack up against the Yankees?" Here the reference is to the columns of chips piled up before the players around a poker table.

- *bottom dollar.* Poker chips also account for the expressions *bottom dollar* and *top dollar. Betting one's bottom dollar* means wagering the entire stack, and the *top dollar*, or chip, is the one that sits atop the highest pile on the table. Indeed, the metaphor of poker chips is so powerful that one of the euphemisms we use for death is *cashing in one's chips.*

- *pass the buck.* How did the expression *pass the buck* come to mean "to shift responsibility"? Why should handing someone a dollar bill indicate that responsibility is in any way transferred?

The *buck* in *pass the buck* was originally a poker term designating a marker that was placed in front of the player whose turn it was to deal the next hand. This was done to vary the order of betting and to keep one person from dealing all the time, thus transferring the disadvantages of being the first to wager and cutting down on the chances of cheating. During the heyday of poker in the nineteenth century, the marker was often a hunting knife whose handle was made of a buck's horn. The marker defined the game as Buckhorn Poker or Buck Poker and gave us the expression *to pass the buck.*

In the Old West, silver dollars often replaced buckhorn knives as tokens, and these coins took on the slang name *buck.* President Harry S. Truman, reputed to be a skillful poker player, adopted the now-famous motto "The buck stops here," meaning that the ultimate responsibility rested with the president.

(See DIE, GOLF, METAPHOR.)

Jason. An amusing pastime is to string together the first letters of people's names as initials of words in meaningful statements. Lee Iacocca's last name, for example, could be said to represent the first letters of "I Am Chairman Of Chrysler Corporation of America."

The name *Jason* is composed of the first letters of five successive months—July, August, September, October, November. If James Jason were a DJ on FM/AM radio, the first letters of all twelve months would be represented sequentially, starting with June:

J. JASON, DJ
FM/AM

John. The name John (or Jon) can be transmogrified phonetically into six different women's names or nicknames simply by changing the internal vowel sound:

Jan   Jane   Jean   Jen   Joan   June

Jovial. Among the literary sources that flow into our English language, mythology is a major tributary. We who are alive today constantly speak and hear and write and read the names of the ancient gods and goddesses and heroes and heroines, even if we don't always know it. For example, *jovial,* an adjective that means "merry, inspiring mirth," comes from *Jove,* the name the ancient Romans gave to the king of their gods because it was a happy omen to be born under the influence of his planet.

Welcome to a pantheon of gods and goddesses, heroes and heroines, and fabulous creatures that inhabit the world of classical mythology and the words that echo them:

- *amazon.* The original Amazons were an ancient nation of female warriors who cut off their right breasts in order to handle their bows more efficiently. *Amazon* originally meant "breastless"; it now means "a strong woman," especially one who works for an online purveyor of books and other products.

- *aphrodisiac, venereal, venerate.* The goddess of love and beauty gives us many words from both her Greek and Roman names, Aphrodite and Venus.

- *herculean.* The great Greek hero Hercules needed all his power to complete twelve exceedingly laborious labors. We use a form of his name to describe a mighty effort or an extraordinarily difficult task.

- *hermaphrodite, mercurial.* A *hermaphrodite* is a plant, animal, or human being possessing both male and female reproductive organs. The word unites the Greek deities Hermes and Aphrodite, who had a son named Hermaphrodite. Because of its fluidity and mobility, quicksilver is identified by the more common label Mercury, the Roman name for Hermes, the winged messenger of the gods. Mercury also bequeaths us the adjective *mercurial,* meaning "swift, eloquent, volatile."

- *odyssey.* Odysseus, the most famous of all of Homer's creations in the *Iliad* and *Odyssey,* spent ten years after the fall of Troy wandering through the ancient world and encountering sorceresses and Cyclopes (monsters with 20/ vision). The wily hero's name lives on in the word we use to describe a long physical or spiritual journey marked by bizarre turns of events.

- *panic.* The frenetic Greek nature god Pan was said to cause sudden fear by darting out from behind bushes and frightening passersby. That fear now bears his name.

- *siren.* The hero Odysseus was tempted by mermaids who perched on rocks in the sea and lured ancient mariners to their deaths. Their piercing call has given us our word for the rising and falling whistle emitted by ambulances, fire engines, and police cars.

- *stentorian.* In Homer's *Iliad,* the Greek herald Stentor was a human public address system, for his voice could be heard all over camp. Today, the adjective form of his name means "loud-voiced, bellowing."

(See CLUE, ECHO, TANTALIZE, WEDNESDAY.)

Keynote. A keynote speaker delivers a keynote address in which he or she develops the underlying theme of the meeting or conference. The term *key note* began as the practice of playing a note before a group, such as a cappella or barbershop, began singing. The note sounded determines the key in which the song will be performed, thus the term *key note*.

Keynote is one example of the music metaphors that play in our language. Aria ready to face the music? Of chorus you are.

When I give a keynote speech, I hope to strike a responsive chord in my audience. I don't blow my own horn or trumpet my achievements. But I am fit as a fiddle, and I don't fiddle around or play second fiddle to anyone.

I'm not a Johnny-one-note who doesn't know his brass from his oboe. I don't play it by ear or soft pedal my commitment or give you a song and dance with a second-string performance. I don't chime in with a bunch of sax and violins. Rather, I, your unsung hero, pull out all the stops and drum up enthusiasm so that my audience will hop on the bandwagon of the amazement of words.

(See METAPHOR, SLAPSTICK.)

Kindergarten is the German for "child's garden." The original compound was *kleinkinderbeschaftigungsanstalt,* which means "institution where small children are occupied," but even the Germans found that to be a mouthful.

Kinnikinnik. This mixture of sumac leaves, dogwood bark, and bearberry smoked by Cree Native Americans in the Ohio Valley presents us with the longest English natural palindromic word.

Among longer English palindromes is the eleven-letter *detartrated,* "separated from or free of tartaric acid," and the ten-letter *detannated,* "separated from or free of tannin."

Beyond English there is *Malayalam,* a Dravidian language related to Tamil and spoken on the Malabar coast of India, presumably in palindromes.

Although it appears in no dictionary, the fifteen-letter Finnish word *saippuakauppias* and the nineteen-letter *saippuakivikauppias,* designating a soap or lye dealer, are, according to native speakers of the language, grammatically sanctioned compound words. They beat the closest English language example by four letters and are recognized by the *Guinness Book of World Records* as the longest palindromic words.

(See ADAM, AGAMEMNON, CIVIC, NAPOLEON, PALINDROME, SENSUOUSNESS, WONTON, *ZOONOOZ.*)

Knight. Hears a rye peace eye maid up inn my idol thyme. Aye rote it four yew two sea Howe homophones Cannes seam sew whiled from there knows write too they're tows. With pried, eye no it will knot boar ewe. Its meant two bee red allowed:

One *night* a *knight* on a *hoarse horse*
Rode out upon a *road.*
This *male wore mail* for *war* and *would*
Explore a *wood* that glowed.

His *tale* I'll tell from head to *tail.*
I'll *write* his *rite* up *right.*
A hidden *site* our hero found,
A *sight* that I shall *cite.*

With *woe* he shouted, *"Whoa!"* as *rain*
Without a *break* did *reign*.
To *brake*, he pulled the *rein*, and like
A shattered *pane* felt *pain*.

The *poor* knight met a *witch, which* made
Sweat *pour* from every *pore*.
He'd never *seen* a *scene* like that.
His *sore* heart couldn't *soar*.

Then they a game for truffles played,
In which he *mined* her *mind*.
To prove who was the *better bettor*
And *find* who should be *fined*.

He *won one* twice, he won *two, too*.
To *grate* on her felt *great*.
To *wrest* the *rest*, he went *for four*,
And, at the *fore, ate eight*.

Due to her loss, the *mourning* witch,
'Midst *morning mist* and *dew*,
Her truffles *missed*. I *know no way*,
Do I, to *weigh* her rue.

Our knight began to *reel*, for *real*.
The *world whirled*, so to speak.
All the *days* of the *week* his *sole soul* felt
The dizzy *daze* of the *weak*.

Our *heir* to knighthood gave it up.
He felt the *fare* not *fair*.
His *wholly holy sword soared* up
As he *threw* it *through* the *air*.

The bell has *tolled*, I'm *told*. The *hour*
To end *our* tale draws nigh.
Without *ado*, I bid *adieu*,
So *by* your leave, *bye-bye*.

(See AIR.)

RICHARD LEDERER

L.A. The full name of Los Angeles is El Pueblo de Nuestra Senora la Reina de Los Angeles de Porciuncula. It can be abbreviated to 3.63 percent of its size: *L.A.*

Laconic. From Laconia, a region in the southwestern peninsula of Greece, we inherit the adjective *laconic,* "using language sparingly." The inhabitants of ancient Laconia were known for their economical use of speech. During a siege of Sparta, the Laconian capital, a Roman general sent a note to the Laconian commander warning that if he captured the city, he would burn it to the ground. From the city gates came this laconic reply: "If."

President Calvin Coolidge, a man of few words, was so famous for saying so little that a White House dinner guest made a bet that she could get him to say more than two words. When she told the president of her wager, he answered laconically: "You lose."

(See BIKINI, HAMBURGER, LIMERICK.)

Latches. Transpose the first and last letters and you get *satchel*—and some satchels actually do sport latches. The longest pairings of this type are the twelve-letter *deprogrammer/reprogrammed* and fourteen-letter *demythologizer/remythologized.*

(See MENTALLY, UNITED.)

Limerick. Let us celebrate the limerick, a highly disciplined exercise in verse that is probably the only popular fixed poetic form indigenous to the English language. While other basic forms of poetry, such as the sonnet and ode, are borrowed from other countries, the limerick is an original English creation and the most quoted of all verse forms in our language.

> The limerick packs laughs anatomical
> Into space that is quite economical.
> But the good ones I've seen
> So seldom are clean,
> And the clean ones so seldom are comical.
> *—Vivian Holland*

Despite the opinion expressed in Holland's limerick about limericks, even the clean ones can be comical. In only five lines, the ditty can tell an engaging story or make a humorous statement compactly and cleverly.

By definition, a limerick is a nonsense poem of five anapestic lines, of which lines one, two, and five are of three feet and rhyme and lines three and four are of two feet and rhyme. Here is the classic limerick stanza:

> da DA da da DA da da DA
> da DA da da DA da da DA
> da DA da da DA
> da DA da da DA
> da DA da da DA da da DA

Unaccented syllables can be added to the beginning and end of any line, resulting in an extremely flexible metrical form.

Although the limerick is named for a county in Ireland, it was not created there. One theory says that Irish mercenaries used to compose verses in limerick form about each other and then join in the chorus of "When we get back to Limerick town, 'twill be a glorious morning."

RICHARD LEDERER

It has been estimated that at least a million limericks—good, mediocre, and indelicate—are in existence today. Among the aristocracy of the genre, the most often quoted limericks of all time, is this creation by Dixon Lanier Merritt, who was known as the dean of Tennessee newspapermen:

> A wonderful bird is the pelican
> His bill will hold more than his belican.
> He can take in his beak
> Enough food for a week,
> But I'm damned if I see how the helican.

Equally clever is this avian limerick, by George S. Vaill, about the inglorious bustard:

> The bustard's an exquisite fowl
> With minimal reason to howl:
> He escapes what would be
> Illegitimacy
> By the grace of a fortunate vowel.

When the limericist experiments with bizarre rhymes and outlandish visuals, the result is a *gimerick* (*gimmick* + *limerick*), as in this interdisciplinary masterpiece:

$$\frac{12 + 144 + 20 + 3(\sqrt{4})}{7} + 5(11) = 9^2 + 0$$

Here's the metrical translation of the equation, which does indeed resolve into 81 = 81:

> A dozen, a gross, and a score
> Plus three times the square root of four,
> Divided by seven
> Plus five times eleven,
> Is nine squared, and not a bit more.

(See BIKINI, HAMBURGER, LACONIC.)

Liverpudlian. Language maven Paul Dickson has coined the word *demonym,* literally "people name," to identify people from particular places. We know that people from Philadelphia are *Philadelphians* and people from New York *New Yorkers.* But what does one call people from Indiana, Connecticut, and Michigan in the United States; Liverpool, Exeter, Oxford, and Cambridge in England; and, in other countries, Florence and Naples, Italy; Hamburg, Germany, and Moscow, Russia? The answers are *Hoosiers, Nutmeggers,* and *Michiganians* (the official name) or *Michiganders; Liverpudlians, Exonians, Oxonians,* and *Cantabridgians;* and *Florentines, Neopolitans, Hamburgers,* and *Muscovites.*

Llama, from Spanish, is the only common English word that begins with a double consonant:

> A one-*L* lama lives to pray.
> A two-*L* llama pulls a dray.
> A three-*L* ama's kind of dire.
> A four-*L* ama's one big fire!

If you went to the mega shopping center to purchase a certain South American ruminant, you would then own *a mall llama,* creating a palindromic string of four consecutive *l*'s.

(See CHTHONIC, LLANFAIRPWLLGWYNGYLLGOGERYCHWYRNDD-ROBWLLLLANTYSILOGOGOCH.)

Llanfairpwllgwyngyllgogerychwyrnddrobwllllantysilogogoch is the Welsh name of a village railway station in Alglesey, Gwynedd, Wales, cited in the *Guiness Book of World Records.* Translated, the name means "Saint Mary's Church in a hollow of white hazel, close to a whirlpool and Saint Ryslio's Church and near a red cave."

In addition to being one of the longest of place-names, the fifty-six-letter cluster contains but one *e.* Hidden in the chain are four consecutive *l*'s, a five-letter palindrome—*ogogo*—and a seventeen-letter stretch without a major vowel—*rpwllgwyngyngyllg.*

The small community of three thousand souls annually attracts a quarter million visitors who take pictures of the railway station festooned with the hippopotomonstrosesquipedalian name.

(See CHARGOGGAGOGGMANCHAUGGAGOGGCHAUBUN-AGUNGAMAUGG, FLOCCINAUCINIHILIPILIFICATION, HIPPOPO-TOMONSTROSESQUIPEDALIAN, HONORIFICABILITUDINITATIBUS, PNEUMONOULTRAMICROSCOPICSILICOVOLCANOKONIOSIS, SUPER-CALIFRAGILISTICEXPIALIDOCIOUS.)

Loll is one of several four-letter words that contain the greatest density of a particular letter. Seventy-five percent of *loll, lull,* and *sass* consists of a single consonant.

(See DEEDED, INDIVISIBILITY.)

Love. The most charming derivation for the use of *love* to indicate "no points" in tennis is that the word derives from the French *l'ouef,* "the egg," because a zero resembles an egg, just as the Americanism *goose egg* stands for "zero." But *un oeuf,* rather than *l'ouef,* would be the more likely French form, and, anyway, the French themselves (and most other Europeans) designate "no score" in tennis by saying "zero."

Most tennis historians adhere to a less imaginative but more plausible theory. These more level heads contend that the tennis term is rooted in the Old English expression "neither love nor money," which is more than a thousand years old. Because love is the antithesis of money, it is nothing.

(See GOLF, SOUTHPAW.)

Mainland. What are the longest words that we can weave by string-ing together a series of two-letter state postal abbreviations? "Stately words" of four letters abound, from *AKIN* (Arkansas + Indiana) to *GAME* (Georgia + Maine) to *ORAL* (Oregon + Alabama) to *WINE* (Wisconsin + Nebraska). About twenty combinations of six letters can be found, from *ALMOND* (Alabama + Missouri + North Dakota) to *INCOME* (Indiana + Colorado + Maine) to *VANDAL* (Virginia + North Dakota + Alabama).

Eight-letter strings are rare as black pearls. In fact, the only com-mon examples of such postal-abbreviation words are *CONCORDE* (Colorado + North Carolina + Oregon + Delaware), *GANYMEDE* (Georgia + New York + Maine + Delaware), *MANDARIN* (Massachu-setts + North Dakota + Arkansas + Indiana), *MEMORIAL* (Maine + Missouri + Rhode Island + Alabama), and–ta da!–*MAINLAND* (Mas-sachusetts + Indiana + Louisiana + North Dakota).

(See MISSISSIPPI.)

Malapropism. When people misuse words in an illiterate but humorous manner, we call the result a *malapropism.* The word echoes the name of Mrs. Malaprop (from the French *mal a propos,* "not appropriate"), a character who first strode the stage in 1775 in Richard Brinsley Sheridan's comedy *The Rivals.* Mrs. Malaprop was a garrulous "old weather-beaten she dragon" who took special pride in her use of the King's English but who, all the same, unfailingly mangled big words: "Sure, if I reprehend anything in this world it is the use of my oracular tongue, and a nice derangement of epitaphs!" She meant, of course, that if she comprehended anything, it was a nice arrangement of epithets.

From *The Rivals,* here are some more of Mrs. M's most malapropriate malapropisms:

- Then, sir, she should have a supercilious knowledge in account;—and as she grew up, I should have her instructed in geometry, that she might know something of the contagious countries.
- She's as headstrong as an allegory on the banks of the Nile.
- Alliterate him, I say, quite from your memory.
- He's the very pineapple of politeness.

The giddy ghost of Mrs. Malaprop continues to haunt the hallowed halls of language. Here are some authentic, certified, unretouched modern-day malapropisms:

- If you wish to submit a recipe for publication in the cookbook, please include a short antidote concerning it.
- I don't want to cast asparagus at my opponent.
- The mountain is named for the Reverend Starr King, who was an invertebrate climber.
- The fun and excitement of childhood are nothing compared to the fun and excitement of adultery.
- I refuse to answer that question. It's too suppository.
- I took up aerobics to help maintain my well-propositioned figure.

(See BLOOPER, CHARACTONYM, MONDEGREEN, SPOONERISM.)

Manatee (from the Carib *manati,* "breast, udder") is the most astounding result of all looping anagrams, words in which the front letter is looped to the back, or the back letter to the front, to form a new word, in this instance *emanate/manatee.*

Other super-duper loopers (also called cyclic transposals):

choice/echoic	gelatin/elating	height/eighth	ought/tough
ether/there	heart/earth	lease/easel	trio/riot

Some triple loopers:

eat/ate/tea	route/outer/utero	stable/tables/ablest
emit/mite/item	sear/ears/arse	stripe/tripes/ripest

And an enlightening three-word looper: *cabaret = a bar, etc.*

You'll *grin* at the *ring* of bright letters,
  Like a *sprite* with *esprit* having fun.
You'll *rove over* anagrams looping.
  You'll laugh till you *ache* at *each* one.
The *heart* of the *earth* is the looper.
  Your face will show *miles* of *smile.*
It's an *echoic choice* that *ought* not to be *tough.*
  Aye, yea, they're not *evil* or *vile.*

(See AYE.)

Marshall. The only name in English that I can think of that can be charaded (cleft) in three places to reveal three different pairs of words:

mar shall   mars hall   marsh all

(See ALKALINE, DAREDEVIL, PASTERN, TEMPERAMENTALLY.)

Maverick. Samuel Augustus Maverick (1803–1870), a San Antonio rancher, acquired vast tracts of land and dabbled in cattle raising. When he neglected to brand the calves born into his herd, his neighbors began calling the unmarked offspring by his name. Today this word has come to designate any nonconformist—anyone who refuses to follow the herd. Pluralized, it's also the name of an NBA team that is often clipped to *Mavs.*

(See GERRYMANDER, SANDWICH, SIDEBURNS, SILHOUETTE, SPOONERISM.)

Mentally. Transposing clusters of letters in words to form new words yields an exclusive group of words. Excluded are reverse compounds, such as *boathouse/houseboat, huntsman/manhunts, birdsong/songbird,* and *shotgun/gunshot;* particle verbs, such as *takeout/outtake, over-*

sleep/sleepover, and *upset/setup*; and repetitions, such as *yo-yo, fifty-fifty*, and *pretty-pretty*.

I call these switcheroos "fortunate reversals." Six-letter exhibits include:

ablest/stable	*bedlam/lambed*	*enlist/listen*
errant/ranter	*ripest/stripe*	*selves/vessel*

seven letters:

ingrain/raining *kingpin/pinking* *redrive/rivered* *respect/spectre*

and eight letters:

barstools/toolbars *mentally/tallymen*

(See LATCHES, UNITED.)

Metalious. Movie stars *Judith Anderson, Bela Lugosi, Rosalind Russell, Blair Underwood,* tennis stars *Gussie Moran* and *Guillermo Vilas,* golfer *Justin Leonard,* and Civil War general *Ambrose Burnside* (who eponymously bequeathed us the word for those sweeping sidewhiskers called sideburns) are among the luminaries whose first and last names together contain all the major vowels. But is there a more compactly voweled surname than that of Grace *Metalious,* author of the mega-selling small-town exposé *Peyton Place*?

(See AMBIDEXTROUS, FACETIOUS, SEQUOIA, ULYSSES SIMPSON GRANT, UNCOPYRIGHTABLE, UNNOTICEABLY.)

Metaphor. This seminal word and concept goes back to the Greek *meta* (μετά), "over, across" + *pheréin* (φέρειν), "to carry." A metaphor, then, is a figure of speech that merges two seemingly different objects or ideas and carries us from one realm of existence to another.

You might have been taught that "*a* is like/as *b*" is a simile ("I'm as jumpy as a puppet on a string") and "*a* is *b*" is a metaphor ("life is a cabaret, old chum"). But almost all metaphors present only the *b*, and the reader or listener infers the *a*. Thus, for example, when you make "a spur-of-the-moment decision," the moment is, figuratively, a rider who leaps upon you, the horse, and digs his or her spurs into your flanks.

We usually think of metaphors as figurative devices that only poets create, but, in fact, all of us make metaphors during almost every moment of our waking lives. As T. E. Hulme observed, "Prose is a museum, where all the old weapons of poetry are kept." That's why I never metaphor I didn't like.

Metaphors be with you!

Much as I hate to stick my neck out on a limb, I'm as happy as a pig in a poke to share with you a selection of my favorite mixed metaphors—miscegenated figurative comparisons guaranteed to kindle a flood of laughter in you. It's time to fish or get off the pot and to take the bull by the tail and look it in the eye:

- A virgin forest is a place where the hand of man has never set foot.
- The bankers' pockets are bulging with the sweat of the honest working man.
- During the Napoleonic era, the crowned heads of Europe were trembling in their shoes.
- I came out of that deal smelling like a bandit.
- I have a mind like a steel sieve.
- They're biting the hand of the goose that laid the golden egg.— *Samuel Goldwyn*
- She was a diva of such immense talent that, after she performed, there was seldom a dry seat in the house.

(See CHIASMUS, HYSTERON PROTERON, IRONY, METONYMY, OXYMORON, PARADOX, ZEUGMA.)

Metonymy. When we use the *crown* to refer to a monarchy, the *brass* to refer to the military, and *suits* to refer to business people and other professionals, we are in each case employing a *metonymy*, a label that stands for something else with which it is closely associated.

When we call an athlete a *jock*, we are shortening the athletic supporter known as the jockstrap and metonymously making it stand for the person's identity. The connection has become so figurative that women, who never wear that equipment, are also called jocks.

(See CHIASMUS, HYSTERON PROTERON, IRONY, METAPHOR, OXYMORON, PARADOX, ZEUGMA.)

Mississippi. How many letters are there in the state name of *Mississippi*? Eleven, of course—but one could also say four—*m, i, s,* and *p*. In letter patterning, *Mississippi* is clearly the best of the state names, rivaled only by *Tennessee*. Both names contain just one vowel repeated four times, three sets of double letters, and only four different letters.

But *Mississippi* has the distinction of containing a seven-letter embedded palindrome–*ississi;* three overlapping four-letter palindromes—

issi, issi, and *ippi;* and a double triple—*ississ.* And each year is crowned a new *Miss Mississippi,* whose title consists of three double triples—*Missmiss, ississ,* and *ssissi.*

Here are some more art-of-the-state insights into the letters in our states:

- *Connecticut.* What begins with a union and ends with a separation? The answer is *Connecticut,* which can be charaded into the oxymoron *Connect I cut.*

- *Hawaii* is the only state with a double vowel. HAWAII is also the longest state whose capital letters are vertically symmetrical and will thus appear the same in a mirror. The other three are IOWA, OHIO, and UTAH.

- *Kentucky* ends with its own postal code.

- *Maine* is the only one-syllable state. The curtailment *Maine/main* is homophonous.

- *Massachusetts* is, with thirteen letters, the longest single-word state name. *North* and *South Carolina* match the length of *Massachusetts* in two words.

- *Minnesota* uses every letter to form the anagram *nominates.*

- *New Mexico* is the longest state name consisting entirely of alternating consonants and vowels (within each word). *Alabama, Arizona, Colorado, Delaware, Oregon, Nevada, Texas,* and *Utah* also adhere to this pattern.

- *New York*'s capital, Albany, ends with the state's postal code.

- It's a foregone conclusion that if you behead and curtail *foregone,* you end up with *Oregon.*

- *South Dakota* is the only state that shares no letters with its own capital—*Pierre.*

(See MAINLAND.)

Mondegreen. To the surprise of many rock-and-roll enthusiasts, Jimi Hendrix sang, "'Scuse me while I kiss the sky," not "'Scuse me while I kiss this guy."

- George Gershwin wrote *Rhapsody in Blue,* not *Rap City in Blue.*

- "Clown control to Mao Zedong" is at least as colorful and imaginative as David Bowie's original lyric, "Ground control to Major Tom."

- And if Davy Crockett was "killed in a bar when he was only three," who was that at the Alamo?

The word *mondegreen* was coined by Sylvia Wright, who wrote about the phenomenon in a 1954 *Harper's* column, in which she recounted hearing a Scottish folk ballad, "The Bonny Earl of Murray." She heard the lyric "Oh, they have slain the Earl of Murray / And Lady Mondegreen." Wright powerfully identified with Lady Mondegreen, the faithful friend of the Bonny Earl. Lady Mondegreen died for her liege with dignity and tragedy. How romantic!

It was some years later that Sylvia Wright learned that the last two lines of the stanza were really "They have slain the Earl of Murray / And laid him on the green." She named such sweet slips of the ear *mondegreens*, and thus they have been called ever since.

Children are especially prone to fresh and original interpretations of the boundaries that separate words in fresh and unconventional ways. Our patriotic and religious songs and vows have been delightfully revised by misspelt youth:

> Jose, can you see
> By the Donzerly light?
> Oh, the ramrods we washed
> Were so gallantly steaming.
> And the rockets' red glare,
> The bombs bursting in there,
> Grapefruit through the night
> That our flag was still rare.
>
>   * * *
>
> I pledge the pigeons to the flag
> Of the United States of America
> And to the republic for Richard Stans,
> One naked individual, underground,
> With liver, tea, injustice for all.
>
>   * * *
>
> Our Father, Art, in Heaven, Harold be Thy name.
> Thy King done come. They will be done
> On earth, as it is in heaven.
> Give us this day our jelly bread,
> And forgive us our press passes
> As we forgive those who press past us.
> And lead us not into Penn Station,
> But deliver us some e-mail . . .

RICHARD LEDERER

When I was a lad in 1943, I adored a popular nonsense song titled *Mairzy Doats*, sung by The Merry Macs. The refrain sounded meaningless:

Mairzy doats and dozy doats and liddle lamzy divey.
A kiddley divey, too, wooden shoe?

Eventually the idea dawned on me that I was listening to a bunch of words with their edges blurred. Turned out most of the lyrics were mondegreens, although that word hadn't yet been invented. The lyrics of the bridge, however, provide a clue:

If the words sound queer and funny to your ear, a little bit jumbled and jivey,
Sing "Mares eat oats and does eat oats and little lambs eat ivy."

That opened up my ears to the last line of the refrain: "A kid'll eat ivy, too, wouldn't you?"

(See BLOOPER, MALAPROPISM, SPOONERISM.)

Mother. The word for *mother* (and *mama* and *mom*) in an astonishing array of languages begins with the letter *m*—*mater* (Latin), *mere* (French), *madre* (Spanish), *mutter* (German), *mam* (Welsh), *mat* (Russian), *ma* (Mandarin), *me* (Vietnamese), *mama* (Swahili), *makuahine* (Hawaiian), and *masake* (Crow Indian). Could it be more than mere coincidence that this pervasive *m* sound for words maternal is made by the pursing of lips in the manner of the suckling babe?

(See BASH, SNEEZE.)

Mumpsimus. *The Century Dictionary* tells "the story of an ignorant priest who in saying his mass had long said *mumpsimus* for *sumpsimus* and who, when his error was pointed out, replied, 'I am not going to change my old *mumpsimus* for your new *sumpsimus*.'"

Mumpsimus, then, denotes stubborn adherence to an erroneous view, as in "He persists in believing the old mumpsimus that a woman's place is in the home."

Napoleon. What do you get when you throw a bomb into a recreation room? Linoleum blown apart.

On a more serious note, gaze upon the palindromic sentence that Napoleon uttered as he paced the shores of the island of Elba in 1814:

Elba Fable
"Able was I ere I saw Elba,"
Napoleon cried like a toy-deprived kid.
Wellington mocked in reply, "Did I
Disable Elba's id? I did!"

(See ADAM, AGAMEMNON, CIVIC, KINNIKINNIK, PALINDROME, SENSUOUSNESS, WONTON, *ZOONOOZ*.)

Nerd. When we think about inventions, we conjure up visions of the wheel, the sail, and the electric light—artifacts that humankind has not always possessed. Words are such an integral part of our consciousness that we believe that they have always existed, like stones and grass and trees. But words are more like weaving and flint tools.

Each new word is inventively spoken or written for the very first time by a particular human being at a particular moment.

Although the identities of most of these wordmakers are lost in the mist of history, we do know who were the creators of a number of neologisms ("new words"). Many of these neologizers are novelists, playwrights, poets, and essayists who are gifted with a keen ear for language, who love to play with words, and who record their fanciful fabrications in print.

We know, for example, that *nerd* first appears in print in 1950 in the Dr. Seuss children's book *If I Ran the Zoo*. Therein a boy named Gerald McGrew makes a great number of delightfully extravagant claims as to what he would do if he were in charge at the zoo. Among these fanciful schemes is:

> And then just to show them, I'll sail to Ka-Troo
> And bring back an IT-KUTCH, a PREEP, and a PROO,
> A NERKLE, a NERD, and a SEERSUCKER, too!

The accompanying illustration for NERD shows a grumpy Seuss creature with unruly hair and sideburns, wearing a black T-shirt— not terribly nerdlike. For whatever reasons, *it-kutch, preep, proo,* and *nerkle* have never been enshrined in any dictionary.

In addition to the lexical creations of Joseph Heller, Charles Dickens, Lewis Carroll, James Barrie, L. Frank Baum, John Milton, Sir Thomas Moore, and William Shakespeare, discussed elsewhere, here's a list of ten authors who have contributed neologisms ("new words") to our language, who have sculpted significance from air and changed the world by changing the word:

• William Tyndale	*scapegoat*	1530
• Ben Jonson	*diary*	1581
• John Dryden	*witticism*	1677
• Jonathan Swift	*yahoo*	1726
• Thomas Jefferson	*belittle*	1797
• Washington Irving	*almighty dollar*	1836
• Harriet Beecher Stowe	*underground railway*	1852
• Herman Melville	*Americana*	1886
• Karel Capek	*robot*	1921
• Stephen Potter	*gamesmanship*	1947

(See CATCH-22, CHARACTONYM, CHORTLE, DOGHOUSE, OZ, PAN-DEMONIUM, WILLIAM SHAKESPEARE.)

No. *What English word seems to you the most useful to the language?* Back in 1931, that question was put to a small panel of eminent novelists, poets, critics, humorists, and educators.

Some of the respondents reasoned that our most useful word must be one of the ten English words most frequently used in conversations, as determined by the word counts of that day. On the basis of frequency alone, *the* was considered our most useful word. Turning to meaning, the panel offered *bread, do, eat, fix, help, man,* and *thing.*

But the greatest number of panelists chose *no* as the most useful word in the English language. It's probably no coincidence that *no* is the first word uttered by more than 50 percent of the world's English-speaking population.

Nonsupports. Here we have the longest word (eleven letters) cobbled entirely of letters from the second half of the alphabet. *Untrustworthy* (thirteen letters) is a frustrating near miss because we can't get the *h* out of there. (Actually, *untrustworthy* is a near hit because a near miss is a hit.)

Soupspoons and the hyphenated *topsy-turvy* are common ten-letter, second-half-of-the-alphabet words.

(See CABBAGE.)

Nother. We hear (seldom see) this "word" only in expressions such as "That's a whole nother matter" and "That's a whole nother ballgame." What is going on here?

Here's what I think. Our English language features a great number of prefixes, such as *pre-* as in *prewar* and suffixes, such as *-ness,* as in *goodness.* Rarely do we encounter infixes, meaning-bearing elements that occupy the middle of a word. When we do, they tend to be naughty, as in the British, *absobloodylutely!,* and the American unprintables—"I'll guarang__d__tee you" and "That's inf__ingcredible!"

So in my view, in "a whole nother ballgame," *whole* is a rare English infix that sits in the middle of the word *another.*

Nth is the best of the one-syllable words that do not include any of the major vowels, *a, e, i, o,* or *u!* In this game you just can't buy a vowel.

With tongue firmly planted in cheek, some call these words that have had a vowel movement "abstemious" words, a facetious label since *abstemious* (along with *facetious*) is stuffed with every major vowel, and in sequence:

by, cry, crypt(s), cyst(s), dry(ly), fly, flyby, fry, glyph(s), gym(s), gyp(s), gypsy, hymn(s), lymph(s), lynch, lynx, my, myrrh, myth(s), nymph(s), ply, pry, pygmy, rhythm(s), shy(ly), sky, sly(ly), spry(ly), spy, sty, sylph(s), synch(s), thy, try, tryst(s), why(s), and *wry(ly).*

One three-syllable word also avoids the major vowels—*syzygy*, which means "the nearly straight-line configuration of three celestial bodies." *Syzygy* is an especially appropriate spelling for such a heavenly three-syllable word.

But *nth*, as in "the nth degree," is triumphantly abstemious because it contains no vowel at all.

A Sonnet to Abstemious Words

Once did a *shy* but *spry gypsy*
Spy a *pygmy,* who made him feel tipsy.
Her form, like a *lynx, sylph,* and *nymph,*
Made all his *dry* glands feel quite *lymph.*

He felt so in *synch* with her *rhythm*
That he hoped she'd *fly* to the *sky* with him.
No *sly myth* would he *try* on her;
Preferring to *ply* her with *myrrh.*

When apart, he would *fry* and then *cry,*
Grow a *cyst* and a *sty* in his eye.
That's *why* they would *tryst* at the *gym,*
By a *crypt,* where he'd write a *wry hymn.*

Her he loved to the *nth* degree,
Like a heavenly *syzygy.*

Now that you're wise to the *y*'s, ask yourself if any other words cavort across the stage of language without spotting any *a, e, i, o,* or *u*—or the minor vowels *y* or *w.*

Hmm. That's one that you can find in some dictionaries, including Scrabble lexicons. I'm not including initialisms, such as *TV* and *Ph.D.*

Shh. Before you grab some *z*'s, give me some time to think. There, you've just spotted another two, along with *brr, pfft,* and *tsk-tsk.*

I sincerely hope that these abstemious words have pleased you, not just to the first, fifth, or tenth degree, but (and embedded in the poem above) to the *nth* degree!

(See RHYTHMS.)

Nuclear. Reverse the first two letters and you get *unclear.*

What *is* clear is that the pronunciation *noo-kyuh-lur* has received much notoriety because a number of presidents, from Dwight David Eisenhower to George W. Bush, have sounded the word that way. The late broadcaster and language commentator Edwin Newman wrote: "The word, correctly pronounced, is too much for a fair part of the population, and education and experience seem to have nothing to do with it."

Noo-kyuh-lur is an example of metathesis, the transposition of internal sounds, as in *Ree-luh-tur* for *Realtor, joo-luh-ree* for *jewelry, hunderd* for *hundred, lahr-niks* for *larynx,* and, more subtly, *cumfter-bull* for *comfortable* and *Wends-day* for *Wednesday.* While the metatheses *cumf-ter-bull* (in which the *r* and the *t* have been transposed) and *Wends-day* (in which the *n* and the *d* have been switched) are fully acceptable and entrenched in our language, cultivated speakers generally consider *noo-kyuh-lur, Ree-luh-tur,* and their ilk to be atrocities.

From Eisenhower (who simply "could not get it right," wrote journalist Edwin Newman) to George W. Bush, *noo-kyuh-lur* has never stopped raising hackles and igniting jeers. *The San Diego Union-Tribune* recently polled its readers to find out the grammar and pronunciation abuses that most seismically yanked their chains and rattled their cages. *Noo-kyuh-lur* was the crime against English mentioned by the greatest number of respondents.

Despite its proliferation, *noo-kyuh-lur* has failed to gain respectability. *Noo-kyuh-lur* may be a sad fact of life, but resistance to it is hardly a lost cause. Although we hear it from some prominent people, it remains a much-derided aberration.

Nut. During a fund drive for WNYC public radio, I fielded questions from New York's finest listeners. At some point, host Leonard Lopate pitched this line: "It costs this station almost $700,000 a year to buy all the national programs you hear each weekend. That's a really big nut to make."

Sure enough, a listener called in to ask the origin of *making the nut*. I love questions like that because I get my audio radiance from my radio audience, and I explained to the listener that when a circus came to town, the sheriff would often remove the nut from a wheel of the main wagon. Because in bygone days these nuts were elaborately and individually crafted, they were well-nigh impossible to replace. Thus, the circus couldn't leave town until the costs of land and utilities rental, easements, and security were paid. It's but a short metaphorical leap to the modern meaning of *making the nut,* "meeting one's expenses."

(See CIRCUS, METAPHOR.)

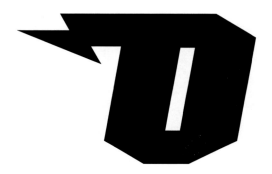

Oil. In the Brooklyn dialect, the word for the black sticky stuff is pronounced "earl," while the noble *earl* is pronounced "oil"—a perfect transposition of sound.

By the way, the origin of *oil* has nothing to do with fossil fuels. The word started out as *élaion* (ἐλαίϝᾱ) in Greek and meant "olive." Popeye's girlfriend applauds this explanation.

(See HOAGIE, Y'ALL.)

OK. What may be the most useful expression of universal communication ever devised, *OK* is recognizable and pronounceable in almost every language on earth.

The late Columbia Professor Allen Walker Read tracked down the first known published appearance of *OK* with its current meaning in the Boston *Morning Post* on March 23, 1839: "The 'Chairman of the Committee on Charity Lecture Balls' is one of the deputation, and perhaps if he should return to Boston, via Providence, he of the Journal, and his train-band, would have the 'contribution box,' et ceteras, o.k.—all correct—and cause the corks to fly, like sparks, upward."

Dr. Read demonstrated that *OK* started life as an obscure joke and through a twist of fate went to the top of the charts on the American hit parade of words. In the 1830s, in New England, there was a craze for initialisms, in the manner of *LOL, OMG, aka,* and *TGIF,* so popular today. The fad went so far as to generate letter combinations of intentionally comic misspellings: *KG* for "know go," *KY* for "know yuse," *NSMJ* for "'nough said 'mong jentlemen," and *OR* for "oll rong." *OK* for "oll korrect" naturally followed.

Of all those loopy initialisms and jocular misspellings *OK* alone survived. That's because of a presidential nickname that consolidated the letters in the national memory. Martin Van Buren, elected our eighth president in 1836, was born in Kinderhook, New York, and, early in his political career, was dubbed "Old Kinderhook." Echoing the "oll korrect" initialism, *OK* became the rallying cry of the Old Kinderhook Club, a Democratic organization supporting Van Buren during the 1840 campaign. Thus, the accident of Van Buren's birthplace rescued *OK* from the dustbin of history.

The coinage did Van Buren no good, and he was defeated in his bid for reelection. But *OK* has become what H. L. Mencken identified as "the most shining and successful Americanism ever invented."

(See CANDIDATE, COOL, FILIBUSTER, HOAGIE, IDIOT, OSTRACIZE, POLITICS, RADAR.)

Orange. A number of words, such as *breadth, depth, fifth, gulf,* and *month,* are famous for being unrhymable. A spectrum of color words— most colorfully *orange, purple,* and *silver*—are often cited as having no words that rhyme with them. But they do.

One Henry Honeychurch Gorringe was a naval commander who in the mid-nineteenth century oversaw the transport of the obelisk Cleopatra's Needle to New York's Central Park. Pouncing on this event, the poet Arthur Guiterman wrote:

> In Sparkhill buried lies a man of mark
>> Who brought the Obelisk to Central Park,
> Redoubtable Commander H.H. Gorringe,
>> Whose name supplies the long-sought rhyme for *orange.*

Or you can bend the rules of line breaks and sound as Willard Espy did:

> Four eng-
> ineers
> Wear orange
> brassieres.

So *orange* is rhymable, as are *purple - curple*: "headquarters, especially of a horse"—and *silver - chilver*: "a ewe lamb."

Orthography—from the Greek *ortho* (ὀρθός): "straight, correct" + *gráphein*: "to write"—is a fancy word for *spelling*. The number of words that cause writers orthographic trouble is relatively small, and they tend to be the common words. According to a swatch of studies, the most frequently misspelled words and word groups are: (1) *there-their-they're*, (2) *to-too-two*, (3) *receive*, (4) *existence-existent*, (5) *occur-occurred-occurrence-occurring*, (6) *definite-definitely-definition*, (7) *separate-separation*, (8) *belief-believe*, (9) *occasion-occasional*, and (10) *lose-losing*.

That line-up doesn't include *its-it's,* which is so frequently messed up that it is a category unto itself, a perfect storm of misspelling and mispunctuation.

A spectre is haunting the English-speaking world—the spectre of the gratuitous apostrophe. *It's* is so often employed as a possessive pronoun, when *its* is the correct choice, that *it's* has become a category of grammatical atrocity unto itself. If you feel that the gratuitous apostrophe (I call it a "prespostrophe") doesn't really make any difference, consider the two sentences below and determine which dog has the upper paw:

(1) A clever dog knows its master.
(2) A clever dog knows it's master.

Speaking of dogs, the most misspelled dog breed is the name for those handsome canines with the short white coat and the dappling of black spots. No, I'm not talking about *Dalmations*. I'm talking about *Dalmatians*, so spelled because the breed is said to have originated in Dalmatia, a peninsula on the Adriatic Sea.

If you think that correct spelling doesn't matter, have a look at these orthographical blunders:

* On Thanksgiving Day we could smell the foul cooking.
* In Pittsburgh they manufacture iron and steal.
* If a tree falls in the dessert, does it make a sound?

- Vestal virgins were pure and chased.
- In midevil times most people were alliterate.
- Joan of Arc was burnt to a steak.
- They gave William IV a large funeral. It took six men to carry the beer.

Ostracize. The verb *to ostracize* means "to exclude from a group by popular consent," and hidden in that verb is an oyster. Rather than clamming up and floundering around, let's go fishing for the animal origin of *ostracize*.

Oysters (from the Greek *óstreon* [ὀστέον], "hard shell") were a staple of the ancient Greek diet. In ancient Athens, a citizen could be banished by popular vote of other citizens, who gathered in the marketplace and wrote down the name of the undesirable on a tile or potsherd. If enough votes were dropped into an urn, the spurned citizen was sent from the city for five or ten years. Because the shards of pottery resembled an oyster, they were called *ostrakismós* (ὄστρακα), the Greek word for "oyster shell," whence our verb for general exclusion.

Centuries after the *ostrakismós*, Italians used small balls or pebbles to vote, "casting" them into one box or another. Hence, the word *ballot*, "a small ball or pebble."

(See BUFFALO, BUTTERFLY, CANARY, CLAM, CRESTFALLEN, DACHS-HUND, DANDELION, HORSEFEATHERS, PARTRIDGE, PEDIGREE, TAD, TURKEY, VACCINATE, ZYZZYVA.)

Out. Here's a little finger exercise. Remember that I'm the teacher, so you must try to do what I ask. Make a circle with the fingers on your left hand by touching the tip of your index finger to the tip of your thumb. Now poke your head through that circle.

If you unsuccessfully tried to fit your head through the small digital circle, you (and almost any reader) thought that the phrase "poke your head" meant that your head was the poker. But if you raised your left hand with the circle of fingers up close to your forehead and poked your right index finger through that circle until it touched your forehead, you realized that the phrase "poke your head" has a second, and opposite, meaning: that the head is the pokee. Such words and compounds are called Janus-faced words or contronyms.

Here are two sentences that will solidify your understanding of how contronyms work:

"The moon is VISIBLE tonight."
"The lights in the old house are always INVISIBLE."

Although the two capitalized words are opposite in meaning, both can be replaced by the same word—*out*. When the moon or sun or stars are out, they are visible. When the lights are out, they are invisible.

Here are some contronymic words that show how words wander wondrously and testify to the fact that nothing in the English language is absolute:

- *with.* alongside; against: *a.* England fought with France against Germany. *b.* England fought with France.
- *clip.* fasten; separate: *a.* Clip the coupon to the newspaper. *b.* Clip the coupon from the newspaper. Similarly, *trim, dust, dress.*
- *fast.* firmly in one place; rapidly from one place to another: *a.* The pegs held the tent fast. *b.* She ran fast.
- *hold up.* support; hinder: *a.* Please hold up the sagging branch. *b.* Accidents hold up the flow of traffic
- *keep up.* continue to fall; continue to stay up: *a.* The farmers hope that the rain will keep up. *b.* Damocles hoped that the sword above his head would keep up.
- *cleave.* separate; adhere firmly: *a.* A strong blow will cleave a plank in two. *b.* Bits of metal cleave to a magnet.
- *sanction.* give approval of; censure: *a.* The NCAA plans to sanction the event. *b.* Should our country impose a new sanction on Syria?
- *oversight.* careful supervision; neglect: *a.* The foreman was responsible for the oversight of the project. *b.* The foreman's oversight ruined the success of the project.
- *burn.* to destroy; to create: *a.* Let's burn the evidence. *b.* Let's burn a CD.
- *wear.* endure through use; decay through use: *a.* This suit will wear like iron. *b.* Water can cause mountains to wear.
- *fix.* restore, remove part of: *a.* It's time to fix the fence. *b.* It's time to fix the bull.

- *take.* obtain; offer: *a.* Professional photographers take good pictures. *b.* Professional models take good pictures.
- *wind up.* start; end: *a.* I have to wind up my watch. *b.* Now I have to wind up this discussion of curious and contrary contronyms.

(See OUTGOING, RAISE.)

Outgoing. What two words in the English language are synonyms but also, without changing anything in the two words, antonyms? The answer is *retiring* and *outgoing.* They're synonyms that mean "leaving the job": "Sally is the retiring Head of Technical Services"; "Sally is the outgoing Head of Technical Services." But they're also antonyms that mean "shy" and "effervescent": "Sally is retiring in social situations"; "Sally is outgoing in social situations."

(See OUT, RAISE.)

Overstuffed houses four consecutive letters of the alphabet, *rstu*, in order. *Overstudious, understudy,* and *superstud* are the only other common words that do that. The more arcane *gymnophobia*, "the fear of nudity," includes the sequence *mnop.*

Oxymoron. An oxymoron is not a big, dumb cow. Rather, an oxymoron is a figure of speech in which two incongruous, contradictory terms are yoked together in a small space. Self-referentially, the word *oxymoron* is itself oxymoronic because it is formed from two Greek roots of opposite meaning—*oxýs* (ὀξύς), "sharp, keen," and *mōros* (μόρος), "foolish," the same root that gives us the word *moron.*

Close kin to *oxymoron* is *sophomore*, a juxtaposition of the Greek *sophós* (σοφία), "wisdom," as in *sophisticated,* "wise in the ways of the world," and the abovementioned *mōros,* "foolish." Many a sophomore is indeed a wise fool.

Other single-word oxymorons include *firewater, spendthrift, wholesome, superette* ("large small"), *Connecticut* ("Connect. I cut."), and the name *Noyes* ("No yes").

Literary oxymorons, created *accidentally on purpose*, include Geoffrey Chaucer's *hateful good*, Edmund Spenser's *proud humility,* John Milton's *darkness visible*, Alexander Pope's "damn with *faint praise*," Lord Byron's *melancholy merriment*, James Thomson's *expressive silence*, Alfred Lord Tennyson's *falsely true*, Ernest Hemingway's *scalding coolness*, and, the most quoted of all, William Shakespeare's "parting is such *sweet sorrow.*"

Among the best two-word oxymora are *jumbo shrimp, military intelligence, political science, good grief, sight unseen, negative growth,* and *flat busted.*

I can only hope that this dissertation on the oxymoron will not go over like a *lead balloon.*

(See CHIASMUS, IRONY, HYSTERON PROTERON, IRONY, META-PHOR, METONYMY, PARADOX, ZEUGMA.)

Oy, *oy vay,* and *oy vay is mir* are Yiddish words that mean literally "Oh, pain." These words also constitute an entire vocabulary. *Oy vay* and *oy* can express any emotion from mild pleasure to vaulting pride, from mild relief to lament through a vale of tears. Albert Einstein's theory of relativity laid the theoretical foundation for the building of the atom bomb. When the great scientist received the news of the mass destruction wrought by the bombs dropped on Hiroshima and Nagasaki, he reacted with two Yiddish words often invoked in such black circumstances: "Oy vay."

When Isaac Bashevis Singer was awarded the Nobel Prize for Literature in 1978, he remarked in his acceptance speech: "The high honor bestowed upon me is also a recognition of the Yiddish language—a language of exile, without a land, without frontiers, not supported by any government, a language which possesses no words for weapons, ammunition, military exercises, war tactics. There is a quiet humor in Yiddish and a gratitude for every day of life, every crumb of success, each encounter of love. In a figurative way, Yiddish is the wise and humble language of us all, the idiom of a frightened and hopeful humanity."

Most of us already speak a fair amount of Yiddish without fully realizing that we do. Almost a hundred Yiddish words have become part of our everyday conversations, including:

- *fin:* slang for five dollar bill, from *finf,* the Yiddish word for "five";
- *glitch:* an error or malfunction in a plan or machine;
- *gun moll:* a double clipping of *gonif's Molly,* Yiddish for "thief's woman";
- *kibitzer:* one who comments, often in the form of unwanted advice, during a game, often cards;
- *maven:* expert;
- *mazuma:* money;

- *mish-mosh:* a mess;
- *schlep:* to drag or haul;
- *schmooze:* to converse informally;
- *schnoz:* nose;
- *yenta:* a blabbermouth, gossip, woman of low origins . . .

. . . and so on through the whole *megillah,* or long, involved story.

Oz. He wrote under the pseudonyms Schuyler Stanton, Floyd Akers, and Edith Van Dyne, but he is best known as L. Frank Baum. In 1900, he sat down to create a children's book about a girl named Dorothy, who was swept away to a fantastic land inhabited by munchkins and witches and a scarecrow, a tin man, and a lion.

The fairy tale began as a bedtime story for Baum's children and their friends and soon spilled over into several evening sessions. During one of the tellings, Baum was asked the name of the strange place to which Dorothy was transported. Glancing about the room, Baum's eyes fell upon the drawers of a filing cabinet labeled "A-N" and "O-Z."

Noting that the letters on the second label spelled out the *ah*s uttered by his rapt listeners, Baum named his fantastic land Oz. Ever since, *The Wonderful Wizard of Oz* has lived in the hearts of children—and grown-ups. Translated into at least thirty languages, it is the best-selling juvenile book of all time.

(See CATCH-22, CHARACTONYM, CHORTLE, DOGHOUSE, NERD, PANDEMONIUM, WILLIAM SHAKESPEARE.)

A **palindrome** (from the Greek *palindromos* [παλίνδρομος], "running back again") is a word, a *word row,* a sentence, or a longer statement that communicates the same message when the letters of which it is composed are read in reverse order. Even if you're a *dud, kook, boob,* or *poop,* palindromes should make you exult, *Ah ha!, Oh, ho!, Hey, yeh!, Yo boy!, Yay!, Wow!, Tut-Tut!, Har-har!, Rah-rah!, Heh-heh!, Hoorah! Har! Ooh!,* and *Ahem! It's time. Ha!*

Prize palindromes exhibit subject-verb structure. Cobbling a subject-verb palindromic statement is harder to pull off than single-word or phrasal palindromes and, hence, more elegant when the result is successful. Moreover, subject-verb syntax inspires the reader to conjure up a clearer image of persons or things in action:

- Nurse, I spy gypsies. Run!
- Sit on a potato pan, Otis.
- Stop! Murder us not, tonsured rumpots!

This matter of imagery is crucial to the greatness of a palindrome. Top-drawer palindromic statements invoke a picture of the world

RICHARD LEDERER

that is a bubble off plumb yet somehow of our world. One *could* warn one's nurse that gypsies are nearby. Someone named Otis *could* sit on a potato pan, and shorn drunkards *could* seek to do us grave bodily harm.

Two of my favorite subject-verb palindromes are *Elk City, Kansas, is a snaky tickle* (and there really is an Elk City, Kansas) and *Doc, note. I dissent. A fast never prevents a fatness. I diet on cod.* But as delightfully loopy as the first specimen is and as astonishing in its length and coherence as the second three-sentence jawdropper is, they do not summon up vivid images to cavort in our mind's eye.

Using the rubrics of elegance, subject-verb structure, and bizarre but vivid imagery, I submit that the greatest palindrome ever cobbled is: *Go hang a salami. I'm a lasagna hog.*

Now that you have read this small disquisition on the art and craft of the palindromes, I hope you have lost any *aibohphobia*, "fear of palindromes," you may have experienced and are now suffused with *ailihphilia*, "a love of palindromes."

(See ADAM, AGAMEMNON, CIVIC, KINNIKINNIK, NAPOLEON, SENSUOUSNESS, WONTON, *ZOONOOZ*.)

Pandemonium. In his epic poem *Paradise Lost,* John Milton invented *Pandemonium*—from the Greek *pan* (Πᾶν), "all," and *daimon* (δαίμων), "evil," literally "a place for all the demons"—as the name of the home for Satan and his devilish friends. Because the devils were noisy, the meaning of *pandemonium,* now lowercased, has been broadened from "the capital of hell" to mean "uproar and tumult."

Pandemonium exhibits the major vowels—*a, e, i, o,* and *u*—in almost alphabetical order. It also can be defined as "what happens when the pandas at the zoo go nuts."

For many lovers of literature, places that exist only between the covers of books are as vivid as places that actually exist on gas station maps, and many of these literary locations dot the maps of our literature:

- *Never Land/Never-Never-Land.* In James M. Barrie's 1904 play *Peter Pan*, the title character presides over an imaginary realm peopled by fairies, mermaids, pirates, and Indians. Barrie's Never Land is a place where little boys never grow up, and the name has become a synonym for an escapist fantasy land. No wonder that Michael Jackson named his Florida Ranch, with its appeal to children, *Neverland.*

- *Shangri-La.* In James Hilton's 1933 novel *Lost Horizon,* the protagonist, Hugh Conway, finds inner peace, love, and purpose in Shangri-La, set in remote Tibet. Popularized by the novel and the 1937 movie, *Shangri-La* has become a name for any isolated, spiritual paradise on earth.

- *Utopia.* In 1516 Sir Thomas More wrote a book about an ideal state. As a name for both the novel and the place, More coined a name from the Greek word parts *ou,* "not," *topos,* "place," and *-ia,* "state of being." The resulting word has come to designate any ideal society—*utopia.* The opposite of a utopia is a *dystopia*—a nightmarish, totalitarian society, such as *Brave New World, 1984,* and *Walden Two,* that erodes the human spirit and desiccates the soul.

- *Wonderland.* On "a golden afternoon," as he called it, an Oxford don named Charles Lutwidge Dodgson began to spin a dreamtale about a little girl named Alice who followed a white rabbit down a hole and into a fantastic world of Cheshire Cats, Mad Hatters, and Red and White Queens. In 1865, the Rev. Dodgson published *Alice's Adventures in Wonderland* under the pseudonym Lewis Carroll. Ever since, a *wonderland* has signified a place lit by magical charm.

(See CATCH-22, CHARACTONYM, CHORTLE, DOGHOUSE, NERD, OZ, WILLIAM SHAKESPEARE.)

Pangram. One of the mightiest challenges for the intrepid logologist is to construct the perfect pangram—a sentence that employs every letter in the alphabet at least once. The most famous exhibit is *The quick brown fox jumps over a lazy dog*, but since that thirty-three-letter statement was created for typists, many shorter ones have bounded onto the stage:

- *Pack my box with five dozen liquor jugs.* (32 letters)
- *Jackdaws love my big sphinx of quartz.* (31)
- *How quickly daft jumping zebras vex.* (30)
- *Quick, wafting zephyrs vex bold Jim.* (29)
- *Waltz, nymph, for quick jigs vex Bud.* (28)
- *Bawds jog, flick quartz, vex nymph.* (27)

And—glory be!—cast your eyes upon four twenty-six-letter Peter Pangrams:

- Mr. Jock, TV quiz Ph.D., bags few lynx.
- The glib czar junks my VW Fox PDQ.
- How JV quartz pyx flings muck bed.
- Vext zing fly jabs cwm Kurd qoph.

The first two of these exhibits make perfect sense but contain two initialisms. The third sentence contains one initialism and an arcane word, *pyx*: a vessel used in the Catholic church. The last is a sentence devoid of initialisms, and it does have a meaning, roughly "An irked, buzzing fly pokes a Hebrew letter written by a valley Kurd." But, to say the least, that pangram is not terribly accessible.

If you can come up with a twenty-six-letter pangram that makes easy sense and doesn't resort to initials, names, and mutant words, wing it to me, and I'll make you famous.

(See UNCOPYRIGHTABLE.)

Paradox. My son Howard and daughter Annie are professional poker players who live and move and have their beings in that window-less, clockless pleasure dome known as Las Vegas. It's an easy life—earning thousands of dollars in a single night just sitting around play-ing card games. But it's a hard-knock life, too, what with the long, sedentary hours; the addictive behavior and secondhand smoke that suffuse the poker rooms; and the times when Lady Luck goes out whoring and your pocketbook and ego get mugged.

How best to catch and crystallize this collide-o-scopic life my chil-dren lead, this life of gorgeous poker rooms and hearts of darkness, of Euclidean clarity and survival of the meanest? Bob "Silver Eagle" Thompson, once tournament director of the World Series of Poker at Binion's Horseshoe casino, said it best: "Poker is a tough way to make an easy living."

That's a paradox, a statement that seems absurd or self-contradic-tory but that turns out to be true. The word *paradox* combines *para,* "against," and *doxos,* "opinion, belief." In its Greek form the word meant "not what you'd expect to be true."

Paradox is a particularly powerful device to ensnare truth because it concisely tells us something that we did not know we knew. It engages our hearts and minds because, beyond its figurative employ-ment, paradox has always been at the center of the human condition. "Man's real life," wrote Carl Jung, "consists of a complex of inexora-ble opposites—day and night, birth and death, happiness and misery, good and evil. If it were not so, existence would come to an end."

Paradox was a fact of life long before it became a literary and rhetorical device. Who among us has not experienced something ugly in everything beautiful, something true in everything false, something female in something male, or, as King Claudius says in Shakespeare's *Hamlet,* "mirth in funeral" and "dirge in marriage"? Who among us is not captured by and captured in Alexander Pope's "An Essay on Man"?:

> Placed on the isthmus of a middle state,
> A being darkly wise and rudely great:
> With too much knowledge on the Sceptic side,
> With too much weakness for the Stoic's pride,
> He hangs between; in doubt to act, or rest,
> In doubt to deem himself a God, or Beast.
> In doubt his mind or body to prefer,
> Born but to die, and reasoning but to err;
>
> . . .
>
> Sole judge of Truth, in endless Error hurled:
> The glory, jest, and riddle of the world!

As I—glory, jest, and riddle—finish writing this entry, I suffer a little death. Something has ended, winked out, never to be begun, shaped, or completed again. But, at the same time, as I approach the end, I think of the poet John Donne, who, four centuries ago, chanted the paradoxology of our lives: "Death, thou shalt die."

Now that I'm ending this small disquisition, I'm a bit immortal, too, because I know that you, in another place and another time, are passing your eyes over these words and sharing my thoughts and emotions long after I have struck the symbols on my keyboard, perhaps even after I have slipped this mortal coil.

(See CHIASMUS, HYSTERON PROTERON, IRONY, METAPHOR, METONYMY, OXYMORON, ZEUGMA.)

Partridge. Believe it or not, the name of this game bird soars up from the Greek *perdesthai,* "to break wind," a humorous comparison to the whirring noise of the bird's wings in flight.

In the seasonal song "The Twelve Days of Christmas," have you ever wondered why the true love sends not only a partridge but an entire pear tree? That's because in the early French version of the song the suitor proffered only a partridge, which in French is rendered as *une pertriz.* A 1718 English version combined the two—

"*a partridge, une pertriz,*" which, slightly corrupted, came out sounding like "a partridge in a pear tree." Through a process known as folk etymology, the partridge has remained proudly perched in a pear tree ever since.

(See BUFFALO, BUTTERFLY, CANARY, CLAM, CRESTFALLEN, DACHSHUND, DANDELION, HORSEFEATHERS, OSTRACIZE, PEDIGREE, TAD, TURKEY, VACCINATE, ZYZZYVA.)

Pastern. The part of a horse's foot between the fetlock and the top of the hoof. In his influential *Dictionary of the English Language*, Samuel Johnson famously misdefined the word as "the knee of a horse." When a woman asked Dr. J to explain why he had botched the definition, he replied, "Ignorance, madam. Pure ignorance."

Logologically—in terms of letter play—*pastern* is the most charadeable of all words in the English language. That is, when you sextuply cleave *pastern* at any point in the word, you will come up with two words.

As you look at the changing two halves, bear in mind that all letters are entries in dictionaries and hence qualify as words, that *ern* is a variant spelling for a long-winged species of sea eagle, that a *paster* is someone who pastes, and that an RN is a registered nurse:

p astern   pa stern   pas tern   past ern   paste RN   paster n

The word *pasterns* can be formed by working from left to right and adding a letter at a time to *p*:

p
pa
pas
past
paste
paster
pastern
pasterns

(See ALONE, MARSHALL, REACTIVATION, STARTLING.)

Pedigree. Even a birdbrain has little trouble figuring out how we derived the noun *crane* for a hoisting machine or the verb *to crane* to depict the act of stretching one's neck to obtain a better view. But it takes an eagle eye to spot the crane hiding in *pedigree.*

Perhaps you are proud of your dog's or cat's or your own pedigree, but did you know that *pedigree* gets its pedigree from the French phrase "foot of the crane" (Latin *pe,* "foot" + *de,* "of" + *grus,* "crane")? Why? Because if you trace a pedigree on a genealogical table, you find that the three-line figures of lineal descent resemble a crane's foot.

(See BUFFALO, BUTTERFLY, CANARY, CLAM, CRESTFALLEN, DACHSHUND, DANDELION, HORSEFEATHERS, OSTRACIZE, PARTRIDGE, TAD, TURKEY, VACCINATE, ZYZZYVA.)

Philodendron. This plant can thank the Greek language for its name: *philo-* "loving" + *dendron,* "tree." Because a philodendron is an evergreen plant that climbs trees, it is a "lover of trees."

The *nickelodeon* got its name from a blending of *nickel,* the cost of admission, and *melodeon,* an old word for a music hall.

Incorrigible punster that I am (don't incorrige me), I have noticed that these two words, and others like them, start with something that sounds like a first name and then comes an *O.*

So, have you heard about

- the Irish botanist Phil O'Dendron;
- the Irish theater owner Nick O'Lodeon;
- the Irish cigarette manufacturer Nick O'Teen;
- the Irish marksman Rick O'Shay;
- the Irish meteorologist Barry O'Metric;
- the Irish printer Mimi O'Graph;
- the Irish playwright Mel O'Drama;
- the Irish poet Ann O'Nymous;
- the Irish linguist Phil O'Logical;
- the Irish singers Mary O'Lanza and Carrie O'Key;
- and the Irish designer for outdoor living Patty O'Furniture?

(See BOLT, PUN.)

A **picayune** was originally a Spanish half real (pronounced "ray-ahl") worth about six cents and circulated throughout the American South. It didn't take long for prices to rise and for inflation to erode the already paltry value of the coin. Up grew the phrase "not worth a picayune," referring to something of little value. Before long, *to be picayune* about a matter came to mean to be petty or picky.

The adjective *picayune* is a mint-condition example of how we metaphorically put our money where our mouth is and our mouth where the money is. *To coin a phrase* (or two), not only does money talk; we talk about money. That's why elsewhere in this book, you'll find small disquisitions about the likes of *bottom dollar, top dollar, jackpot, pass the buck,* and *talent.* That's why if you *throw in your two cents,* I'll give you *a penny for your thoughts* and you'll be *short-changed.*

Hey, my own thoughts may *not be worth a red cent* or *a plugged nickel,* but I promise not *to take any wooden nickels* or *nickel and dime you to death.* I may be *as phony as a three-dollar bill,* but I *look like a million dollars*—all green and wrinkled.

What about the ubiquitous financial metaphor *scot-free?* The compound has nothing to do with Scotland or the Scottish people. Even before Shakespeare's day, a scot was a municipal tax paid to a sheriff or bailiff. So for centuries those who got off scot-free managed to avoid paying their taxes. Their progeny still walk the earth.

You can *bank on* my expertise; *it's like money in the bank,* and *you can take it to the bank.* No longer will you be *penny wise and pound foolish* and unable *to make head or tail* of expressions such as *don't take any wooden nickels.* During the centennial celebration of America, in Philadelphia, commemorative tokens made of wood sold for five cents. Such coins were accepted as legal tender while the festivities were in progress. But once the show was over, their value disappeared. That's why, beginning in the late nineteenth century, the advice *Don't take any wooden nickels* became the popular equivalent of "Don't be a sucker."

(See METAPHOR.)

Pneumonoultramicroscopicsilicovolcanokoniosis. This hippopoto-monstrosesquipedalian word is the longest enshrined in *Merriam Webster's Third New International Dictionary* and, since 1982, the longest in the *Oxford English Dictionary.* The word describes a miners' disease caused by inhaling too much quartz or silicate dust. Among its forty-five letters and nineteen syllables occur nine *o*'s, surely the record for a letter most repeated within a single word; six *c*'s; and but one *e.*

Here's a limerick about superultrahypermultimagnamega words:

A Gimerick

It's true that I have halitosis,
At least it's not pneumonoultramicroscopicsilicovolcanokoniosis.
 Thus, rather than floccinaucinihilipilification,
  I feel hippopotomonstrosesquipedalian elation
That's supercalifragilisticexpialidocious.

The longest words that we are likely to encounter in general text are the twenty-two letter *counterrevolutionaries* and *deinstitutionalization*. Then again, there's the bumper sticker with a twenty-seven-letter, eleven-syllable adverb: "He's not dead. He's just electroencephalographically challenged."

(See CHARGOGGAGOGGMANCHAUGGAGOGGCHAUBUN-AGUNGAMAUGG, FLOCCINAUCINIHILIPILIFICATION, HIPPOPOTOMON-STROSESQUIPEDALIAN, HONORIFICABILITUDINITATIBUS, LLANFAIR-PWLLGWYNGYLLGOGERYCHWYRNDDROBWLLLLANTYSILOGOGOCH, SUPERCALIFRAGILISTICEXPIALIDOCIOUS.)

Poetry. Reverse the two halves and you get *Try Poe.* Not a bad idea.

Edgar Allan Poe possesses one of the most misspelled middle names in literary history. It's not *Alan* or *Allen;* it's *Allan*, the last name of the family that took him in as a child.

Poe's "The Raven" is one of the best-known poems in American literature. It's dexterous internal rhymes, restless trochaic meter, and "Nevermore" refrain have inspired a parade of parodies, one of the best being "Ravin's of a Piute Poet Poe," by C. L. Edson, which begins:

Once upon a midnight dreary—eerie, scary—I was wary;
I was weary, full of sorry, thinking of my lost Lenore.
Of my cheery, eerie, faery, fiery dearie—nothing more.

I lay napping when a rapping on the overlapping coping
Woke me—grapping, yapping, groping—I went hopping,
Leaping!, hoping that the rapping on the coping
Was my little lost Lenore.

That, on opening the shutter, to admit the latter critter,
In she'd flutter from the gutter, with her bitter eyes aglitter.
So I opened wide the door—what was there?
The dark weir and the drear moor—or, I'm a liar!:
The dark mire, the drear moor, the mere door . . .
And nothing more.

Polish. A capitonym is a word that changes meaning and pronunciation when it is capitalized, as illustrated in these quatrains:

Job's Job

In *August,* an *august* patriarch,
Was *reading* an ad in *Reading,* Mass.
Long-suffering *Job* secured a *job*
To *polish* piles of *Polish* brass.

Herb's Herbs

An *herb* store owner, name of *Herb,*
Moved to *rainier* Mt. *Rainier.*
It would have been so *nice* in *Nice,*
And even *tangier* in *Tangier.*

Here are a dozen more capital capitonyms:

Begin/begin	Degas/degas	Messier/messier
Breathed/breathed	Guy/guy	Millet/millet
Colon/colon	Levy/levy	Natal/natal
Concord/concord	Lima/lima	Ravel/ravel

(See BOLT, ENTRANCE.)

Politics. The word *politics* derives from *poly,* "many," (as in *polygamy, polytheism,* and *polyglot*) and *tics,* which are blood-sucking parasites. Just kidding. In truth, *politics* issues from the Greek word *pólitēs* (πολίτης), "city, citizen."

Here's a story about what may be the most brilliant use of language ever in the field of politics:

The 1950 Florida Democratic primary for the Senate pitted incumbent Claude Pepper against then-Congressman George Smathers. Here's my expansion of a statement that, according to political folklore, appeared in unsigned pamphlets and in actual stump orations that Smathers trotted around the North Florida pinelands.

Pepper lost the race but went on to a long and distinguished service in the House. Smathers retired from the senate in 1971, vigorously denying responsibility until the end but acknowledged that the tale had "gone into the history books." Whether apocryphal or authentic, the "speech" provides a lively example of how a politician can sling muddle at opponents without getting taken to court:

My fellow citizens, it is my patriotic duty to inform you of some disturbing facts about my opponent.

Are you aware of the fact the senator is a known sexagenarian? He is a flagrant Homo sapiens who for years has been practicing celibacy all by himself. He has been seen on repeated occasions masticating in public restaurants. In fact, my opponent is a confessed heterosexual who advocates and even participates in social intercourse in mixed company.

His very home is a den of propinquity. The place is suffused with an atmosphere of incense, and there, in the privacy of his own residence, he practices nepotism and extroversion with members of his own family.

Now let's take a closer look at the salubrious acts committed by members of the senator's family.

It is a controvertible fact that his father, who died of a degenerative disease, made his money publishing phonographic magazines and distributing literature about horticulture.

His mother was a known equestrienne who nourished colts on her country estate and practiced her diversions out in the field.

His daughter, who is powerfully attracted to sects, is a well-known proselyte who accosts lay people outside of churches and plies them with hoary platitudes.

His son matriculates openly at Harvard University and is a member of an all-male sextet.

For many years his sister was employed as a floorwalker, and she practiced her calling in some of our city's best department stores.

His brother is so susceptible to moral suasion that he has been advocating oral hygiene for the masses.

And at this very moment the senator's wife is off in wicked New York City living the life of a thespian and performing her histrionic acts before paying customers, many of whom are heroine addicts.

Now I ask you: Do you want a man with such an explicable and veracious reputation occupying public office? Under his influence, our youth might convert to altruism. Clearly a vote for my opponent is a vote for the perpetuation of all we hold dear. A vote for me is a vote for the very antithesis of the American Way.

(See CANDIDATE, FILIBUSTER, IDIOT, INAUGURATE, MALAPROPISM, OK, OSTRACIZE.)

Posh. One of the most persistent apocryphal etymologies is the recurrent wheeze that *posh,* "elegant, swanky," is an acronym for "p(ort) o(ut), s(tarboard) h(ome)," a beguiling bit of linguistic legerdemain that has taken in a company of estimable scholars. When British colonial emissaries and wealthy vacationers made passage to and from India and the Orient, they often traveled along the coast of Africa on the Peninsular and Oriental Steam Navigation Company line. Many of these travelers sought ideal accommodations "away from the weather," on the more comfortable or shady side of the ship. By paying for two staterooms—one portside out, the other starboard home—the very rich could avoid the blazing sun and strong winds both ways, an act of conspicuous consumption that has become synonymous with anything luxurious and ultrasmart.

While the abundant inventiveness here deserves at least a sitting ovation, this etymology of *posh* is, well, bosh. For one thing, neither the travelers' literature of the period nor the records of the famous Peninsular and Oriental Steam Navigation Company show a jot of reference to *posh.* For another, an examination of the deck plans of the ships of the period reveals that the cabins were not placed on the port and starboard sides. For a third, *posh* does not show up in print until 1918.

The editors of the *Oxford English Dictionary* say nothing of any connection with the location of cabins on ships and either ignore or reject outright the acronymic theory, and all Merriam-Webster dictionaries list the origin as "unknown." Moreover, the monsoon winds that blow in and out of the Asian heartland shift from winter to summer. This fickle phenomenon changes the location of the sheltered and exposed sides of a ship so that in a given season the ideal location can be starboard out, portside home (hence, *soph*). More likely and more mundanely, *posh* hails from a British slang word of the same spelling that means "a dandy."

(See COP, GOLF.)

Potpourri has come to mean an assortment of pleasant objects in one place, such as a mixture of dried petals and spices kept in an open bowl so that their aroma can be enjoyed. But the etymological antecedents of *potpourri* are more putrid than pleasant.

Pot is clipped from the Latin *potare,* "to drink" (as is *potion*). To *pot* was added an offshoot of the Latin *putrere,* "to be rotten," the same word from which wafts *putrid, putrescent,* and (yuck) *pus.* Early

Spanish had an expression *olla podrida,* literally "rotten pot." The French borrowed it, and from there it passed into English in the early 1600s.

Preamble. Every first-year Latin student learns that the verb *ambulare* means "to walk" and that the common prefix *pre-* (as in *prefix*) derives from a Latin preposition meaning "in front of" or "before." Thus, a preamble is something that comes walking before something else. In the case of our Constitution, the Preamble is a short, but very important, philosophic statement that walks before the actual Articles of Constitution.

Prelate is beheaded one letter at a time in this reverential ditty:

> The *prelate* did *relate* a tale
> Meant to *elate* both you and me.
> We stayed up *late* and *ate* our meal,
> "*Te* deum" sang in key of *E.*

(See ALONE, PASTERN, REACTIVATION, STARTLING.)

Preposition. It's easy to see that the word for words that link other words to a sentence, such as *in, by,* and *under,* means "put before." A preposition does indeed come before its object, as in "*before* its object."

The most pervasive of all grammar commandments may be the one against using a preposition to end a sentence with. Frankly, that injunction doesn't have a leg to stand on. Ending a sentence with a preposition is a construction many famous writers are fond of.

Note that all three sentences in the previous paragraph feature terminal prepositions, yet they are perfectly natural statements. The anti-terminal preposition "rule" is a bogus restriction that reposes in no reputable grammar book. In fact, this destructive piece of gossip is so out of whack with the realities of English style that it has engendered the four most famous grammar jokes in the canon.

The most widely circulated anecdote about the terminal preposition involves Sir Winston Churchill, one of the greatest of all English prose stylists. As the story goes, an officious editor had the audacity to "correct" a proof of Churchill's memoirs by revising a sentence that ended with the outlawed preposition. Sir Winston hurled back at the editor a memorable rebuttal: "This is the sort of arrant pedantry up with which I will not put!"

A variation on that story concerns a newspaper columnist who responded snappily to the accusation that he was uncouthly violating the terminal preposition "rule": "What do you take me for? A chap who doesn't know how to make full use of all the easy variety the English language is capable of? Don't you know that ending a sentence with a preposition is an idiom many famous writers are very fond of? They realize it's a colloquialism a skillful writer can do a great deal with. Certainly it's a linguistic device you ought to read about."

For the punster there's the set-up joke about the prisoner who asks a female guard to marry him on the condition that she help him escape. Here we have a man attempting to use a proposition to end a sentence with.

Then there's the one about the little boy who has just gone to bed when his father comes into the room carrying a book about Australia. Surprised, the boy asks: "What did you bring that book that I didn't want to be read to out of from about Down Under up for?"

Now that's a sentence out of which you can get a lot.

My favorite of all terminal preposition stories involves a boy attending public school and one attending private school who end up sitting next to each other in an airplane. To be friendly, the public schooler turns to the preppie and asks, "What school are you at?"

The private schooler looks down his aquiline nose at the public school student and comments, "I happen to attend an institution at which we are taught to know better than to conclude sentences with prepositions."

The boy at public school pauses for a moment and then says: "All right, then. What school are you at, dingbat!"

(See PRONOUN, VERB.)

Preposterous is one of those words where the meaning is photographically laid out in front of us. The Latin parent word is *praeposterus*, "before-after," suggesting that what should come first comes last and what should come last first, the verbal and proverbial cart before the horse.

(See HYSTERON PROTERON, WORD.)

Preventive. In many horror films, malignant monsters, from giant insects to blobs of glop, writhe about. Unfortunately, such grotesque mutations are not limited to science fiction; they are constantly spawning in our language. We English speakers seem possessed by a desire to use a bloated form of certain words when a more compact form will do. These elongated versions are called "needless variants" and "unnecessary doublets," and should be assiduously avoided.

Please allow me to orient, not orientate, you to the strategies for avoiding the affectation of gratuitous syllabification:

Use *accompanist,* not *accompanyist; analysis,* not *analyzation; archetypal,* not *archetypical; brilliance,* not *brilliancy; combative,* not *combatative; compulsory,* not *compulsorary; connote,* not *connotate; desalination,* not *desalinization; empathic,* not *empathetic; grievous,* not *grievious; heart rending,* not *heart-rendering; mischievous,* not *mischievious; regardless,* not *irregardless; skittish,* not *skitterish; spayed,* not *spayded;* and, in most instances, *sewage,* not *sewerage.*

These choices constitute a form of preventive maintenance of our English language. True, *preventative* does repose in many dictionaries, but *preventive,* especially as an adjective, is generally viewed as the preferred form. That's why the impeccable Henry W. Fowler, in *Modern English Usage,* remarks that "*preventative* is a needless lengthening of an established word, due to oversight and caprice." That's why *preventive* is about five times as common as *preventative* in modern print sources.

Prince. What English word is singular, but if you add an *s,* it becomes plural, and if you add another *s,* it becomes singular again, with a sex change? You got it: *prince-princes-princess.* A second answer that conforms to this pattern but involves an arcane word is *ogre-ogres-ogress.*

But wait. There's more! What English word is singular, but if you add an *s,* it becomes plural, and if you add another *s,* it becomes a singular word that can make the first two words vanish?

The solution: *care-cares-caress.*

Pronoun. Forged from the Latin *pro,* "in place of" + *nomen,* "noun or name," a pronoun replaces a noun. Because pronouns change form in ways that nouns don't, they create more grammatical atrocities than any other part of speech:

- "Me and Mary went to the movies," which should be "Mary and I went to the movies."
- "Thank you for voting for Scott and I," which should be "Thank you for voting for Scott and me."
- "They were amazed at me running for school board," which should be "They were amazed at my running for school board."
- "I kept the secret between Heather and myself," which should be "I kept the secret between Heather and me."

We can list pronouns in the order of one to ten letters: *I, we, you, they, their, myself, himself, yourself, ourselves, themselves.*

Here's an unusual use of pronouns to make a point about our lives:

This is a story about four people—Everybody, Somebody, Anybody, and Nobody.

There was an important job to be done, and Everybody was sure that Somebody would do it. Anybody would have done it, but Nobody did it.

Somebody got angry about that because it was Everbody's job. Everybody thought Anybody could do it, but Nobody realized that Everybody wouldn't do it.

It ended up that Everybody blamed Somebody when Nobody did what Anybody could have done.

(See PREPOSITION, VERB.)

Pumpernickel is etymologically baked from the German *pumpern,* "to break wind," and *Nickel,* "devil, demon, goblin." The idea is that those who eat the heavy, dark, hard-to-digest rye bread are liable to be smitten by a diabolical flatulence.

(See CAKEWALK, COMPANION, COUCH POTATO, HOAGIE, SALARY, SANDWICH, TOAST.)

Pun. No one is sure of the origin of the word *pun,* but the best guess is that *pun* is a shortening of the Italian *puntiglio,* "a small or fine point." Punnery is largely the trick of compacting two or more ideas within a single word or expression. Punnery challenges us to apply the greatest pressure per square syllable of language. Punnery surprises us by flouting the law of nature that pretends that two things cannot occupy the same space at the same time. Punnery is an exercise of the mind at being concise.

In addition *to blend words* and *spoonerisms*, both illuminated elsewhere in this book, puns can be divided into the following categories:

- *homographs:* two or more words with the same spelling but different meanings, as in "Show me where Stalin is born, and I'll show you a communist plot"—*George S. Kaufman*; "A committee is a group of people who keep minutes and waste hours."—*Milton Berle*

- *homophones:* two or more words with the same sound but different spellings and meanings, as in "A naked grizzly is a bare bear"; "A pony with a sore throat is a hoarse horse."

- *double-sound puns:* two or more words that are spelled and sounded differently, as in "May the farce be with you!"; "Every four years Americans exhibit a collective case of electile dysfunction."

Using the criteria of verbal pyrotechnics, humor, and popularity of the play on words, I present my picks for the top ten English-language puns of all time. Sharpen your pun cells, O pun pals. Let's get to wit:

10. Time flies like an arrow. Fruit flies like a banana.

9. Take my wife—please!—*Henny Youngman*

8. A good pun is like a good steak—a rare medium well done.

7. As one frog croaked to another: "Time's fun when you're having flies!"

6. Outside of a dog, a book is a man's best friend. Inside of a dog, it's too dark to read.—*Groucho Marx*

5. Cowboy singer Roy Rogers went bathing in a creek. Along came a cougar and, attracted by the smell of new leather, began nibbling on one of Roy's brand new boots, which were sitting by the edge of the water. Dale Evans entered the scene, and noting the critter chomping her husband's footwear, fired her trusty rifle in the air, scaring the cougar away.

    She turned to her husband and asked, "Pardon me, Roy. Was that the cat that chewed your new shoe?"

4. What did the Buddhist priest say to the hot dog vendor? "Make me one with everything." And the same holy man said to his dentist, "I wish to transcend dental medication."

3. Two ropes walked into an old western saloon. The first rope went up to the bar and ordered a beer. "We don't serve ropes in this saloon," sneered the bartender, who picked up the rope, whirled him around in the air, and tossed him out into the street.

"Oh, oh. I'd better disguise myself," thought the second rope. He ruffled up his ends to make himself look bigger and twisted himself into a circle. Then he too sidled up to the bar.

"Hmmm. Are you one of them ropes?" snarled the bartender.

"I'm a frayed knot."

2. You better watch out, or my karma will run over your dogma.

And the number-one pun of all time, created by the incomparable Dorothy Parker:

1. I'd rather have a bottle in front of me than a frontal lobotomy.

(See BOLT, DAFFYNITION, PHILODENDRON, SPOONERISM, SWIFTY, WITZELSUCHT.)

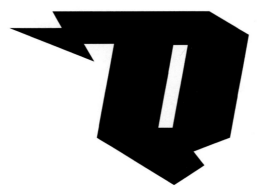

Q-Tips. Cotton swabs are called cotton buds in England and ear buds in South Africa. The *Q* in *Q-Tips* stands for "Quality."

All twenty-six letters can be used as kickoffs to everyday words:

A-frame	G-string	n-type	U-turn
B-movie	H-bomb	O-ring	V-neck
C-section	iPhone	P-wave	W particle
D-day	J-bar	Q-Tip	X-ray
E-mail	K ration	R-month	Y chromosome
F-stop	L dopa	S corp	Z-coordinate
	M phase	T-shirt	

(See A, EXPEDIENCY, I, S, W, X.)

Queue. Here we gaze upon a word that can have its last four letters curtailed and still retain its original pronunciation. Performing the same stunt with its first four letters beheaded is *aitch*. *Queueing* is also the only common word in English that houses five consecutive vowels.

(See A, I, X, W.)

Quintessence reflects the ancient Greek view of the universe. Empedocles posited that everything was composed of four elements— earth, air, fire, and water. Aristotle added to these basic elements a fifth (*quinta*) essence, which he called ether. This *quintessence* was the purest and most concentrated of all because it made up all the heavenly bodies. Hence, the quintessence of something is its purest and most concentrated form.

William Shakespeare's disillusioned Hamlet uses the word that way when he laments, "What a piece of work is a man, how noble in reason, how infinite in faculties. . . . And yet, to me, what is this quintessence of dust?"

(See SEPTEMBER.)

Radar, which sounds like a Spanish infinitive, is actually an acronym for "*ra*dio *d*etecting *a*nd *r*anging." *Radar* is also a palindrome, an appropriate pattern for a device that bounces pulses of radio waves back and forth.

An acronym is a word-making device coined from two Greek roots: *akros*, "topmost, highest," and *onyma*, "word, name." Because acronyms are generally fashioned from the capital letters, or tops, of other words, the label is appropriate.

Technically, an acronym is a series of "high letters" that are pronounced as words, as in CARE (Committee for American Remittances Everywhere), NAFTA (North American Free Trade Agreement), MADD (Mothers Against Drunk Driving), and *NIMBY* (not in my back yard). Some acronyms actually become words—*AWOL:* "absent without leave," *snafu:* "situation normal, all fouled up," and *scuba:* "self-contained underwater breathing apparatus."

Close kin to the acronym is the initialism, in which each component is sounded as a letter, as in YMCA, *TGIF, LOL, OMG,* and *OK.* The art of initialisms goes back centuries before the development of the English language. The Romans wrote *SPQR* for *Senatus populusque Romanus,* "Roman senate and people," therein expressing their democratic conception of the State. At the end of a friendly letter they signed *SVBEEV, Si vales bene est, ego vale:* "I'm quite well, and I do hope that you are, too."

The abundant proliferation of initialisms in America can be dated from the "alphabet soup" government agencies created by Franklin Delano Roosevelt during the New Deal, among them the WPA (Works Progress Administration), CCC (Civilian Conservation Corps), and FDIC (Federal Deposit Insurance Corporation). It is perhaps more than coincidence that Roosevelt was our first chief executive to be known by his initials only: *FDR.*

(See OK.)

Raise/Raze are the only homophones in the English language that are opposites of each other. Coming close are *oral* and *aural, petalous* and *petalless,* and *reckless* and *wreckless.*

(See OUT, OUTGOING.)

Reactivation is the longest common word that can be transdeleted. That is, from the twelve-letter reactivation we can pluck out any letter, one at a time, and then form successively smaller anagrams, until but a single letter remains:

> reactivation
> ratiocinate
> recitation
> intricate
> interact
> tainter
> attire
> irate
> tare
> art
> at
> a

(See ALONE, PASTERN, PRELATE, STARTLING.)

A **Rebus** is a word picture in which letters are manipulated for their visual features to represent a word or expression. *Rebus,* from the Latin "by things," appears in the phrase *non verbis sed rebus,* "not by words but by things." Hence, *r/e/a/d/i/n/g* yields *reading between the lines*, *slobude* turns out to be *mixed doubles*, and *HIJKLMNO* must be *water* because it is "*H* to *O*."

Here are some rebuses about food. Can you deduce their meanings?:

gesg	eggs	may	me	me	me	knee
	easy	aaa	al	al	al	a lot of

The answers are *scrambled eggs, eggs over easy, mayonnaise, three square meals,* and *a lot of baloney.*

And here are some more classics, with answers immediately following:

mind	poFISHnd	paid	**blood** water	I right I	ssa
matter		I'm			
		worked			

Answers: *mind over matter, big fish in a small pond, I'm overworked and underpaid, blood is thicker than water, right between the eyes,* and *ass backwards*

And here are a stratospherically clever British rebus and translation:

If the B mt put :	If the grate be empty, put coal on.
If the B . putting :	If the grate be full stop putting coal on.
Don't put : over a - der	Don't put coal on over a high fender.
You'd be an * it	You'd be an ass to risk it.

(See EXPEDIENCY.)

Redundancy. We are adrift in a sea of American redundancies. The sea is a perfectly appropriate metaphor here, for the word *redundancy* is a combination of the Latin *undare,* "to overflow" and *re-,* "back," and literally means "to overflow again and again," which may itself be a bit redundant. It may come as an *unexpected surprise* (even more surprising than an expected surprise) that the ancient Greeks had a name for this rhetorical blunder—*pleonasmós* (πλεονασμός). Redundancies, or pleonasms, are the flip side of oxymorons. Instead of yoking together two opposites, we say the same thing twice.

Of all the adspeak that congests my radio, TV, and mailbox the one that I *hate with a passion* (how else can one hate?) is *free gift.* Sometimes I am even offered a *complimentary free gift.* I sigh with relief, grateful that I won't have to pay for that gift.

My *fellow colleagues* and *fellow classmates,* I am here in *close proximity* (rather than a proximity far away) to tell you the *honest truth* (not to be confused with the dishonest truth) about the *basic fundamentals* (aren't all fundamentals fundamentally basic?) of redundancies. As an *added bonus* (aren't all bonuses added?), my *past experience,* which is a lot more reliable than my present or future experience, tells me that redundancies *surround us on all sides* and will not go away. Trust me. I come under no *false pretenses* (only true ones).

The rise of initialisms through the twentieth century and into the computer age has generated new kinds of letter-imperfect redundancies—*ABM missile, AC or DC current, ACT test, AM in the morning, BASIC code, CNN network, DOS operating system, GMT time, GRE examination, HIV virus, HTML language, ICBM missile, ISBN number, MAC card, OPEC country, PIN number, PM in the evening, ROM memory, SALT talks (or treaty), SAT test, SUV vehicle,* and *VIN number.* In each of these initialisms, the last letter is piled on by a gratuitous noun. *ATM machine* turns out to be a double redundancy: *machine* repeats the *M,* and the *M* repeats the *A.* If you agree with my observation, *RSVP please.*

(See OXYMORON, TAXICAB.)

Reek. *Stink* and *stench* were formerly neutral in meaning and referred to any smell, as did *reek,* which once had the innocuous meaning of "to give off smoke, emanate." In fact, an old term for the act of smoking meats was "to reek them."

William Shakespeare wrote his great sonnet sequence just at the time that *reek* was beginning to degrade. The Bard exploited the double meaning in his whimsical Sonnet 130:

> My mistress' eyes are nothing like the sun,
> Coral is far more red than her lips' red.
> If snow be white, why then her breasts are dun,
> If hair be wires, black wires grow on her head.
> I have seen roses damasked, red and white,
> But no such roses see I her on her cheeks.
> But in some perfume there is more delight
> Than in the breath that from my mistress reeks.

Reek is embedded in a famous Marx Brothers' pun. Chico Marx once took umbrage upon hearing someone exultantly exclaim, "Eureka!" Chagrined, Chico shot back, "You doan smella so good yourself!"

(See AWFUL.)

Restaurateurs. By far the longest (thirteen letters) balanced word, that is, a word in which a single middle letter, acting as a fulcrum, is surrounded by an identical set of letters. In *restaurateurs,* the middle *r* is both preceded and followed by the letters *aerstu.*

If one sets the requirement that the surrounding letters must appear in the same order on both sides of the midpoint, the champion words are *eighty-eight* and *artsy-fartsy,* both eleven letters. Runners up, but perhaps more impressive because they are not obvious repetitions, are the nine-letter *outshouts* and *outscouts.* The seven-letter *ingoing* is also nicely camouflaged.

(See HOTSHOTS, INTESTINES, SHANGHAIINGS.)

Retronym. Have you noticed that a number of simple nouns have recently acquired new adjectives? What we used to call, simply, "books," for example, we now call *hardcover books* because of the production of paperback books. Now *e-books* are starting to dominate the market. What was once simply a guitar is now an *acoustic guitar* because of the popularity of electric guitars. What was once just soap is now called *bar soap* since the invention of powdered and liquid soaps.

Frank Mankiewicz, once an aide to Robert Kennedy, invented a term for these new compounds. He called them *retronyms,* using the classical word parts *retro,* "back," and *nym,* "name or word." A retronym is an adjective-noun pairing generated by a change in the meaning of the noun, usually because of advances in technology. Retronyms, like retrospectives, are backward glances.

When I grew up, there were only Coke, turf, and mail. Nowadays, Diet Coke, artificial turf, and e-mail have spawned the retronyms *real Coke, natural turf,* and *snail mail.* Once there were simply movies. Then movies began to talk, necessitating the retronym *silent movies.* Then came color movies and the contrasting term *black-and-white movies.* Now *3-D movies* are contrasted with *2-D movies.* I remember telephones that we all dialed. When push-button phones came onto the market, *rotary telephones* became the retronym. Then, with the conquest of the market by cell phones, *land lines* entered our parlance.

May the following retronyms never come to pass—*teacher-staffed school, non-robotic product, non-performance-enhanced athletic contest, monogamous marriage,* and *two-parent family.*

A **rhopalic** is a sentence in which each word is progressively one letter or one syllable longer than its predecessor. This word derives from the Greek *rhopalos*, for a club or cudgel, thicker toward one end than the other.

Here's a rhopalic letter sentence from the great Dmitri Borgmann: *O to see man's stern, poetic thought publicly expanding recklessly imaginative mathematical inventiveness, openmindedness unconditionally superfecundating nonantagonistical, hypersophisticated, interdenominational interpenetrabilities.*

Now here's a syllabic rhopalic by me that employs more accessible words: *I never totally misinterpret administrative, idiosyncratic, uncategorizable, overintellectualized deinstitutionalization.*

(See HIPPOPOTOMONSTROSESQUIPEDALIAN.)

Rhythms. The longest word lacking an *a, e, i, o,* or *u, rhythms* boasts two syllables, yet only one vowel. Also syllabically efficient are *schism* (and any other kind of ism, from *fascism* to *romanticism), chasm, dirndl, fjord, subtly, massacring,* and *Edinburgh,* each characterized by fewer vowels than syllables.

(See Nth.)

Right started out in life as an adjective that meant "straight, lawful, true, genuine, just good, fair, proper, and fitting." Only later did *right* come to signify the right hand or right side. Ever since, right suggests rectitude, to which it is etymologically related:

- You are in the right about this issue.
- Throckmorton is the boss's right-hand man.
- Her left hand doesn't know what the right one is doing.

The bias toward the right side extends beyond English. One who is skilled is *dexterous,* from the Latin *dexter,* meaning "right, on the right hand," and *adroit,* from the French *a droit,* "to the right."

On the other hand—the left one, of course—language appears to libel the left-handed:

- On the dance floor, Taylor seems to have two left feet.
- That sounds like a left-handed compliment to me.
- When it comes to grammar, I feel out in left field.

Bias against the left-handed minority is embedded in many languages. *Sinister,* the Latin for "left, on the left hand," yields the darkly threatening *sinister* in English, while the French word for "left hand" is *gauche*, the debasement of which is *gawky*.

Apparently, it is not only doorknobs, school desks, athletic gear, musical instruments, can openers, and flush handles on toilets that favor the right-handed majority.

(See HAND.)

Rode is one of a handful of one-syllable words in English that morph into a three-syllable word with the addition of a single letter—*rode-rodeo*. Others: *are-area, came-cameo, gape-agape, lien-alien*, and *smile-simile*.

Run. What could be so amazing about this plain, little word? Turns out it's actually our longest word, in the sense that with 645—you read right: 645—meanings, *run* takes up more room in our biggest, fattest dictionaries than any other word. But how many meanings can *run* have beyond "to move rapidly on alternate feet"? Well, you can run a company, run for the school board, run the motor of your car, run a flag up a pole, run up your debts, run your stocking, run your mouth, run a fence around a property, run an idea past a colleague, run an antagonist through with your sword, run an ad in a newspaper, run into a childhood friend, never run out of meanings for *run*—and your nose can run and your feet can smell.

If you need a fancy term for multiple meanings of a word, it's *polysemy*. *Run* takes up half again as much space as its nearest polysemous competitor, *put*, which itself is far more polysemous than the third word in this race, *set*. So the three "longest" words enshrined in our dictionaries are each composed of three letters.

Rounding out the top ten most polysemous words—each but a single syllable—are, alphabetically, *cast, cut, draw, point, serve, strike,* and *through*.

S. If you look at a real-world dictionary that features little half moons cut into the edge of pages, you'll probably find that only one of them displays just one letter, and that letter is *s*. That's because *s* starts more English words than any other letter in the alphabet. The versatile *s* is also used to mark plural nouns (*cats*), third-person singular verbs (*walks*), and possessive nouns and pronouns (*men's clothing, hers*).

S is all too frequently overused. It's *daylight saving time*, not *daylight savings time*; *in regard to*, not *in regards to*; *a way to go*, not *a ways to go*; the book of *Revelation*, not the book of *Revelations*; *number-crunching*, not *numbers-crunching*; and *brinkmanship*, not *brinksmanship*.

(See A, I, Q-TIPS, SILENT, W, X.)

Salary. The ancients knew that salt was essential to a good diet, and centuries before artificial refrigeration, it was the only chemical that could preserve meat. Thus, a portion of the wages paid to Roman soldiers was "salt money," with which to buy salt, derived from the

Latin, *sal*. This stipend came to be called a *salarium*, from which we acquire the word *salary*. A loyal and effective soldier was quite literally worth his salt. Please don't take my explanations with a grain of salt. That is, you, who are the salt of the earth, don't have to sprinkle salt on my etymologies to find them tasty.

(See CAKEWALK, COMPANION, COUCH POTATO, HOAGIE, PUMPERNICKEL, SANDWICH, TOAST.)

Sandwich. In order to spend more uninterrupted time at the gambling tables, John Montagu, Fourth Earl of Sandwich, ordered his servants to bring him an impromptu meal of slices of beef slapped between two slices of bread. Thus, America's favorite luncheon repast was rustled up to feed a nobleman's gambling addiction.

(See BIKINI, CAKEWALK, COMPANION, COUCH POTATO, DACHSHUND, GERRYMANDER, HAMBURGER, HOAGIE, LACONIC, MAVERICK, PUMPERNICKEL, SALARY, SIDEBURNS, SILHOUETTE, SPOONERISM, TOAST, TURKEY.)

Scent is, I believe, the only word in the English language that conforms to these specifications: Think of a five-letter word in which you can delete the first letter and retain a word that sounds just like the first word, then restore the first letter, and then delete the second letter and retain a word that sounds just like the other two words. And the three words possess totally distinct meanings. Those words are *scent, cent,* and *sent*.

And *scent* is an exceedingly punnable sound: Have you heard about the successful perfume manufacturer? His business made a lot of *scents/cents/sense*.

(See AIR, WHERE.)

Scintillating shines forth from the Latin *scintilla*, "spark," and means "to give off sparks." Personally, I never sin in the morning, but I often scintillate at night.

Scintillating, is one of a number of adjectives that compare intelligence to light. Other such metaphors include *bright, brilliant, dazzling,* and *lucid*.

Clever is another intriguing descriptor for intelligence, harking back to the Old English *cleave* and *cleaver*. That history leads us to a second metaphoric cluster, one that likens intelligence to the edge of a knife, as with *acute, incisive, keen,* and *sharp.*

(See METAPHOR.)

Scuttlebutt. On sailing ships of yesteryear the "butt" was a popular term for the large, lidded casks that held drinking water. These butts were equipped with "scuttles," openings through which sailors ladled out the water. Just as today's office workers gather about a water cooler to exchange chitchat and rumor, crewmen stood about the scuttled butts to trade *scuttlebutt.*

To help you learn the ropes and get your bearings with seafaring metaphors, take a turn at the helm. The coast is clear for you to sound out the lay of the land by taking a different tack and playing a landmark game. Don't go overboard by barging ahead, come hell or high water. If you feel all washed up, on the rocks, in over your head, and sinking fast in a wave of confusion, try to stay on an even keel. As your friendly anchorman, I won't rock the boat by lowering the boom on you.

Now that you get my drift, consider how the following idioms of sailing and the sea sprinkle salt on our tongues: *shape up or ship out, to take the wind out of his sails, the tide turns, a sea of faces, down the hatch, hit the deck, to steer clear of, don't rock the boat, to be left high and dry, to harbor a grudge,* and *to give a wide berth to.*

In "Sea Fever" (1902), the poet John Masefield sang:

> I must down to the seas again
> To the lonely sea and the sky,
> And all I ask is a tall ship
> And a star to steer her by.

Relatively few of us go down to the seas any more, and even fewer of us get to steer a tall ship. Having lost our intimacy with the sea and with sailing, we no longer taste the salty flavor of the metaphors that ebb and flow through our language:

- *by and large.* To ancient mariners this compound was a command that meant "sailing slightly off the wind," in contrast to *full and by.* When we say *by and large* today, we mean "in general; for the most part" because we do not wish to sail directly into the topic.
- *taken aback.* This phrase probably conjures up in your mind an image of a person caught off guard and staggering backwards. But the origin of the phrase is nautical, too: Sailing by and large left an

inexperienced helmsman in less danger of being taken aback, which meant "to catch the wind on the wrong side of the sails."

- *leeway.* The lee is the side of the ship sheltered from the wind. Hence, when we make things easy for others, we give them *leeway.*

- *governor.* A governor steers "the ship of state," so it is appropriate that the word *governor* sails into the great harbor of English from the Greek *kybernân* (κυβερνάω), "steersman, pilot."

- *touch and go.* Old salts used to describe a ship in shallow water that touches bottom from time to time has been extended to designate any precarious situation as *touch and go.* A much worse situation is one in which a ship strikes bottom and is held tight, unable to proceed. Today we use the expression *hard and fast* to identify any rigid rule or opinion.

- *take down a peg.* Ships' colors used to be raised and lowered a peg at a time. The higher the colors, the greater the honor. Nowadays, we diminish others' self-esteem by *taking them down a peg.*

- *between the devil and the deep blue sea.* In sailing parlance *devil* is not he of the forked tail but a nautical term for the seam between two planks in the hull of a ship, on or below the water line. Anyone who had to caulk such a "devil" was figuratively caught between a rock and a hard place, or *between the devil and the deep blue sea.*

- *three sheets to the wind.* For sailors, *sheets* refer to the lines attached to the lower corner of a sail. When all three sheets of an old sailing vessel were allowed to run free, they were said to be "in the wind," and the ship would lurch and stagger like a person inebriated. That's why we call an unsteady state of drunkenness *three sheets to the wind.*

- *under the weather.* Feeling seasick on shipboard can force one to go below deck to recover. On deck, a sailor wouldn't want to toss his cookies in his own face; below deck he would encounter less pitch and roil. That's where we get the expression *under the weather,* meaning "to feel yucky."

- *the bitter end.* Seafaring folk called that part of the cable that is to the rear of the windlass *bitt,* and the turn of the cable around the bitts the *bitter.* When a ship rides out a gale, the cable is let out to just the place that this entry has reached—*the bitter end.*

(See DOLDRUMS, FATHOM, FORECASTLE, METAPHOR.)

Sensuousness. Some palindromic letter patterns repose inside a word, anchored there by other letters. Five-letter anchored palindromes are relatively common, including this dozen:

b*anana*	*dissid*ent	h*angna*il	p*ropor*tion
bre*athta*king	di*visiv*e	he*lple*ss	*rever*e
c*hoco*holic	e*vergre*en	p*etite*	sy*nony*m

Step right up to a dozen six-letter anchored palindromes:

br*aggar*t	*grammar*	mo*delled*	st*accat*o
*diffid*ent	k*nitting*	pos*sesses*	*tinnit*us
fiddl*edeede*e	mi*sdeed*s	sh*redder*	un*essen*tial

Now, here now are one last dozen anchored palindromes, each of seven letters:

*assessa*ble	*igniting*	mo*notono*us	reco*gnizing*
*footstoo*l	in*terpret*	pa*cifica*tion	re*divide*
hu*llaball*oo	*locofoco*	pr*ecipice*	*selfles*s

But the grand champion of all anchored palindromes—ahead of its closest competitor by four letters—is the eleven-letter sequence embedded in *sensuousness*.

Note that words such as *banana, petite, revere, grammar, igniting, locofoco,* and *redivide* spell themselves backwards when the first letter is looped to the back of the word.

(See ADAM, AGAMEMNON, CIVIC, KINNIKINNIK, NAPOLEON, PALINDROME, WONTON, *ZOONOOZ*.)

September, with its derivation from the Latin *septem,* looks as if it should be the seventh month of the year. And October (*octo*), November *(novem)*, and December (*decem*) appear in their structure to be the eighth, ninth, and tenth months. And they were, when the Roman lunar calendar started the year in March at harvest time.

But all that changed in 46 B.C., when January became the first month of the new Julian calendar, making September, October, November, and December the ninth, tenth, eleventh, and twelfth months of the year.

Several other numbers embedded in our words are deceiving:

- *Unique* reflects the Latin *unus,* "one," but many people use *unique* to mean not "one of a kind," but simply "unusual," as in "You have a very unique opportunity to support a worthy cause."

- *Siesta,* from the Latin compound *sexta hora,* literally means "the sixth hour after sunrise, i.e. "noon", but the *siesta* now refers to a rest period that can occur at any time of day.

- *Decimate* once described the nasty habit of the Romans of maiming or killing one out of every ten captives or mutineers. Now *decimate* means "to destroy," with no connection to the number ten.

- The first meaning of *quarantine,* from the Italian *quarantina,* was a period of forty days during which a widow had the right to continue living in her deceased husband's house, especially if the residence was to be seized for debt. Soon the word took on a related meaning—the forty days in which a ship suspected of carrying disease had to remain in isolation. And soon after that, *quarantine* broadened to signify any period of sequestering, and the reference to "forty" has vanished.

(See QUINTESSENCE.)

Sequoia is the shortest common word (seven letters) in which each major vowel appears once and only once. Eight-letter exhibits include *dialogue* and *equation. Sequoia* is further distinguished by a string of four consecutive vowels.

A rare variant of the verb *meow* is *miaou,* and the past tense of that verb is *miaoued*—five consecutive major vowels and each one different!

Do many words include the major vowels *a, e, i, o,* and *u? Unquestionably*—and that word is your best answer. Ross Eckler crafted the following sentence to demonstrate that the major vowels can occur, exactly once each, in just about any order: "Unsociable housemaid discourages facetious behaviour."

(See AMBIDEXTROUS, FACETIOUS, METALIOUS, ULYSSES SIMPSON GRANT, UNCOPYRIGHTABLE, UNNOTICEABLY.)

Set, anagrammed twice thrice, yields the triplet *testes, tsetse,* and *sestet.*

(See ANAGRAM, COMPASS, DANIEL, EPISCOPAL, ESTONIA, SILENT, STAR, STOP, TIME, WASHINGTON, WILLIAM SHAKESPEARE.)

Sex. The same letter cluster may yield different meanings and etymologies. For example, the *sex* in *sex* means "state of being either male or female," from the Latin *sexus*. The *sex* in *sextet* means "six," as in the Latin. The *sex* in *sexton* means "sacred," from Medieval Latin *sacristan*. And the *sex* in *Essex, Wessex,* and *Sussex* shows that they are the parts of England where the East, West, and South Saxons lived.

Shanghaiings is the longest reasonably familiar word (twelve letters) that consists entirely of letter pairs—two *s*'s, two *h*'s, two *a*'s, two *n*'s, two *g*'s, and two *i*'s.

Among eight-letter exhibits are *appeases, hotshots, reappear, signings,* and *teammate.* Among ten-letter runners up we find *arraigning, horseshoer,* and *intestines.* In many of these isogrammatical words, the two halves contain the same letters and hence are anagrams of each other.

(See HOTSHOTS, INTESTINES, RESTAURATEURS.)

Shiftgram. Take the word *add* and promote each letter by one letter in the alphabet. You'll get *bees.* When pairs of words are yoked together by promoted letters, we call them shiftgrams. Among shifty pairs that are semantically related we find:

cheer + 7 = *jolly*   *etch* + 12 = *pens*   *ice* + 2 = *keg*   *irk* + 13 = *vex*
dazed + 15 = *spots*   *green* + 13 = *terra*   *inkier* + 7 = *purple*   *oui* + 10 = *yes*
and *USA* + 12 = *gem*!

In *gnat* +13 = *tang*, the two words are mirror images.

Glory be, *God* is the grandest of all shiftgram clusters:

God + 8 = *owl*   *owl* + 4 = *sap*   *sap* + 4 = *wet*   *wet* + 10 = *God*

(See STAR.)

Sideburns. A century before Elvis Presley, the handsome face of Civil War general Ambrose E. Burnside was adorned by luxuriant side-whiskers sweeping down from his ears to his clean-shaven chin. The two halves of the general's last name somehow got reversed and pluralized, and the result was *sideburns.*

(See CROSSWORD, GERRYMANDER, MAVERICK, SANDWICH, SIL-HOUETTE, SPOONERISM.)

Silent. I *enlist* you to be *silent* and *listen* to the *inlets* of my *tinsel* words. That's five six-letter anagrams.

Now let's listen to the sounds of silence. All twenty-six of our letters are mute in one word or another. Here's an alphabet of such contexts to demonstrate the deafening silence that rings through English orthography:

A: *bread, marriage, pharaoh* N: *column, hymn, monsieur*
B: *debt, subtle, thumb* O: *country, laboratory, people*
C: *blackguard, indict, yacht* P: *cupboard, psychology, receipt*
D: *edge, handkerchief, Wednesday* Q: *lacquer, racquet*
E: *more, height, steak* R: *chevalier, forecastle, Worcester*
F: *halfpenny* S: *debris, island, viscount*
G: *gnarled, reign, tight* T: *gourmet, listen, tsar*
H: *ghost, heir, through* U: *circuit, dough, gauge*
I: *business, seize, Sioux* V: *fivepence*
J: *marijuana, rijsttafel* W: *answer, two, wrist*
K: *blackguard, knob, sackcloth* X: *faux pas, grand prix, Sioux*
L: *half, salmon, would* Y: *aye, prayer*
M: *mnemonic* Z: *rendezvous*

Now consider the opposite phenomenon, words in which a letter is sounded even though that letter is not included in the spelling. In *Xerox,* for example, the letter *z* speaks even though it doesn't appear in the base word. Behold, then, a complete alphabet of silent hosts:

A: *bouquet* G: *jihad* N: *comptroller* U: *ewe*
B: *W* H: *nature* O: *beau* V: *of*
C: *sea* I: *eye* P: *hiccough* W: *one*
D: *Taoism* J: *margin* Q: *cue* X: *decks*
E: *happy* K: *quay* R: *colonel* Y: *wine*
F: *ephemeral* L: *W* S: *civil* Z: *xylophone*
  M: *grandpa* T: *missed*

(See A, I, Q-TIPS, S, W, X.)

Silhouette. Long ago in prerevolutionary France there lived one Etienne de Silhouette, a controller-general for Louis XV. Because of his fanatical zeal for raising taxes and slashing expenses and pensions, he enraged royalty and citizens alike, who ran him out of office within eight months.

At about the same time that Silhouette was sacked for his infuriating parsimony, the method of making cutouts of profile portraits by throwing the shadow of the subject on the screen captured the fancy of the Paris public. Because the process was cheap and one that cut back to absolute essentials, the man and the method, in the spirit of ridicule, became associated. Ever since, we have called shadow profiles *silhouettes*, with a lowercase *s*.

(See GERRYMANDER, MAVERICK, SANDWICH, SIDEBURNS, SPOONERISM.)

Slapstick comedy owes its name to the double lath that clowns in seventeenth-century pantomimes wielded. The terrific sound of the two laths slapping together on the harlequin's derriere banged out the word *slapstick*.

One of those puppet clowns was Punch, forever linked to his straightwoman Judy. The Punch that was so pleased in the cliché *pleased as Punch* is not the sweet stuff we quaff. That phrase in fact alludes to the cheerful singing and self-satisfaction of the extroverted puppet.

From the art of puppetry we gain another expression. Puppetmasters manipulate the strings or wires of their marionettes from behind a dark curtain. Unseen, they completely control the actions of their on-stage actors. Whence the expression *to pull strings*.

Because entertainment is such a joyful, enriching part of our world, show business metaphors help our language to get its act together and get the show on the road. At the opportune moment, these sprightly words and expressions stop *waiting in the wings* and *step out into the limelight*. The first limelights were theatrical spotlights that used heated calcium oxide, or quicklime, to give off a light that was brilliant and white but not hot. Ever since that bright idea, *to be in the limelight* has been a metaphor for being in the glare of public scrutiny. Such show biz metaphors become *a tough act to follow,* but their act is followed again and again.

As my last act, I shine the spotlight on a few individual words and expressions that were born backstage and onstage:

- *Claptrap* was originally a theatrical trick or device designed to attract (trap) applause (clap) in a theater. It might have been a showy line, such as "Britannia rules the waves!" Or it might have been a machine that made a clapping sound before canned applause was invented. Thus, *claptrap* compares a clap trapper to "shallow, showy, cheap sentiment expressed solely for effect."

- *Desultory* descends from the Latin *de-*, "from," and *salire*, "to leap." The Roman *desultors*, or leapers, were circus performers who jumped from one moving horse to another. They were soon compared to people who fitfully jumped from one idea to another in conversation or one goal to another in their lives.

- *Explode* comes from the Latin *explodere*, "to chase away by clapping one's hands." In ancient Rome, disgruntled theatergoers would clap loudly to show their dissatisfaction with the performance on stage.

- *Hanky-panky* is possibly created, with the aid of reduplication, from the magician's handkerchief, or "hanky," a prop for trickery and sleight of hand. Or *hanky-panky* may be an alteration of *hocus-pocus*.

- *Hypocrite* is an offspring of the Greek *hypókrites* (ὑποκρίτης), a stage actor who, by the nature of his occupation, pretended to be someone other than himself. By extension, a hypocrite pretends to beliefs or feelings he doesn't really have.

- *Person* also steps from the stage into our everyday parlance. In Greek and Roman theater, actors played more than one role during a performance simply by donning a *persona* ("mask") to change character. Eventually, *persona* came to mean the role an individual assumes in life and, later, the individual himself.

You're as real trouper to have stayed with this entry to the very end. Note that the spelling isn't the military *trooper,* but *trouper,* a member of a theater company. *A real trouper* now means "one who perseveres through hardships without complaint."

(See KEYNOTE, METAPHOR.)

Slay is an irregular verb that declines as *slay-slew-slain*. *Slay* generates nine "illusory declensions." These are triads of words that aren't tenses of the same verb but that look like them because they follow the spelling pattern of *slay-slew-slain:*

bray	brew	brain	gray	grew	grain	spay	spew	Spain
dray	drew	drain	may	mew	main	stay	stew	stain
fay	few	fain	pay	pew	pain	stray	strew	strain

(See TEMP, VERB.)

RICHARD LEDERER

Sleeveless is the best example of a pyramid word, containing one occurrence of one letter, two occurrences of a second letter, and so on. Six-letter, 1-2-3 examples abound:

acacia	bowwow	hubbub	pepper
banana	cocoon	mammal	tattoo
bedded	horror	needed	wedded

Ten-letter, four-layer pyramids are wondrous monuments. Packed in *sleeveless* are one *v*, two *l*'s, three *s*'s, and four *e*'s. The strata in *Tennessee's* are one *t*, two *n*'s, three *s*'s, and four *e*'s. From *peppertree* grow one *t*, two *r*'s, three *p*'s, and four *e*'s.

(See TEMPERAMENTALLY.)

Smith. The largest category of last names began as descriptions of the work people did. In the telephone directories of the world's English-speaking cities, *Smith*, which means "worker," is the most popular last name by a large margin over its nearest competitors, Jones and Johnson (both of which are patronymics, "son of John"). And it is no wonder when you consider that the village smith, who made and repaired all objects of metal, was the most important person in the community. Two common expressions that we inherit from the art of blackmithery are *strike while the iron is hot* and *too many irons in the fire*.

International variations on *Smith* include *Smythe, Schmidt, Smed, Smitt, Faber, Ferrier, LeFebre, Ferraro, Kovacs, Manx, Goff,* and *Gough*. Versions of *Tailor* (*Taylor*) include *Schneider, Sarto, Sastre, Szabo, Kravitz, Hiatt, Portnoy,* and *Terzl*.

It is easy to trace the occupational origins of surnames such as *Archer, Baker, Barber, Brewer, Butler, Carpenter, Cook, Draper, Farmer, Fisher, Forester, Gardener, Hunter, Miller, Potter, Sheppard, Skinner, Tanner, Taylor, Weaver,* and *Wheeler*. Other surnames are not so easily recognized but, with some thought and research, yield up their occupational origins. My last name is an example. *Lederer* means "leather maker," the German equivalent of *Tanner* and *Skinner*.

Here are two dozen surnames paired with the occupations they subtly signify:

Bailey - bailiff	*Keeler* - bargeman
Baxter - baker	*Lardner* - keeper of the cupboard
Brewster - brewer	*Mason* - bricklayer
Chandler - candle maker	*Porter* - doorkeeper
Clark - clerk	*Sawyer* - carpenter
Cohen - priest	*Schumacher* - shoemaker
Collier - coal miner	*Scully* - scholar
Cooper, Hooper - barrel maker	*Stewart* - sty warden
Crocker - potter	*Thatcher* - roofer
Faulkner - falconer	*Travers* - toll-bridge collector
Fletcher - arrow maker	*Wainwright* - wheel maker
Hayward - keeper of fences	*Webster* - weaver

(See APTRONYM, ELIZABETH, JOHN.)

Smithery. When anagrammed, *smithery* contains no fewer than seventeen pronouns: *I, me, my, he, him, his, she, her, hers, it, its, ye, they, them, their, theirs,* and *thy.*

(See ANAGRAM, DANIEL, SPARE, STAR, STOP, THEREIN, WILLIAM SHAKESPEARE.)

Sneeze. Why do so many words beginning with *sn-* pertain to the nose—*snot, sneeze, snort, snore, sniff, sniffle, snipe, snuff, snuffle, snarl, snitch, snoot, snout, sneer,* and *snicker*? Maybe it's that the *s* sound widens your nostrils and lifts up your nose in a way that no other sound can.

And why are so many other *sn-* words distasteful and unpleasant—*snafu, snap, sneak, snide, snobby, snitch, snit, snub, snafu, snoop, snipe, snake, snotty, snooty,* and *snaggle tooth*? To appreciate the nasal aggression inherent in *sn-*, form the sound and note how your nose begins to wrinkle, your nostrils flare, and your lips draw back to expose your threatening canine teeth.

(See BASH, MOTHER.)

Southpaw. You may well know that a *southpaw* is a slang term for a left-handed person, but do you know why? The answer can be found in our great American pastime, baseball.

Most early baseball diamonds were laid out with the pitcher's mound to the east of home plate. With the westward orientation of home plate the batter wouldn't have to battle the afternoon sun in his eyes. As a result, as a right-handed pitcher wound up, he faced north—and a left-handed pitcher south. *South + paw* ("hand") = *southpaw.*

(See GOLF, LOVE.)

Spare. As well as being marvelously beheadable—*spare/pare/are/ re/e*—and curtailable—*spare/spar/spa*—*spare* is the most anagrammable of all English words. Juggle *spare* and you get *apers, pares, parse, pears, rapes, reaps,* and *spear,* along with the rarer *apres, asper, prase,* and *presa.*

Longer words are also productive:

- The seven-letter *allergy* brings forth *gallery, largely,* and *regally.*
- The eight-letter *triangle* tings out with *alerting, altering, integral,* and *relating.*
- Even ten-letter words offer up this remarkable trigram: *Discounter introduces reductions.*
- Disputes between New York and Los Angeles can be described with two twelve-letter anagrams: *intercoastal altercations.*
- With a switch of just two letters, the eighteen-letter *conversationalists* and *conservationalists* is the longest non-scientific anagram.

(See ANAGRAM, COMPASS, DANIEL, EPISCOPAL, ESTONIA, SET, STAR, STOP, TIME, WASHINGTON, WILLIAM SHAKESPEARE.)

Speech. Garnering twelve Academy Award nominations and four Oscars, including Best Picture, *The King's Speech* was by far the most honored film of 2010. Among its many excellencies is the double entendre in its title. The word *Speech* in *The King's Speech* means the speaking of George VI, the stammerer who did not want to become king. At the same time and in the same space, the word *Speech* means the particular address, in 1939, that King George VI delivered to his British subjects exhorting them to join in battle against the Germans.

In other words, *Speech* in the context of this triumphant film is an accordion word. Some of our most intriguing words, such as *speech,* are double-duty words that can expand and contract like an accordion. We know how big or small they are by their context.

Take the accordion word *time. Time* can refer to vast periods, as in "Over time, humans have built civilization." Or *time* can refer to a few hours: "We had a good time at the Quimbys' party." Or *time* can be a specific moment: "What time is it?"

Then there's the word *animal,* which can be used at two levels in a hierarchy of inclusion: First, *animal* can mean anything living that does not grow from the earth, as in "animal, vegetable, or mineral." In this context *animal* includes human beings, beasts, birds, fishes, and insects. Second, *animal* can refer to beasts only, in contrast with human beings, as in "man and the animals share dominance of the earth."

The use of *man,* above, yields another accordion word. Although the noun has come under increasing attack as sexist, *man* is still employed to refer both to all of humankind, as in Jacob Bronowski's *The Ascent of Man,* and to only the male members of our species, as in "man and woman." Similar is the word *gay,* which can designate all homosexuals, as in "gay rights," or only male homosexuals, as in "the gay and lesbian community."

Business started out as a general term meaning literally "busyness." After several centuries of life, *business* picked up the narrower meaning of "commercial dealings." In 1925 Calvin Coolidge used the word in both its generalized an specialized senses when he stated, "The chief business of the American people is business." We today can see the word starting to generalize back to its first meaning in phrases like "I don't like this funny business one bit."

In the examples that follow, I list the broader meaning first and the narrower meaning second:

- *American*: (1) a native or inhabitant of North or South America (2) a citizen of the United States.
- *body*: (1) the entire person, especially when dead: "They removed the body" (2) the main part of a person, as distinguished from head and limbs: "He took a hard right to the body."
- *country*: (1) a nation: "I am proud of my country." (2) the rural areas of a nation: "town and country."
- *day*: (1) an era: "In my day, we shoveled coal to heat the house." (2) a 24-hour span: "What day do I start work?" (3) the daylight hours of a 24-hour span: "day and night." The second and third meanings work together in Bill Hicks's quip "I sleep eight hours a day. And at least ten at night."
- *dress (n.)*: (1) apparel, clothing: "Describe the dress of the early puritans." (2) a garment for females: "Jane bought a new dress."
- *drink (n.)*: (1) any liquid suitable for swallowing: "I'd like a drink of cold water," (2) alcoholic liquid: "You've had too many drinks."

- *earth*: (1) our planet: "dominion over all the earth" (2) soil: "rich earth."
- *verse*: (1) poetry. (2) a stanza in a poem.

Samuel Goldwyn once observed, "A verbal contract isn't worth the paper it's written on." Obviously the movie mogul used *verbal* to mean "oral," as do most speakers of American English. But *verbal* (Latin *verbum,* "word") communication involves words spoken or written, as in "I'm trying to improve my verbal skills." In this sense, Goldwyn's Goldwynism isn't so funny after all.

Spoonerism. The Reverend William Archibald Spooner entered the earthly stage near London on July 22, 1844, born with a silver spoonerism in his mouth. He set out to be a bird-watcher but ended up instead as a word-botcher. That's because he tended to reverse letters and syllables, often with unintentionally hilarious results. For example, he once supposedly lifted a tankard in honor of Queen Victoria. As he toasted the reigning monarch, he exclaimed, "Three cheers for our queer old dean!"

That was appropriate because Dr. Spooner became a distinguished master and warden of New College at Oxford University. But because of his frequent tips of the slung, he grew famous for his tonorous rubble with tin sax. In fact, these switcheroos have become known as spoonerisms.

The larger the number of words in a language, the greater the likelihood that two or more words will rhyme. Because the English language embraces a million words, it is afflicted with a delightful case of rhymatic fever. A ghost town becomes a *toast gown.* A toll booth becomes a *bowl tooth.* A bartender becomes a *tar bender.* And motion pictures become *potion mixtures.*

More rhymes mean more possible spoonerisms. That's why English is the most tough and rumble of all languages, full of thud and blunder. That's why English is the most spoonerizable tongue ever invented. That's why you enter this entry optimistically and leave it misty optically.

In honor of Dr. William Archibald Spooner's tang tongueled whiz and witdom, here's a gallimaufry of tinglish errors and English terrors:

Dr. Spooner's Animal Act

Welcome, ladies; welcome gents.
 Here's an act that's so in tents:
An absolute sure-fire parade,
 A positive pure-fire charade—
With animals weak and animals mild,
 Creatures meek and creatures wild,
With animals all in a row.
 I hope that you enjoy the show:

Gallops forth a curried horse,
 Trotting through a hurried course.
Ridden by a loving shepherd
 Trying to tame a shoving leopard.
Don't think I'm a punny phony,
 But next in line's a funny pony.
On its back a leaping wizard,
 Dancing with a weeping lizard.

Watch how that same speeding rider
 Holds aloft a reading spider.
Now you see a butterfly
 Bright and nimbly flutter by,
Followed by a dragonfly,
 As it drains its flagon dry.
Step right up; see this mere bug
 Drain the drink from his beer mug.

Lumbers forth a honey bear,
 Fur as soft as bunny hair.
Gaze upon that churning bear,
 Standing on a burning chair.
Gently patting a mute kitten,
 On each paw a knitted mitten.
Watch as that small, running cat
 Pounces on a cunning rat.

See a clever, heeding rabbit
 Who's acquired a reading habit,
Sitting on his money bags,
 Reading many bunny mags,
Which tickle hard his funny bone,
 As he talks on his bunny phone.
He is such a funny beast,
 Gobbling down his bunny feast.

RICHARD LEDERER

Gasp in awe as winking seals
Sit atop three sinking wheels.
Don't vacillate. An ocelot
Will oscillate a vase a lot.
There's a clever dangling monkey
And a stubborn, mangling donkey
And—a gift from our Dame Luck—
There waddles in a large lame duck.

That's Dr. Spooner's circus show.
With animals all in a row,
(As you can see, we give free reign
To this metrical refrain.)
Now hops a dilly of a frog
Followed by a frilly dog.
Hear that hoppy frog advise:
"Time's fun when you're having flies!"

That's a look at spoonerisms in one swell foop. Just bear in mind: Don't sweat the petty things, and don't pet the sweaty things. And let's close with a special toast: Here's champagne to our real friends and real pain to our sham friends!

(See GERRYMANDER, MALAPROPISM, MAVERICK, PUN, SANDWICH, SIDEBURNS, SILHOUETTE.)

Squirreled is the longest one-syllable word (eleven letters), if you indeed pronounce it monosyllabically.

The lengthiest two-syllable words come to thirteen letters:

breakthroughs   breaststrokes   straightedged   straightforth

The twelve-letter *spendthrifts* merits a merit badge because it may the longest word that is pronounced exactly as it is spelled.

(See STRENGTHS.)

Star is truly a star among words. Spell *star* backwards, and you get *rats*.

Next, we'll twice progress from inside to outside, in the order of 2-1-3-4 and 3-4-2-1, and we derive *tsar* and *arts*. Star and its reversal, *rats*, are the only two English words that can do that.

Now, let's transport the *s* to the back of *star*, and *tars* appears.

For more fun, let's promote each letter in *star* by one. Voila! We find the shiftgram *tubs*: $s + 1 = t$, $t + 1 = u$, $a + 1 = b$, and $r + 1 = s$.

The Latin word for "star" is *stella*, whence the name *Stella*, the adjective *stellar*, and the noun *constellation*.

(See ANAGRAM, COMPASS, DANIEL, DISASTER, EPISCOPAL, ESTO-NIA, SET, SHIFTGRAM, SILENT, SPARE, STOP, TIME, WASHINGTON, WIL-LIAM SHAKESPEARE.)

Startling is a nine-letter word that remains a word each time one of its letters is removed, from nine letters down to a single letter:

startling
starting
staring
string
sting
sing
sin
in
I

Similarly:

stringier
stingier
stinger
singer
singe
sine
sin
in
I

Other nine-letter words that can be transdeleted one letter at a time to form one word at a time include *cleansers, discusses, drownings, replanted, restarted, scrapping, splatters, startling, strapping, trappings,* and *wrappings*.

(See ALONE, PASTERN, PRELATE, REACTIVATION.)

Stop. The STOP you see on traffic signs yields six different words that begin with each of the letters in STOP:

Our landlord *opts* to fill our *pots*
Until the *tops* flow over.
Tonight we *stop* upon this *spot*.
Tomorrow *post* for Dover.

(See ANAGRAM, COMPASS, DANIEL, EPISCOPAL, ESTONIA, SET, STAR, WASHINGTON, WILLIAM SHAKESPEARE.)

Strengthlessness is the longest common univocalic word—one that contains just one vowel repeated (sixteen letters, three *e*'s). Next come *defenselessness* (fifteen letters, five *e*'s), then *sleevelessness* (fourteen letters, five *e*'s).

Assesses is the longest word (eight letters) with one, and only one, consonant repeated throughout, five times in eight letters.

(See ABRACADABRA, DEEDED, MISSISSIPPI.)

Strengths. One of a number of nine-letter words of one syllable and the longest containing but a single vowel. Among its strengths is the fact that it ends with five consecutive consonants.

Nine-letter, one-syllable words with more than one vowel include:

scratched   *screeched*   *scrounged*   *squelched*   *stretched*

(See SQUIRRELED.)

Supercalifragilisticexpialidocious is a thirty-four letter word invented for the film version of *Mary Poppins* (1964) that has become our best known really, really big word. Etymologically, this is not entirely a nonsense word:

super: "above"   *cali:* "beauty"   *fragilistic:* "delicate,"
expiali: "to atone"   *docious:* "educable"

Stitched together, *supercalifragilisticexpialidocious* means "atoning for extreme and delicate beauty [while being] highly educable."

The word has also inspired what I believe to be the most bedazzling syllable-by-syllable set-up pun ever devised:

One of the greatest men of the twentieth century was the political leader and ascetic Mahatma Gandhi. His denial of the earthly pleasures included the fact that he never wore anything on his feet. He walked barefoot everywhere. Moreover, he ate so little that he developed delicate health and very bad breath. Thus, he became known as a *super callused fragile mystic hexed by halitosis*!

(See CHARGOGGAGOGGMANCHAUGGAGOGGCHAUBUN-AGUNGAMAUGG, FLOCCINAUCINIHILIPILIFICATION, HIPPOPOTOMON-STROSESQUIPEDALIAN, HONORIFICABILITUDINITATIBUS, LLANFAIR-PWLLGWYNGYLLGOGERYCHWYRNDDROBWLLLLANTYSILOGOGOCH, PNEUMONOULTRAMICROSCOPICSILICOVOLCANOKONIOSIS.)

Sweet-toothed is a hyphenated example of a word containing three adjacent double letters.

(See BOOKKEEPER.)

Swifty. Starting in 1910, boys grew up devouring the adventures of Tom Swift, a sterling hero and natural scientific genius created by Edward Stratemeyer. Many of Tom's inventions predated technological developments in real life-—electric cars, seacopters, and houses on wheels. In fact, some say that the Tom Swift tales laid the groundwork for American science fiction.

In Stratemeyer's stories, Tom and his friends and enemies didn't always just say something. Occasionally they said something *excitedly, sadly, hurriedly,* or *grimly.* That was enough to inspire the game called Tom Swifties. The object is to match the adverb with the quotation to produce, in each case, a high-flying pun. Here are my favorite Tom Swifties (says Lederer puntificatingly):

- "My pants are wrinkled," said Tom ironically.
- "I dropped my toothpaste," said Tom crestfallen.
- "I lost my flower," said Tom lackadaisically.
- "My favorite statue is the Venus de Milo," said Tom disarmingly.
- "I love reading *Moby-Dick*," said Tom superficially.
- "I'll take the prisoner downstairs," said Tom condescendingly.
- "I'm sorry that my jet propulsion system didn't get the rocket to the moon," said Tom apologetically.
- "My stereo is finally fixed," said Tom ecstatically.
- "What I do best on camping trips is sleep," said Tom intently.
- "I manufacture table tops," said Tom counterproductively.
- "That's a really ugly river beast," said Tom hypocritically.
- "I'm going to kill Dracula," said Tom painstakingly.

- "Be sure to feed kitty her cod liver oil," said Tom catatonically.
- "In order to join the Airborne Medical Corps, I had to earn a Ph.D. and an M.D.," said Tom paradoxically.

(See DAFFYNITION, PHILODENDRON, PUN, SPOONERISM.)

A **synonym** (from the Greek "same name or word") is a word that has an identical or similar meaning to another word. Some wag has defined a synonym as "the word you use in place of the word you'd really like to use but can't spell."

You should not be aghast, amazed, appalled, astonished, astounded, bewildered, blown away, boggled, bowled over, bumfuzzled, caught off base, confounded, dumbfounded, electrified, flabbergasted, floored, flummoxed, overwhelmed, shocked, startled, stunned, stupefied, surprised, taken aback, thrown, or thunderstruck by the o'erflowing cornucopia of synonyms in our marvelous language. Boasting a million words—more than four times the number in any other language—English possesses the richest vocabulary in history.

If you don't believe me, please read the following announcement:

> I regret to inform you that yesterday, a senior editor of *Roget's Thesaurus* assumed room temperature, bit the dust, bought the farm, breathed his last, came to the end of the road, cashed in his chips, cooled off, croaked, deep sixed, expired, gave up the ghost, headed for the hearse, headed for the last roundup, kicked off, kicked the bucket, lay down one last time, lay with the lilies, left this mortal plain, met his maker, met Mr. Jordan, passed away, passed in his checks, passed on, pegged out, perished, permanently changed his address, pulled the plug, pushed up daisies, returned to dust, slipped his cable, slipped his mortal coil, sprouted wings, took the dirt nap, took the long count, traveled to kingdom come, turned up his toes, went across the creek, went belly up, went to glory, went the way of all flesh, went to his final reward, went west—and, of course, he died.

The opposite of a *synonym* is an *antonym*; that is, *synonym* and *antonym* are antonyms. Aside from the usual antonymic pairings—*black* and *white, good* and *bad, rich* and *poor, fat* and *thin*—antonyms can be formed anagrammatically, in which case they are called *antigrams*:

cheater/teacher	fluster/restful	Satan/Santa
filled/ill-fed	listen/silent	united/untied
	marital/martial	

and by deleting internal letters:

animosity/amity	feast/fast	resign/reign
avoid/aid	friend/fiend	resist/rest
communicative/mute	inattentive intent	spurns/spurs
courteous/curt	injured/inured	stray/stay
cremate/create	intimidate/intimate	threat/treat
deify/defy	patriarch/pariah	un-huh/uh-uh
encourage/enrage	pest/pet	vainglorious/valorous
exist/exit	prurient/pure	wonderful/woeful

Now that you know how to transdelete letters from the middle of words, I hope that I no longer intimidate you. Simply remove the *id* from the middle of *intimidate*, and the result is *intimate*.

(See DRUNK.)

RICHARD LEDERER

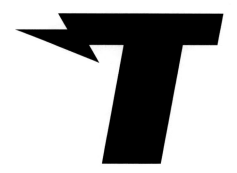

Tad. Biologically, a tadpole is a larval amphibian. Etymologically, *tadpole* is formed from the Middle English *tode,* "toad" + *polle*, "head" because a tadpole looks like a toad that is all head, with the limbs to grow out later. The clipped form *tad* swam into American English around 1915 with the meaning "a small amount," as in "a tad of sugar" and "a tad chilly."

(See BUFFALO, BUTTERFLY, CANARY, CAPER, CLAM, CRESTFALLEN, DACHSHUND, DANDELION, HORSEFEATHERS, OSTRACIZE, PARTRIDGE, PEDIGREE, TURKEY, VACCINATE, ZYZZYVA.)

Tantalize. One of the vilest of villains in Greek mythology's was King Tantalus, who served the body of his young son to the gods. They soon discovered the king's wicked ruse, restored the dead boy to life, and devised a punishment to fit the crime. They banished the king to Hades, where he is condemned to stand in a sparkling pool of water with boughs of luscious fruit overhead; when he stoops to drink, the water drains away through the bottom of the pool, and when he wishes to eat, the branches of fruit sway just out of his grasp. Ever since, when something presents itself temptingly to our view, we say that we are tantalized.

(See CLUE, ECHO, JOVIAL, WEDNESDAY.)

Taxicab is the best example of a redundant word, in which the two halves of a word mean exactly the same thing. Other specimens include *bunny rabbit, forefront, oleomargarine, Ouija, pussycat, soda pop, sum total,* and *tabby cat.*

(See REDUNDANCY.)

Temp is the best of "pseudo-comparatives"—words that can add both an *-er* and *-est* but that don't relate at all to true comparisons of adjectives. That is, the triad of *temp/temper/tempest* looks like the *small/smaller/smallest* adjective model, but it isn't a true progression of adjectives. Other examples: *be/beer/beest; hon/honer/honest; mole/molar/molest, p/per/pest,* and *pry/prior/priest. Deter/detest* and *infer/infest* are the ultimate heartbreakers—comparatives and superlatives, but with no basewords.

(See SLAY.)

Temperamentally. Medieval philosophers believed that four qualities—hot, cold, moist, and dry—coalesced in varying quantities to form the nature of things. The Latin word for this mixture was *temperamentum*; if anyone became temperamental, the mixture was apparently a bubble off plumb.

In addition, the word *temperamentally* is a blazing sun in the heavens of letter play. I say that because it's the densest example of a snowball word, one that can be cleft into one-, two-, three-, four-, and five letter words: *t em per amen tally.*

(See ALKALINE, DAREDEVIL, MARSHALL, SLEEVELESS.)

Thai. In the triad *Thai, thigh,* and *thy,* the first two letters of each word are spelled the same but sounded differently, while the remaining letters are each spelled differently but pronounced the same—*eye.*

Therein. Lurking in *therein* are ten words with letters adjacent and in order:

the	there	here	herein	re
he	her	ere	rein	in

(See BLOSSOM.)

Thingamabob. When we don't know what something is called, we have at least thirty synonyms to identify "that object I don't know the name for":

dingus	gigamaree	thingamajig
doofunny	gimmick	thingamajigger
dohickey	gizmo	thingamaree
dojigger	hickey	thingammy
dojiggy	hootenanny	thingum
domajig	hootmalalie	thingy
domajigger	jigger	whatzy
doodad	such-and-such	whatchamacallit
dowhackey	thingamabob	whatzit
flumadiddle	thingamadoodle	widget

(See ZARF.)

Thunder. The English poet and playwright John Dennis is best known for first sneering, "A pun is the lowest form of wit." In 1709, Dennis's tragedy, *Appius and Virginia*, turned out to be a tragic failure among critics and playgoers alike. The play bombed even though Dennis had invented for it a device that generated the roaring of thunder as part of the staging.

Shortly after the premature closing of Dennis's play, Shakespeare's *Macbeth* came to London. Dennis attended an early performance, where he heard his own thunder machine roar during the three witches' opening scene on the heath. The upstaged Dennis exclaimed: "My God! The villains will not play my play, but they will steal my thunder!" And that's where we get the expression "to steal my thunder," meaning "to be robbed of deserved glory."

(See KEYNOTE, METAPHOR, SLAPSTICK.)

Time. William Shakespeare spoke of people who "run before the clock," as if the hands of the clock would sweep them away if they did not hustle their bustles. In the English-speaking world so many of us seem to be working harder and taking fewer and shorter vacations. The Oxford English Corpus list of word frequencies confirms that obsession with time and productivity by revealing that *time* is the most frequently used noun in our language. *Year* is ranked third, *day* fifth, *work* sixteenth, and *week* seventeenth.

In his poem "To His Coy Mistress," the English poet Andrew Marvell wrote, "But at my back I always hear/Time's winged chariot hurrying near." According to the Oxford English Corpus frequency list, time's winged chariot is running us over.

Time is also a perfect anagram, a word whose letters can be juggled so that each new word begins with a different letter from the original word: "Now is the *time* to *emit* information about an *item* that may help you a *mite*."

Have you ever noted how ambiguous are statements that involve time?

- "Let's push up [or back] that appointment by two days." Does that mean that the appointment will now be two days earlier or later?

- "I'll see you next Wednesday." Is that the Wednesday coming up, or the one after that?

- "Our biannual meeting is very important." Does that meeting take place twice a year or every other year?

- "The boss will see you momentarily." Will the boss see you in a moment or for a moment?

- "Since 1988, the company has been in the forefront of technological creativity." Does that innovativeness include 1988?

- "The train arrives at 12 a.m." Is that noon or midnight?

It's amazing that we English speakers ever get any place on time.

Toast. In the days of Queen Elizabeth I and William Shakespeare, people would place slices of spiced toast into their tankards of ale or glasses of wine to improve the flavor and remove the impurities. The drink itself became a "toast," as did the gesture of drinking to another's good health.

Centuries later, an eastern farmer in the United States who had decided to move west would stop by the local tavern to say good-bye to friends and neighbors. They would toast him with *Here's mud in your eye,* which meant "May you find soft, rich, dark, and moist soil that will be thrown up as specks of mud as you plow it."

(See CAKEWALK, COMPANION, COUCH POTATO, HOAGIE, PUMPER-NICKEL, SALARY, SANDWICH.)

Towhead. This form of *tow* descends from an Old English word that means "flax." A towhead is a youngster—usually male, but not necessarily so—with white or pale yellow hair the color of flax. Avoid confusing *tow* with *toe,* as in this newspaper photo caption "Linda Tinyon clutched her toe-headed son during the storm." Even worse: "Linda Tinyon clutched her two-headed son during the storm."

(See BLOOPER.)

Triskaidekaphobia. Do you have an undomesticated phobia? No? Think again. Does your stomach want to scream when it and you arrive at the zenith of a Ferris wheel? Does your head retract turtlelike into your body when the lightning flashes and the thunder cracks? Do you tremble at the sight of a snake or a rat or a spider or a cockroach?

Humankind is beset with a host of fears and has managed to assign names to more than a thousand of them. Phobos, "fear," was the son of Ares, the god of war, and was the nephew of Eris, goddess of discord, and brother to Deimos, "dread." The names of our deepest dreads generally include the Greek root *phobia* (φόβος), "fear or hatred," affixed to another Greek root. The two most common fears are *acrophobia,* a morbid fear of heights, and *claustrophobia,* a morbid fear of enclosed spaces. Things could be worse. Count your blessings that you aren't stuck with *pantophobia*—the morbid fear of everything.

Among this class of fears that go bump in our minds, my favorites include *triskaidekaphobia*: fear of the number thirteen (*tris,* "three" + *kai,* "and" + *deka,* "ten" + *phobia,* "fear"); *pentheraphobia*: fear of your mother-in-law; *pteronophobia*: fear of being tickled by feathers; and—I'm not making this up—*arachibutyrophobia*: the dread of peanut butter sticking to the roof of your mouth.

When Franklin Roosevelt declaimed, in his 1933 inaugural address, "The only thing we have to fear is fear itself," he was warning against *phobophobia*, the fear of being afraid. Knowing that all our terrors have names may be a kind of magic that helps us to hold them at bay and to experience less fear about fear itself.

Trivia is borrowed from the Latin word spelled the same way and composed of *tri,* "three" + *via,* "roads" = "the place where three roads meet." At such crosswords, travelers would exchange idle chitchat and stories; whence and hence, the current meaning, "commonplace things of little or no importance."

Trivium took on a more metaphorical significance in the Middle Ages, when it referred to the three roads to knowledge—grammar, rhetoric, and logic. Rounding out the liberal arts was the *quadrivium*—arithmetic, geometry, astronomy, and music.

Writer James Joyce is said to have said, "My puns are not trivial. They are quadrivial."

Turkey. Centuries ago, the Pilgrims found in America a wild fowl somewhat similar in appearance to a guinea fowl they had known back in England, a fowl that acquired its name because it was first imported by way of Turkey. As the (probably apocryphal) tale spins out, back in the early colonial days, a white hunter and a friendly Native American made a pact before they started out on the day's hunt. Whatever they bagged was to be divided equally between them. At the end of the day, the white man undertook to distribute the spoils, consisting of several buzzards and turkeys. He suggested to his fellow hunter, "Either I take the turkeys and you the buzzards, or you take the buzzards and I take the turkeys." At this point the Native American complained, "You talk buzzard to me. Now talk turkey." And ever since, *to talk turkey* has meant "to tell it like it is."

(See BIKINI, BUFFALO, CANARY, CAPER, CLAM, CRESTFALLEN, DACHSHUND, HAMBURGER, HORSEFEATHERS, OSTRACIZE, PARTRIDGE, PEDIGREE, TAD, VACCINATE, ZYZZYVA.)

Typewriter. When we seek to find the longest word that can be typed on a single horizontal row of a standard typewriter keyboard, we naturally place our fingers on the top row of letters—*qwertyuiop*—because five of the seven vowels reside there. From that single row we can type seven ten-letter words: *pepperroot, pepperwort, peppertree, perpetuity, proprietor, repertoire,* and—ta da!—*typewriter.*

Ulysses Simpson Grant and *Rutherford Birchard Hayes* are the only presidential names that contain *a, e, i, o,* and *u* with a *y* to boot.

- *Eisenhower* is the only presidential surname that contains four syllables.

- *Nixon.* Reverse the last two letters and you get a double negative—*nix no.*

- *Obama* is the only presidential surname that begins with *O* and that begins and ends with a vowel.

- *Pierce, Grant, Ford, Bush, Carter,* and (in Britain) *Hoover* are all common words when uncapitalized.

- *Roosevelt, Coolidge, Hoover,* and *Roosevelt* are presidential surnames containing *oo.* All these men occupied the Oval Office in the twentieth century, three of them sequentially.

- *James Madison* is the only president whose first and last names alternate between consonants and vowels.

- *Rutherford B. Hayes's* first name contains the last name of *Gerald Ford. Andrew* and *Lyndon Johnson's* last name contains the first name of four other presidents—*Adams, Quincy Adams, Tyler,* and

Kennedy. The middle names of *Ronald Wilson Reagan* and *William Jefferson Clinton* match the last names of two of their predecessors.

(See OK, WASHINGTON.)

Uncopyrightable. An isogram is a single word in which no letter of the alphabet appears more than once—an iso(lated pan)gram. Among fairly common English words, the fifteen-letter *uncopyrightable* is the longest. In *uncopyrightable* each major vowel plus *y* appears once and only once.

The less familiar *dermatoglyphics* (the science of skin patterns, especially fingerprints) also sports fifteen letters. *Ambidextrously* is a satisfying fourteen-letter isogram; it too contains each major vowel plus *y*.

The longest isographic duo is *blacksmith-gunpowdery* (twenty letters), the longest trio (twenty-two letters) *frowzy-humpbacks-tingled,* which is also a plausible sentence.

(See FACETIOUS, METALIOUS, PANGRAM, SEQUOIA, ULYSSES SIMPSON GRANT, UNNOTICEABLY.)

Underground. It's shockingly easy to turn your *mentor* into your *tormentor*: Simply clone the *tor* at the end and graft the offspring on to the beginning of the word. Even more subtly, buried in *underground* are the letters *und* at both the beginning and the end. And, if you accept *undergrounder* as a word, you have an entity beginning and ending with *under.*

Many other words begin and end with the same trigram, including:

*anti*oxid*ant*	*ent*ertainm*ent*	*mes*dames	*red*iscover*ed*
*bed*aub*ed*	*ion*ization	*mic*rocos*mic*	*res*tores

(See HOTSHOTS.)

United. In an installment of Johnny Hart's comic strip *B.C.,* one caveman screams at another, "No, no, no, no! I distinctly said to *gird* your *loins!*" The other cave guy has drawn a grid on a lion. The humor of this episode arises from the fact that a number of words transform into other words when two adjacent letters are switched—*trial/trail, diary/dairy, silver/sliver, closets/closest, infraction/infarction,* and, of course *gird/grid* and *loins/lions.*

RICHARD LEDERER

With the same interchange of neighboring letters, *united* becomes its opposite—*untied*. *Complaint* and *compliant* form near opposites, as do *sacred* and *scared*. Depending on your point of view, *marital* and *martial* may be antonyms or synonyms.

(See LATCHES, MENTALLY.)

Up. It's time to catch up on *up*, the ever-present two-letter word that may have more meanings than any other and, at times, no meaning at all. It's easy to understand *up* when it means skyward or toward the top of a list. And clearly there are crucial differences between *call* and *call up* and *beat* and *beat up*. But I have to wonder why we warm ourselves up, why we speak up, why we shower up, why a topic comes up, and why we crack up at a joke.

Let's face up to it: We're all mixed up about *up*. Usually the little word is totally unnecessary. Why do we light up a cigar, lock up the house, polish up the silverware, and fix up the car when we can more easily and concisely light, lock, polish, and fix them?

At times, verbs with *up* attached mess up our heads and screw up our minds with bewildering versatility. To look up a chimney means one thing, to look up a friend another, to look up to a friend yet another, to look up a word something else. We can make up a bed, a story, a test, our face, and our mind, and each usage has a completely different meaning.

At other times, *up*-verbs are unabashedly ambiguous. When we wind up our watch, we start it; when we wind up a meeting, we stop it. When we hold up our partners on the tennis court, are we supporting or hindering them? How, pray tell, can we walk up and down the aisle at the same time and slow up and slow down at the same time?

What bollixes up our language worse than anything else is that *up* can be downright misleading. A house doesn't really burn up; it burns down. We don't really throw up; we throw out and down. We don't pull up a chair; we pull it along. Most of us don't add up a column of figures; we add them down.

And why it is that we first chop down a tree, and then we chop it up?

Maybe it's time to give up on the uppity *up*.

AMAZING WORDS   185

Vaccinate. For centuries, smallpox was a scourge of humanity, scarring and killing millions, Edward Jenner, a British doctor, noticed that milkmaids did not generally get smallpox and theorized that the pus in the blisters that these women developed from cowpox protected them from the more virulent smallpox. In 1796, Jenner found that inoculating people with a serum containing the lymph gland fluid of cows infected with cowpox virus prevented the similar smallpox. That's why *vaccine, vaccination,* and *vaccinate* contain the Latin name for "cow," *vacca.*

To err is human, to explore cow etymologies is bovine. *Pecu* is the Latin word for "herd of cattle," and because the ancients often expressed the value of an estate by the number of cattle therein, early metal coins were stamped with a bull's head. From this association of wealth with cattle we inherit the words *pecuniary,* "pertaining to money"; *impecunious,* "without money"; *peculate,* "to embezzle"; and *peculiar,* "that which is one's own."

Egregious literally means "apart from the herd," from the Latin *ex-,* "out of," and *grex,* "flock." *Grex* is also the source of *gregarious,* or "sociable."

RICHARD LEDERER

(See BUFFALO, BUTTERFLY, CANARY, CLAM, CRESTFALLEN, DACHS-HUND, DANDELION, HORSEFEATHERS, OSTRACIZE, PARTRIDGE, PEDI-GREE, TAD, ZYZZYVA.)

Vacuum. Latin is alive and well and living in our everyday vocabu-lary—in fact, more than three hundred Latin words in English that are unchanged by a single letter in the twenty centuries that span the two languages. These pristine Latin entries include: *actor, basis, cam-era, circus, doctor, elevator, epitome, exit, focus, formula, gusto, honor, interest, janitor, labor, memorandum, minimum, motor, narrator, op-era, prior, quota, rancor, recipe, splendor, stimulus, tribunal, transit, trivia, ulterior,* and *vacuum*—all words that are written exactly the same way today as they were by the emperor Nero.

Vacuum is the most common of double-*u* words, joined by the likes of *continuum, Equus, muumuu,* and *residuum.*

Ventriloquist. One who is skilled in the art of throwing his or her voice so that it appears to emanate from a source other than the speaker. Appropriately, the roots of *ventriloquist* are the Latin *ven-tris,* "belly" + *loqui,* "speaker." In other words, a ventriloquist is a "belly speaker."

I'm thinking of writing a book titled *Ventriloquism for Dummies.*

Verb. Verbs are the sparkplugs of our sentences and take their name from *verbum,* the Latin word for *word.*

Have you heard the one about the man who went to trial for hav-ing pulled a woman down a street by the hair? When the judge asked the arresting officer, "Was she drugged?" the policeman answered, "Yes sir, a full block." Or the one about the woman who asked a Boston cab driver where she could get scrod. "I didn't know that the verb had that past tense," muttered the cabbie.

Both jokes rely on the fact that verb tenses in English are cra-zy, fraught with a fearful asymmetry and puzzling unpredictability. Some verbs form their past tense by adding -*d,* -*ed,* or -*t*—*walk, walked; bend, bent.* Others go back in time through an internal vowel change—*begin, began; sing, sang.* Another cluster adds -*d* or -*t* and undergoes an internal vowel change—*lose, lost; buy, bought.* And still others don't change at all—*set, set; put, put.* No wonder, then, that our eyes glaze and our breath quickens when we have to form the past tense of verbs like *dive, weave, shine, sneak,* and *babysit.*

An English teacher spent a lot of time marking grammatical errors in her students' written work. She wasn't sure how much impact she was having until one overly busy day when she sat at her desk rubbing her temples.

A student asked, "What's the matter, Mrs. Bennett?"

"Tense," she replied, describing her emotional state.

After a slight pause the student tried again: "What was the matter? What has been the matter? What will be the matter? What might have been the matter?"

The past tenses of verbs in our language cause so many of us to become tense that I've written a poem about the insanity:

A Tense Time with Verbs

The verbs in English are a fright.
 How can we learn to read and write?
Today we speak, but first we spoke;
 Some faucets leak, but never loke.
Today we write, but first we wrote;
 We bite our tongues, but never bote.

Each day I teach, for years I've taught,
 And preachers preach, but never praught.
This tale I tell; this tale I told;
 I smell the flowers, but never smold.

If knights still slay, as once they slew,
 Then do we play, as once we plew?
If I still do as once I did,
 Then do cows moo, as they once mid?

I love to win, and games I've won;
 I seldom sin, and never son.
I hate to lose, and games I've lost;
 I didn't choose, and never chost.

I love to sing, and songs I sang;
 I fling a ball, but never flang.
I strike that ball, that ball I struck;
 This poem I like, but never luck.

I take a break, a break I took;
 I bake a cake, but never book.
I eat that cake, that cake I ate;
 I beat an egg, but never bate.

I often swim, as I once swam;
I skim some milk, but never skam.
I fly a kite that I once flew;
I tie a knot, but never tew.

I see the truth, the truth I saw;
I flee from falsehood, never flaw.
I stand for truth, as I once stood;
I land a fish, but never lood.

About these verbs I sit and think.
These verbs don't fit. They seem to wink
At me, who sat for years and thought
Of verbs that never fat or wrought.

(See PREPOSITION, PRONOUN, SLAY, WOMEN.)

Verbivore. I conjured up this word about twenty years ago for the title of my book *Adventures of a Verbivore,* and it has now made a home for itself in the vocabulary of lexiphiles, logolepts, and wordaholics. Carnivores eat flesh and meat; piscivores eat fish; herbivores consume plants and vegetables; verbivores devour words. I am such a creature. My whole life I have feasted on words—ogled their appetizing shapes, colors, and textures; swished them around in my mouth; lingered over their many tastes; let their juices run down my chin. Now that you have progressed this far in this book, you are a clearly a fellow verbivore.

Veterinarian. The verb *to vet* means "to examine credentials, manuscripts, or other documents as a veterinarian examines an animal, hoping to give it a clean bill of health." The noun *veterinarian* came about because the first veterinarians treated only animals that were old (Latin *vetus,* as in *veteran*), that is, old enough and experienced enough to perform work such as pulling a plow or hauling military baggage.

Most occupational titles are self-explanatory: A teacher teaches, a preacher preaches, a gardener gardens, and a writer writes. But the origins of some job names are more obscure. *Veterinarian* is one example. *Janitor* is another, deriving from the Roman god Janus, who guarded doorways. A *professor* is "one who makes public declarations," while the first *deans* were military officers in charge of ten (*decem*) soldiers. Those *soldiers* were so called because they were paid in Roman coins called *solidi*.

When Geoffrey Chaucer wrote in his Prologue to *The Canterbury Tales*, "a clerk ther was of Oxenford," the poet was referring to a clergyman or cleric, the first meaning of the word *clerk*. In the Middle Ages, literacy was largely confined to the clergy, but *clerk* gradually became the name for bookkeepers, secretaries, and notaries—anyone who could read or write.

Here are some more vocational names and their not-so-apparent derivations:

- *broker*. One who broaches (opens) casks of wine.
- *bursar*. One who controls the purse (*bursa*).
- *chauffeur*. One who stokes the fires of a steam engine.
- *coroner*. An officer of the crown (*corona*).
- *grocer*. One who sells by the gross.
- *nurse*. One who nourishes.
- *orthopedist*. One who corrects (the bones of) children.
- *pastor*. A spiritual herdsman.
- *plumber*. One who works with lead (*plumbum*).
- *secretary*. One to whom secrets are entrusted.

W is the shortest three-syllable word in English. All other letters of the alphabet are sounded with a single syllable. None of the letters in *double-u* is a *w*.

(See A, I, Q-TIPS, S, SILENT, X.)

Washerayetagemud. Okay, this isn't a word, but it is a letter chain in which each group of three consecutive letters—*was, ash, she, her, era, ray, aye, yet, eta, tag, age, gem, emu,* and *mud*—forms a word with no word repeated. An analogous chain of four-letter words is *tsaridesk*.

Washington. George Washington is truly the father of his country when it comes to place names:

our nation's capital	one monument
a state	thirty-three counties
a bridge	121 cities and villages
seven mountains	nine universities and colleges
ten lakes	eight streams

In honor of our first president, here's a stately sonnet composed by David Shulman way back in 1936. Each line is an anagram of all the letters in the title, yet the lines are cast in reasonable meter and each couplet rhymes:

Washington Crossing the Delaware

A hard, howling, tossing, water scene;
Strong tide was washing hero clean.
How cold! Weather stings as in anger.
O silent night shows war ace danger!

The cold waters swashing on in rage.
Redcoats warn slow his hint engage.
When general's star wish'd "Go!"
He saw his ragged continentals row.

Ah, he stands—sailor crew went going,
And so this general watches rowing.
He hastens—Winter again grows cold;
A wet crew gain Hessian stronghold.

George can't lose war with 's hands in;
He's astern—so, go alight, crew, and win!

(See ANAGRAM, DANIEL, ULYSSES SIMPSON GRANT, WILLIAM SHAKESPEARE.)

Wednesday is spelled so peculiarly because it descends from an Old English word that meant "Woden's day," Woden being the great storm god in Norse mythology who corresponds to the Roman deity Mercury. Woden was the father of *Tyr*, who bequeaths us the name *Tuesday*.

From *Thor*, the strongest and bravest of the Norse gods and counterpart to the Roman Jupiter, we get Thursday, and from Woden's wife *Frigg*, the goddess of marriage, we receive *Friday*.

(See CLUE, ECHO, JOVIAL, TANTALIZE.)

Where is a reverse image of *scent*. Remove the first letter and you get a four-letter word with a different vowel sound. Restore that letter and then delete the second letter. Now you have another four-letter word with yet another vowel sound. Those words are *where-here-were*.

(See SCENT.)

Whippersnapper may be the snappiest sounding word in English. When we say *whippersnapper*, we forcible expel the two double *p*'s from our lips like a watermelon seed. The word, which means "a cheeky young man," was originally a *whip snapper*, an idle youth who had nothing better to do than to stand around snapping his whip.

Widow. A number of masculine words add a suffix to become feminine, such as *prince-princess, major-majorette, hero-heroine,* and *czar-czarina*, but *widower* is the only common word in the English language in which the feminine form constitutes the base and the addition of a suffix creates the male form. That's because, of course, there survive considerably more widows than widowers.

William Shakespeare. What do these six sentences have in common?

- Has Will a peer, I ask me.
- I swear he's like a lamp.
- We all make his praise.
- Wise male. Ah, I sparkle!
- Hear me, as I will speak.
- Ah, I speak a swell rime.

Each is an anagram that uses all the letters in the name *William Shakespeare* and captures a luminous truth: Peerless Will Shakespeare shines through the centuries and inspires our praise.

Here's another wonderment about the name *William Shakespeare*:

In 1610, the year of the most intensive work on the translation of the King James Bible, Shakespeare was forty-six years old. Given this clue, we turn to the Forty-sixth Psalm as it appears in the King James Bible. Count down to the forty-sixth word from the beginning and then count up to the forty-sixth word from the end, excluding the cadential *Selah*:

God is our refuge and strength, a very present help in trouble.
Therefore will not we fear, though the earth be removed,
and though the mountains be carried into the midst of the sea;
Though the waters thereof roar and be troubled,
though the mountains shake with the swelling thereof. Selah.
There is a river, the streams whereof shall make glad the city of God,
the holy place of the tabernacle of the Most High.

God is in the midst of her; she shall not be moved:
God shall help her, and that right early.
The heathen raged, the kingdoms were moved:
he uttered his voice, the earth melted.
The Lord of hosts is with us; the God of Jacob is our refuge. Selah.
Come, behold the works of the Lord,
what desolations he hath made on earth;
He maketh wars to cease unto the end of the earth;
he breaketh the bow, and cutteth the spear in sunder;
he burneth the chariot in the fire.
Be still, and know that I am God:
I will be exalted among the heathen, I will be exalted in the earth.
The Lord of hosts is with us; the God of Jacob is our refuge. Selah.

If you counted accurately, your finger eventually lit upon the two words *shake* and *spear*. Shakespeare. Whether or not he created the translated majesty of the forty-sixth psalm, he is in it. Whether the embedded *shake spear* is a purposeful plant or the product of happy chance, the name of the world's most famous poet reposes cunningly in the text of the world's most famous translation.

But most wondrous of all is that reading Shakespeare is like witnessing the birth of our English language. Consider the following list of fifty representative words that, as far as we can tell, Shakespeare was the first to use in writing. So great is his influence on his native tongue that we find it hard to imagine a time when these words did not exist:

accommodation	courtship	hurry	perusal
aerial	critic (and critical)	impartial	pious
amazement	dexterously	indistinguishable	premeditated
apostrophe	dishearten	invulnerable	radiance
assassination	dislocate	lapse	reliance
auspicious	dwindle	laughable	road
baseless	eventful	lonely	sanctimonious
bedroom	exposure	majestic	seamy
bump	fitful	misplaced	sneak
castigate	frugal	monumental	sportive
clangor	generous	multitudinous	submerge
countless	gloomy	obscene	useless
	gnarled	pedant	

(See ANAGRAM, CATCH-22, CHARACTONYM, CHORTLE, NERD, PANDEMONIUM, WASHINGTON.)

Willy-nilly is a version of the phrase "Will I, nill I?"—*nill* being an obsolete word that means "not to will, to refuse." A close cousin is *shilly-shally,* echoing the repetition of "Shall I, shall I?"

When a sound or syllable in a word repeats itself with little or no change, the resulting combination is often what linguists call a reduplication. More than two thousand reduplications enliven our English language, and they come in three varieties:

- *rhymes*: fuddy-duddy, hocus-pocus, humdrum, okeydokey, super duper
- *vowel shifts*: chitchat, flim-flam, flip-flop, pitter-patter, zigzag
- *repetitions:* goody-goody, fifty-fifty, no-no, tom-tom, yo-yo

A number of rhyming reduplications shine forth with scintillating origins:

- *Namby-pamby* was the title of a poem written by Henry Carey in 1726 ridiculing Ambrose Phillips's poetic endeavors by altering his first name.
- The *hob* in *hobnob* is a projection from a fireplace used to warm beverages; the *nob* is a table on which the drinks are placed, an appropriate setting for hobnobbing.
- A *hodgepodge* (earlier hotchpotch) was originally a stew of many ingredients and has broadened in meaning to signify a widely varied concoction, a mess.
- Many linguists attribute *nitty-gritty* to the Black English expression "nits like grits," that is, "lice (nits) as hard as grits."

Witzelsucht has been identified as a psychological syndrome characterized by an unremitting urge to make bad puns and to laugh at them uncontrollably. It's good to put a name to my magnificent obsession.

(See PUN.)

Women. A pair of animals died at a small zoo, and the owner wrote to the animal supply company to order replacements.

"Dear Company," he wrote. "Please send me two mongooses," and then grew nervous that *mongooses* was not the correct plural form. So he composed a second draft—"Dear Company: Please send me two mongeese" and then fretted that *mongeese* was not the correct plural form.

Finally, he sent this request: "Dear Company: Please send me a mongoose, and, while you're at it, please send me another mongoose."

Turns out that *mongooses* is the proper plural because *mongoose* is Hindi and is thus made plural in the regular way. In fact, only seven common nouns, all of which go back to Old English, become plural by changing a vowel in their middle. Three are animals—*goose-geese, mouse-mice,* and *louse-lice;* two are parts of the body—*tooth-teeth* and *foot-feet;* and two are people—*man-men* and *woman-women.*

The last transformation is the most unusual because in *woman-women,* the first vowel also changes sound, even though the *o* stays the same.

Irregular plurals in the English language include Greek endings—*phenomenon-phenomena, crisis-crises;* Latin endings—*medium-media, addendum-addenda; alumnus-alumni;* Old English endings—*ox-oxen, child-children;* and plurals exhibiting no apparent change—*sheep-sheep, moose-moose.*

Here are more transmogrifying plurals:

- *Rhinoceros* (built from two Greek roots that mean "nose horn") boasts four plural forms—*rhinoceros, rhinoceroses, rhinocerosi,* and, more rarely and academically, *rhinocerotes.*
- *Kine* is the only plural that contains no letter in common with its singular—*cow.* Sure, *kine* is archaic, but we're allowed to have archaic and eat it too.
- *Axes* is the plural of both *axe* and *axis. Bases* is the plural of both *base* and *basis.*

(See VERB.)

Wonton. Of all the palindromic statements that inhabit the logological universe, the one you might actually utter, presumably in a Chinese restaurant, is "Wonton? Not now."

(See ADAM, AGAMEMNON, DESSERTS, NAPOLEON, PALINDROME, SENSUOUSNESS, *ZOONOOZ.*)

Word is an autological word, one that expresses a property that it also possesses itself. That is, *word* is itself a word. Most words aren't what they signify. For example, *book* isn't a book, and there isn't anything especially happy about *happy. Preposition* isn't a preposition, and *sentence* isn't a sentence. Words such as *big* and *monosyllabic* turn out to be the opposite of what they mean. *Big* isn't big at all, and, although *monosyllabic* refers to words of but a single syllable, *monosyllabic* is composed of five syllables.

Here's a line-up of my favorite autological words. Can you identify why each one is self-referential?:

boldface	grandiloquent	sesquipedalian
CAPITALIZED	*italics*	trochee
English	lowercased	typeset
esoteric	noun	unhyphenated
euphonious	oxymoron	visible
four	pentasyllabic	wee

(See PREPOSTEROUS.)

Words. Loop the *s* from the back to the front and your *words* become your *sword*. The day we put away our sword and use words instead will be the day we become truly civilized.

How many words are there in English? This apparently simple question turns out to be surprisingly complicated. The answer partly depends on what you count as English words and where you go looking for them.

One place, of course, is "the dictionary." In the United States, Noah Webster's 1806 dictionary included about 37,000 words, but his 1828 edition contained about 70,000. *The Century Dictionary,* which appeared in 1889, held about 200,000, and by 1911, the editors found it necessary to add 100,000 more. Merriam-Webster's *Third New International Dictionary,* published in 1961, lists more than 450,000 words and the *Oxford English Dictionary* some 616,500. One thing is certain: Modern English has the largest and richest word-hoard of any human language ever known.

But no one can be sure how many words there are in English. As good as our lexicographers are at catching and exhibiting words, no dictionary can be complete. There are well over a million organic and inorganic chemical compounds, each with its own distinctive name, along with several million insects that have been named, with millions more flying or crawling around yet unlabeled. In fact, three-quarters of our words belong to specialized fields such as medicine, psychology, and technology or to trade jargons. Dictionaries for general use simply have no room for most of these words.

Among the half-million words that repose in our biggest, fattest American dictionaries how many belong to the average speaker? To answer this question, we must distinguish between two kinds of vocabulary, those words we recognize or recall and those we actually use. The average person possesses a vocabulary of 10-20,000 words but actively uses only a small fraction of these, the others being recognition or recall vocabulary. In fact, a number of linguists claim that nine words make up twenty-five percent of our speech. The most popular of these are *the, of, and, a, to, in, it, for,* and *he.*

A literate adult may recognize sixty thousand or more words, the most learned of us a hundred thousand. The surprising fact remains that the most articulate verbivore interacts with only one-fifth of the total official word stock and actually employs a far smaller fraction. The most verbal among us are still semiliterate.

The increasing complexity of society and the rapid growth of technology have led to an explosion in the number of words at our disposal. More new words were added to English between 1850 and 1950 in the field of chemistry alone than Old English acquired from all sources in five hundred years.

The accelerating growth of English will increase the gap between the individual's vocabulary and the total number of words in the language. Our language is a classic case of conspicuous consumption—or perhaps we should say non-consumption—because so many words remain unemployed. Fortunately, we seldom miss the words we never use and can get along without them. But we should count our linguistic blessings. In language, an embarrassment of wealth is preferable to an embarrassment of poverty.

Various studies report that women speak an average of seven thousand to thirty thousand words a day and men an average of three thousand to twelve thousand words a day. In all such studies, women speak an average of two-and-a-half to three times more words each day than do men. That's because women speak more rapidly, devote more brain power to conversation, and constantly have to repeat themselves to men.

RICHARD LEDERER

X is one of our most versatile letters. *X* marks the spot; is an ancient symbol for Christ; and represents the Roman numeral ten, a strike in bowling, a kind of ray, a signature, and a kiss.

In the Middle Ages, when most people were unable to read or write, documents were often signed with an X, indicating that in Christ's name the signer was the person he claimed to be. Kissing the X became an oath to fulfill obligations specified in the document, and that's why the X has come to represent a kiss as well as a signature.

Because the Greek letter *chi* is the first letter for the Greek word for Christ, the word *Xmas,* "Christ's mass," has been commonly used in Europe for centuries. *Xmas,* then, is not an attempt to "take the Christ out of Christmas." It's a legitimate term first used by the Greek Orthodox Church.

According to *The X-Files,* the letter *X* can be pronounced in at least ten different ways, depending on context:

eks: X-ray	*gz*: exist	*kris*: Xmas	*z*: xylophone
eksh: sexual	*gzh*: luxurious	*ks*: hex	__: faux pas
	k: except	*ksh*: anxious	

(See A, I, Q-TIPS, S, SILENT, W.)

Xerox. Do you talk or write about "xeroxing" a document no matter what machine you use to do the photocopying? Beware: Anyone who lowercases and verbifies *Xerox* runs the risk of hearing from the Xerox Corporation, which spends a bundle every year to persuade the public not to say or write *xerox* when they mean "photocopy."

The Johnson & Johnson Company writes admonishing letters to any periodical that prints expressions like "band-aid diplomacy" or "band-aid economics." Although *band-aid* has come to stand for any medicinal plastic strip or merely cosmetic remedy, it is a registered trademark and, by law, should be capitalized.

And, if you describe any plastic flying disk as a frisbee, you could get whammed by the Wham-O Manufacturing Company of San Gabriel, California. The idea for the plastic saucers came from the aerodynamic pie tins once manufactured for the Frisbie Bakery in Bridgeport, Connecticut, and the name *Frisbee* remains a registered asset.

For decades the Coca-Cola Company has been playing legal hardball to protect its name. While the courts have allowed other purveyors of soft drinks to use the name *Cola* because it is descriptive of the product, the Supreme Court decided in 1930 that the combination *Coca-Cola* and the clipped form *Coke* are the exclusive property of the company.

It is both ironic and paradoxical that the more successful a product, the more likely that its name will become an eponym and lose its privileged status as a result of lawsuits by competitors. The term for this kind of commercial demise is "genericide." Victims of genericide include *aspirin, cellophane, celluloid, corn flakes, cube steak, dry ice, escalator, formica, heroin, kerosene, lanolin, linoleum, linotype, milk of magnesia, mimeograph, pogo stick, raisin bran, shredded wheat, thermos, trampoline, yo-yo,* and *zipper*. These words have made such a successful journey from uppercase brand name to lowercase noun that it is difficult to believe that they were ever "owned" by a particular outfit.

Among product names that are threatened by genericide but that have so far survived legal onslaughts and are still registered are *Baggies, Beer Nuts, Cuisinart, Fig Newtons, Jeep, Jell-O, Jockey Shorts, Kitty Litter, Kleenex, Levi's, Life Savers, Mace, Magic Marker, Novocain, Ping-Pong, Polaroid, Popsicle, Post-It Notes, Q-Tips, Realtor, Rollerblade, Scotch Tape, Styrofoam, Technicolor,* and *Vaseline.*

If you don't believe that they are registered trademarks, look on packages containing these items, and you will still see a symbol of their registered status, such as *TM* or *R,* following each brand name.

(See BRAND.)

RICHARD LEDERER

Y'all, an elision of "you all," is the pronoun that southerners use when they speak to more than one other person. Most of us crave a second-person-plural pronoun to go with a second-person-singular pronoun—the equivalent of *thou* and *ye* in Middle English and *Usted* and *Ustedes* in Spanish—but all we have at our disposal is *you* and *you*. In the United States, aside from *you*, *y'all* is the most popular pronoun for a bunch of *you*'s, followed by *you guys, youse, yins, you 'uns,* and *you lot.*

> Y'all gather 'round from far and near,
>> Both city folk and rural,
> And listen while I tell you this:
>> The pronoun *y'all* is plural.

> If I should utter, "Y'all come down,
>> Or we-all shall be lonely,"
> I mean at least a couple folks,
>> And not one person only.

If I should say to Hiram Jones,
"I think that y'all are lazy,"
Or "Will y'all let me use y'all's knife?"
He'd think that I was crazy.

Don't think I mean to criticize
Or that I'm full of gall,
But when we speak to one alone,
We all say *you*, not *y'all*.

(See COOL, HOAGIE, OK.)

Yankee. As the traditional saying goes, to a foreigner, a Yankee is an American. To a southerner, a Yankee is a northerner. To a northerner, a Yankee is a New Englander. To a New Englander, a Yankee is from Vermont. And to a Vermonter, a Yankee is someone who eats apple pie for breakfast.

The first verse of "Yankee Doodle," as often sung today, runs:

Yankee Doodle went to town,
Riding on a pony.
Stuck a feather in his hat
And called it macaroni.

The original Yankees were Dutch settlers who had come to the new world, and *Yankee* may derive from the Dutch *Jan Kaas*, "Johnny Cheese." *Yankee* migrated from an ethnic insult against the Dutch to New Englanders in general when the song began life as a pre-Revolutionary creation originally sung by British military officers. The intent of "Yankee Doodle" was to mock the ragtag, disorganized New Englanders with whom the British served in the French and Indian War.

Doodle first appeared in the early seventeenth century and derives from the Low German word *dudel,* meaning "fool" or "simpleton." The macaroni wig was in high fashion in the 1770s and became contemporary slang for foppishness. The last two lines of the verse implied that the unsophisticated Yankee bumpkins thought that simply sticking a feather in a cap would make them the height of fashion. The colonists liked the tune of "Yankee Doodle" and adopted it as a robust and proud marching song. What was once a derisive musical ditty became a source of American pride.

(See FILIBUSTER.)

RICHARD LEDERER

Yeoman. English spelling is characterized by what is called the phoneme-grapheme chasm, a great gulf between the way words sound and the way they look. To illustrate, here's a twenty-three word sentence in which every word but one contains a long *oh* sound, yet each word spells that sound differently:

Although yeoman folk owe pharaoh's Vaud bureau's depot hoed oats, chauvinistic Van Gogh, swallowing cognac oh so soulfully, sews grossgrained, picoted, brooched chapeaux.

(See EINSTEIN, GHOTI, HICCOUGH.)

Zarf. Few people know that the holder for a paper cone coffee cup is called a *zarf*. Here are my favorite thingamabobs that have names you probably never knew existed:

- *aglet.* The little plastic tip of a shoelace.
- *chimb.* The rim of a barrel.
- *dingbat.* A cute little typesetter's mark or ornament, such as the bullet point to the left of each item in this section.
- *escutcheon.* The decorative metal plate around a keyhole, drawer pull, or doorknob.
- *ferrule.* The metal band that holds an eraser to a pencil or the metal tip of an umbrella.
- *harp.* The small metal hoop that supports a lampshade.
- *muntins.* The frames for holding window panes.
- *neb.* The curved end of the handle of a knife.
- *pintel.* The vertical post that runs through a door hinge.
- *punt.* The indentation at the bottom of some wine bottles that provides added strength to the vessel but reduces the holding capacity.

(See THINGAMABOB.)

Zeugma. In addition to wanting to fill in and out the "Z" cluster of this book, I love how *zeugma* sounds and looks. *Zeugma* (ζεῦγμα), from a Greek word meaning "yoke," is also one of my favorite figures of rhetoric. Zeugma features the omission of a verb, creating a striking yoking of two nouns:

> Or stain her Honor, or her new Brocade . . .
> Or lose her Heart, or necklace at a Ball.
> —*Alexander Pope*

When I am speaking on behalf a large-hearted organization, I sometimes declare zeugmatically, "ABC Charity validates your parking and your humanity."

Zeugma is one of dozens of figures of speech and rhetoric in the bestiary collected by the ancient Greeks. Among other specimens:

- *alliteration.* The repetition of initial consonant sounds. Dollars to doughnuts, our English language contains a treasure trove and kit and caboodle of tried-and-true, bright-eyed-and-busy-tailed, bread-and-butter, bigger-and-better, cream-of-the-crop, fit-as-a-fiddle, hale-and-hearty, picture-perfect, shipshape alliterative expressions, all of them good as gold and worth a pretty penny.

- *enallage.* A rhetorically effective mistake in grammar, as in "We was robbed!"—*Jimmy Jacobs*; "If it ain't broke, don't fix it."

- *isolcolon.* Parallelism of grammatical forms, as in "The bigger they are, the harder they fall."; "government of the people, by the people, for the people . . ."—*Abraham Lincoln*

- *litotes.* A deliberate understatement that helps make a point, as in "Last week I saw a woman flayed, and you will hardly believe how much it altered her appearance."—*Jonathan Swift*

- *paraprosdokian.* Derived from two Greek roots that mean "an unexpected outcome," this figure of speech is characterized by a surprising left-hand turn at the end of a statement that produces a humorous or dramatic effect, as in "I've had a perfectly wonderful evening, but this wasn't it."—*Groucho Marx*; "When I die, I want to die like my grandfather did—peacefully in his sleep, not screaming like all the passengers in the car he was driving."—*Bob Monkhouse*

- *simile.* A comparison between two essentially different objects or ideas expressly indicated by words such as *like* or *as,* as in "My love is like a red, red rose."—*Robert Burns*

One Judge Martin J. Sheehan of Kenton Circuit Court, Kentucky, rejoiced similitudinously in the settlement of a case that had been scheduled to go to trial earlier:

> And such news of an amicable settlement having made this court happier than a tick on a fat dog because it is otherwise busier than a one-legged cat in a sand box and, quite frankly, would have rather jumped naked off of a twelve-foot step ladder and into a five-gallon bucket of porcupines than have presided over a two-week trial of the herein dispute, a trial which, no doubt, would have made the jury more confused than a hungry baby in a topless bar and made the parties and their attorneys madder than mosquitoes in a mannequin factory.

> It is therefore ordered and adjudicated by the court that the jury trial scheduled herein for July 13, 2011, is hereby canceled.

- *synecdoche.* The substitution of a part for the whole, as in "Dad, why don't Mom and you watch the tube tonight so that I can borrow the wheels?"

(See CHIASMUS, HYSTERON PROTERON, IRONY, METAPHOR, METONYMY, OXYMORON, PARADOX.)

Zoology. Being both a bird watcher and a word botcher, I took my three granddaughters to the San Diego Wild Animal Park, where we attended "Frequent Flyers," the famous bird show. Our family enjoyed various avians strutting their stuff on the ground, hawks swooping down from the sky, and a gray parrot squawking and squeaking all sorts of sound effects.

In their ongoing narrative, two of the Wild Animal Park's trainers kept pronouncing the name of the San Diego Zoological Society as *ZOO-uh-LAHJ-i-kul society.* After the performance, I mentioned to the two young women in private that there are two, not three, *o*'s in *zoological* so the proper sounding is *ZOH-uh-LAHJ-i-kul.* They told me they knew that but had been instructed by their bosses to say *ZOO-uh-LAHJ-i-kul* because people wouldn't understand the proper pronunciation. Glug. Talk about the dumbing down of America.

Pronunciation maven Charles Harrington Elster points out that there is no *zoo* in *zoology,* no *noun* in *pronunciation,* no *point* in *poinsettia,* no *sick* in *psychiatrist,* no *spear* in *experiment,* no *wine* in *genuine* or *sanguine,* no *berry* in *library,* no *shoe* in *eschew,* no *art* in *arctic,* no *ant* in *defendant,* no *foe* in *forward* and *foreword,* no *pair* in *comparable*, no *day* in *deity*, no *sea* in *oceanic*, no *she* in *controversial*, no *punk* in *pumpkin*, no *eve* in *evolution*, no *pen* in *penalize*, no *pitch* in *picture*, no *pole* in *police*, no *pot* in *potpourri*, no *ex* in *espresso*, no *Arthur* in *arthritis*, no *Bert* in *sherbet*, no *sees* in *species*, no *deer* in *idea*, no *ram* in *ignoramus*, no *tang* in *orangutan*, no *mitten* in *badminton*, no *tie* in *tyrannical*, no *lock* in *lilac*, no *port* in *rapport*, no *beast* in *bestial*, no *doe* in *docile*, no *beau* in *boutique*, no *owner* is *onerous*, no *spite* in *respite*, no *oh* in *myopic*, no *brew* in *brooch*, no *over* in *hover*, no *reek* in *recluse*, no *sewer* in *connoisseur*, no *sees* in *processes*, no *nix* in *larynx*, no *home* in *homicide*, no *gal* in *gala*, no *mire* in *admirable*, no *chick* in *chic*, no *click* in *clique*, no *me* or *Lee* in *melee*, no *ray* in *lingerie*, no *dye* in *dais*, no *oral* in *pastoral, pectoral, electoral*, and *mayoral*, no *air* in *err*, no *restaurant* in *restaurateur*, no *stray* in *illustrative* or *menstruation*, no *spar* in *disparate*, no *rounded* in *drowned*, no *vice* in *vice versa*, no *nominee* in *ignominy*, no *mash* in *machination*, no *spire* in *respiratory*, no *late* in *prelate*, no *pray* in *prelude*, no *magnet* in *magnate*, no *dare* in *modernity*, no *eye* in *Iran* and *Iraq*, no *you* in *jaguar* and *February*, no *pew* in *Pulitzer*, no *clue* in *Ku Klux Klan*, no *Poe* in *impotent*, no *cane* in *Spokane*, no *cue* in *coupon* and in *nuclear*, and no *anus* in *Uranus*.

ZOONOOZ. Among the many attractions of San Diego, where I am fortunate enough to live, are our zoo and wild animal park. Since 1920 the magazine published by our zoological society has been titled *ZOONOOZ*. It's a bedazzling, beguiling, and bewitching name because it's a palindrome right side up, upside down, and both ways in a mirror:

> *ZOONOOZ! ZOONOOZ!* burning bright
> In the forests of the night.
> What immortal hand or eye
> Could frame thy dazzling symmetry?

Topsy-turvy words like *ZOONOOZ* that can retain their appearance upside down are called *ambigrams*:

| dip | dollop | mow | NOON | pod | suns | SWIMS |

(See ADAM, AGAMEMNON, CIVIC, KINNIKINNIK, NAPOLEON, PAL-INDROME, SENSUOUSNESS, WONTON.)

Zounds. English speakers apparently take deeply to heart the biblical commandment not to take the Lord's name in vain and Christ's injunction to eschew all swearing, either by heaven or by earth. Have you ever noticed how many different ways we have come up with to avoid saying *God* and *damnation?*: *gosh, golly, goodness gracious, good grief, good gravy, by gar, by golly, by gum, dad gum, doggone, gol dang, gol darn, dear me* (an approximation of the Italian *Dio mio,* "my God"), *jumpin' Jehoshaphat* ('jumping Jehovah"), *begorrah, great Scott, gosh all fishhooks* ("God almighty"), *by gorey, by Godfrey,* and W.C. Fields' *Godfrey Daniels.*

Older and more elegant stratagems for skirting the name of the Almighty include *egad* ("ye gods"), *odds bodkins* (a shortening of "God's body"), *gadzooks* ("God's hooks," the nails of the cross), *drat* ("God rot"), *'sblood* ("God's blood"), and *zounds* ("God's wounds").

Who needs to shout "hell!" when Sam Hill (euphemism for "damn hell") is available to help us cuss ("curse") in a socially acceptable manner? Sam Hill was not a particular person, but "Sam Hill" expressions, such as *what the Sam Hill!* and *mad as Sam Hill,* grew up in the American West in the 1830s. Sam Hill was a trusty friend of frontiersmen, especially when they needed to clean up their language in the presence of womenfolk. One can count among additional surrogates for *hell* the words *heck, hey, Halifax, Hoboken,* and *Jesse* ("if you don't watch out, you're going to catch Jesse."

We live in a culture in which calling out the name of Jesus Christ in church is a sign of moral rectitude; but, once outside, we have to find ways of not quite saying that name. Among those taboo euphemisms we find *gee, gee whiz* ("Je-sus"), *gee whillikers, jesum crow, Christmas, holy cow, holy crow, holy Christmas, cripes, criminey, crikey, by Jingo, by Jiminy, Jiminy Cricket, Jiminy Christmas, Judas Priest,* and even *jeepers creepers.*

(See EUPHEMISM.)

Zyzzyva. A genus of tropical South American snouted weevil discovered in Brazil. No longer than an ant, this insect could be labeled "the lesser of two weevils."

With the first five of its seven letters being *z* or *y, zyzzyva* is the last word in many dictionaries. And, except for the Index, it's the last word of this book.

(See BUFFALO, BUTTERFLY, CANARY, CLAM, CRESTFALLEN, DACHSHUND, DANDELION, HORSEFEATHERS, OSTRACIZE, PARTRIDGE, PEDIGREE, TAD, TURKEY, VACCINATE.)

RICHARD LEDERER

INDEX

The indented, italicized words repose in the entries for other words.

A

a, 1
abecedarian, 2
abracadabra, 2
ace, 3
Adam, 3
  Adam's apple
aegilops, 4
Agamemnon, 4
ague, 4
ahoy, 4
ai, 4
air, 4–5
akimbo, 5
  monogamous words
alimony, 5
alkaline, 6
alone, 6
amateur, 6
ambidextrous, 6
  ambidextrously, ambisinister
anagram, 6–7
  aptagram
anger, 7–8
anthology, 8–9
  *daffodil, narcissus, orchid,
  poinsettia, precocious, tulip*
archetypal, 9
arf, 9
arm, 10
ashtray, 10
asinine, 10
assassin, 10
atone, 10
@, 10–11
awful, 11
aye, 11

B

balderdash, 12–13
  *gibberish, double Dutch, flapdoodle,
  folderol, mumbo-jumbo, hocus-
  pocus, poppycock*
bash, 13–14
bated, 14
bathroom, 15
bear/bull, 15
Bible, 15–16
  *maudlin, scapegoat, shibboleth,
  talent*
bikini, 16
bildungsroman, 17
blooper, 17
blossom, 18
  kangaroo words
Bolt, 19–20
  aptronym
bookkeeper, 20
boss, 20
brand, 20–21
  *Advil, Avis, Avon, Camry, Dial,
  Evian, Kools, Look, Tic Tacs, Tums,
  Tulsa, Tylenol, Visa, Wal-Mart,
  Yamaha*
buffalo, 21–22
  buff
butterfly, 22

C

cabbage, 23
  boldface, cabbageheaded, feedback
cakewalk, 24
  a piece of cake, take the cake
caliber, 24–25
  *bite the bullet, a flash in the pan,
  go off half cocked, lock, stock, and
  barrel, loose cannon, point blank,
  ramrod, skinflint, snapshot, stick to
  your guns*

Index

canary, 26–27
candidate, 27
  ambitious
caper, 27
  cabriolet, get your goat, goatee,
carnival, 28
  bonfire, enthusiastic, excruciating,
  fan, holiday, red-letter day, short
  shrift
casino, 29
catch-22, 29
catchphrase, 30
charactonym, 30
Chargoggagoggmanchauggagoggchaubunagungamaugg, 30
chiasmus, 30–31
chocoholic, 31
chortle, 32
Christchurch, 32
chthonic, 32–33
circus, 33–34
  argot, back yard, bull, dog and pony
  show, donniker, doors, cherry pie,
  first-of-May, grease joint, hump,
  jump, kinker, mud show, painted
  pony, rube, spec, straw house,
  stripes, towner
CIVIC, 34
clam, 34–35
  happy as a clam, harp on, naked as a
  jaybird, the proof is in the pudding
cliché, 35
  stereotype
clue, 35–36
cockamamie, 36
cockney, 36–37
companion, 37
  lady, lord, upper crust
compass, 38
congress, 38
convict, 39
cool, 39–40
  slang
cop, 40
corpse, 40
couch potato, 40
covivant, 41
crestfallen, 41
  cockpit, get your hackles up, well-
  heeled
crossword, 42

D

Dachshund, 43–44
  hot dog
daffynition, 44
dandelion, 44–45
  indent, indenture
Daniel, 45
daredevil, 45–46
deadline, 46
deeded, 46
denouement, 47
desserts, 47
die, 47
  at sixes and sevens, make no bones
  about it, on a roll
disaster, 47–48
  asterisk, asteroid, astronomer, dog
  days, eccentric, honeymoon, lunatic
disgruntled, 49
doghouse, 49
doldrums, 50
doornail, 50–51
doublespeak, 51
drunk, 52
  intoxicated

E

ecdysiast, 53
echo, 53–54
  narcissistic
eerie, 54
  Ouija
egress, 54
Einstein, 55
elbow, 55
electric, 56
Elizabeth, 56
encyclopedia, 56
enervate, 56–57
  wherefore
English, 57
entrance, 57–59
  heteronym
Episcopal, 59
  Presbyterian
Estonia, 59–60
  Etaoin Shrdlu
etymology, *vii*
euphemism, 60–61
  dysphemism

expediency, 61
   grammagram
   eye, 62–63
   autopsy, daisy, daylights, iris, pupil,
   supercilious

F

facetious, 64
fathom, 65
filibuster, 65
finger, 66
   prestidigitator, rule of thumb,
   thumb
fired, 66–67
first, 67–68
   eleven, fifteen, five, four, one, one
   billion, one thousand, one million,
   ten, thirteen, TWENTY-NINE, two
floccinaucinihilipilification, 68
focus, 68
forecastle, 69

G

galore, 70
gargoyle, 70
gay, 70–71
gerrymander, 71–72
   Dagwood sandwich, goon, on the
   fritz, mickey mouse, milquetoast,
   wimpy
ghoti, 72
gobbledygook, 73
golf, 73–74
   stymie
good-bye, 74
groak, 74
gry, 74–75
   hazardous

H

had, 76
hallmark, 76–78
   acid test, cut and dried, masterpiece,
   millstone, retail, touchtone, the
   whole nine yards
hamburger, 78–79
   frankfurter
hand, 79–80
   caught red-handed, handicap, hand
   over fist, handsome, wash your
   hands of the matter, win hands down

harrowing, 80–81
   by hook or by crook, cultivated,
   fertile, haywire, make hay while the
   sun shines, nip in the bud, tough
   row to hoe, windfall
hear, 81
heart, 81
   discouraged, warms the cockles of
   your heart
hiccough, 82
hijinks, 83
hippopotomonstrosesquipedalian, 83
   hapax legomenon
hoagie, 83–84
honorificabilitudinitatibus, 84
horsefeathers, 85–86
   don't look a gift horse in the mouth,
   straight from the horse's mouth
hotshots, 86
humerus, 86–87
   canthus, frenum, lunula, opisthenar,
   philtrum, purlicue, thenar, tragus,
   uvula, vomer
humor, 87
hurricane, 87
hysterical, 88
hysteron proteron, 88

I

I, 89
idiot, 90
   vote
inaugurate, 90
indivisibility, 90–91
infantry, 91
infinite, 91
inflammable, 91–92
intestines, 92
iota, 92
irony, 92–93
   dramatic irony, situational irony,
   verbal irony
irregardless, 93

J

jackpot, 94–95
   blue-chip, bottom dollar, the buck
   stops here, four-flusher, pass the
   buck, stack up, top dollar
Jason, 95–96
John, 96

jovial, 96–97
  amazon, aphrodisiac, herculean,
  hermaphrodite, mercurial, odyssey,
  panic, siren, stentorian

K
keynote, 98
kindergarten, 99
kinnikinnik, 99
knight, 99–100

L
L.A., 101
laconic, 101
latches, 102
limerick, 102–103
  gimerick
linguistics, *viii*
Liverpudlian, 103–104
llama, 104
Llanfairpwllgwyngyllgogerychwyrnddrobwllllantysilogogoch, 104
logology, *viii*
loll, 105
love, 105

M
mainland, 106
malapropism, 107
manatee, 107–108
Marshall, 108
  charade
maverick, 108
mentally, 108–109
Metalious, 109
metaphor, 109–110
  mixed metaphor
metonymy, 110
Mississippi, 110–111
mondegreen, 111–113
mother, 113
mumpsimus, 113

N
Napoleon, 114
nerd, 114–115
  neologism
no, 116
nonsupports, 116
nother, 116
nth, 116–118
  syzygy

nuclear, 118
nut, 118–119

O
oil, 120
OK, 120–121
orange, 121–122
orthography, 122–123
  Dalmatian, it's
ostracize, 123
  ballot
out, 123–125
  burn, cleave, clip, contronym, fast,
  fix, hold up, keep up, oversight,
  sanction, take, wear, wind up, with
outgoing, 125
overstuffed, 125
oxymoron, 125–126
oy, 126–127
  fin, glitch, gun moll, kibitzer, ma-
  ven, mazuma, mish-mosh, schlep,
  schmooze, schnoz, yenta
Oz, 127

P
palindrome, 128–129
pandemonium, 129–130
  dystopia, Never Land/Never-Never-
  Land, Shangri-La, Utopia, Wonder-
  land
pangram, 130–131
paradox, 131–132
partridge, 132
pastern, 133
pedigree, 133–134
philodendron, 134
picayune, 134–135
  don't take any wooden nickels, scot-
  free
pneumonoultramicroscopicsilicovolcanokoniosis, 135–136
poetry, 136–137
  Edgar Allan Poe
polish, 137
politics, 137–138
posh, 139
potpourri, 139–140
preamble, 140
prelate, 140
preposition, 140–141
preposterous, 141

preventive, 142
prince, 142
pronoun, 142–143
pumpernickel, 143
pun, 143–145
    double-sound pun, homograph,
    homophone

Q
Q-Tips, 146
queue, 146
quintessence, 147

R
radar, 148–149
    acronym, initialism
raise/raze, 149
reactivation, 149
rebus, 149–150
redundancy, 150–151
    pleonasm
reek, 151
restaurateurs, 152
retronym, 152
rhopalic, 153
rhythms, 153
right, 153–154
    adroit, dexterous, gauche, left,
    sinister
rode, 154
run, 154
    polysemy

S
s, 155
salary, 155–156
sandwich, 156
scent, 156
scintillating, 156–157
    clever
scuttlebutt, 157–158
    between the devil and the deep blue
    sea, the bitter end by and large,
    governor, leeway, take down a
    peg, taken aback, three sheets to
    the wind, touch and go, under the
    weather
sensuousness, 159
September, 159–160
    decimate, quarantine, siesta, unique
sequoia, 160

set, 160
sex, 160–161
    Essex, sacristan, sextet, sexton
shanghaiings, 161
shiftgram, 161
sideburns, 161
silent, 162
silhouette, 162
slapstick, 163–164
    claptrap, desultory, explode, hank-
    panky, hypocrite, in the limelight,
    person, pleased as Punch, pull
    strings
slay, 164
sleeveless, 165
Smith, 165–166
smithery, 166
sneeze, 166
southpaw, 166–167
spare, 167
speech, 167–169
    American, animal, business, coun-
    try, day, dress, drink, earth, gay,
    man, time, verse, verbal
spoonerism, 169–171
squirreled, 171
star, 171–172
    constellation, Stella, stellar
startling, 172
    stringier
stop, 172–173
strengthlessness, 173
strengths, 173
supercalifragilisticexpialidocious, 173
sweet-toothed, 174
Swifty, 174–175
synonym, 175–176
    antigram, antonym

T
tad, 177
tantalize, 177–178
taxicab, 178
temp, 178
temperamentally, 178
Thai, 178
therein, 179
thingamabob, 179
thunder, 179
time, 180
toast, 180

towhead, 181
triskaidekaphobia, 181–182
trivia, 182
turkey, 182
typewriter, 182

U

Ulysses Simpson Grant, 183–184
uncopyrightable, 184
underground, 184
united, 184–185
up, 185
usher, *vii–viii*

V

vaccinate, 186–187
egregious, gregarious, impecunious,
peculate, peculiar, pecuniary
vacuum, 187
ventriloquist, 187
verb, 187–189
verbivore, 189
veterinarian, 189–190
broker, bursar, chauffeur, clerk,
coroner, grocer, janitor, nurse, ortho-
pedist, pastor, plumber, professor,
secretary, soldier

W

w, 191
washerayetagemud, 191
Washington, 191–192
Wednesday, 192
Thursday, Friday
where, 192
whippersnapper, 193
widow, 193

William Shakespeare, 193–195
willy-nilly, 195
hobnob, hodgepodge, namby-pamby,
nitty gritty
witzelsucht, 195
women, 195–196
axes, bases, kine, rhinoceros
wonton, 196
word, 196–197
words, 197–198

X

x, 199
Xmas
Xerox, 200
Band-Aid, Coca-Cola, Frisbee,
genericide

Y

y'all, 201
Yankee, 202
Yankee doodle
yeoman, 203

Z

zarf, 204
aglet, dingbat, escutcheon, ferrule,
harp, muntins, neb, pintelpunt
zeugma, 205–206
alliteration, enallage, isolcolon,
paraprosdokian, simile, synecdoche
zoology, 206–207
ZOONOOZ, 207
ambigram
Zounds, 208
Sam Hill
zyzzyva, 208

RICHARD LEDERER